Lecture Notes in Computer Science

Lecture Notes in Artificial Intelligence 15924
Founding Editor

Jörg Siekmann

Series Editors

Randy Goebel, *University of Alberta, Edmonton, Canada*
Wolfgang Wahlster, *DFKI, Berlin, Germany*
Zhi-Hua Zhou, *Nanjing University, Nanjing, China*

The series Lecture Notes in Artificial Intelligence (LNAI) was established in 1988 as a topical subseries of LNCS devoted to artificial intelligence.

The series publishes state-of-the-art research results at a high level. As with the LNCS mother series, the mission of the series is to serve the international R & D community by providing an invaluable service, mainly focused on the publication of conference and workshop proceedings and postproceedings.

Tianqing Zhu · Wanlei Zhou · Congcong Zhu
Editors

Knowledge Science, Engineering and Management

18th International Conference, KSEM 2025
Macao, China, August 4–7, 2025
Proceedings, Part VI

Editors
Tianqing Zhu
City University of Macau
Macau, China

Wanlei Zhou
City University of Macau
Macau, China

Congcong Zhu
City University of Macau
Macau, China

ISSN 0302-9743 ISSN 1611-3349 (electronic)
Lecture Notes in Artificial Intelligence
ISBN 978-981-95-3071-7 ISBN 978-981-95-3072-4 (eBook)
https://doi.org/10.1007/978-981-95-3072-4

LNCS Sublibrary: SL7 – Artificial Intelligence

© The Editor(s) (if applicable) and The Author(s), under exclusive license
to Springer Nature Singapore Pte Ltd. 2026

This work is subject to copyright. All rights are solely and exclusively licensed by the Publisher, whether the whole or part of the material is concerned, specifically the rights of translation, reprinting, reuse of illustrations, recitation, broadcasting, reproduction on microfilms or in any other physical way, and transmission or information storage and retrieval, electronic adaptation, computer software, or by similar or dissimilar methodology now known or hereafter developed.
The use of general descriptive names, registered names, trademarks, service marks, etc. in this publication does not imply, even in the absence of a specific statement, that such names are exempt from the relevant protective laws and regulations and therefore free for general use.
The publisher, the authors and the editors are safe to assume that the advice and information in this book are believed to be true and accurate at the date of publication. Neither the publisher nor the authors or the editors give a warranty, expressed or implied, with respect to the material contained herein or for any errors or omissions that may have been made. The publisher remains neutral with regard to jurisdictional claims in published maps and institutional affiliations.

This Springer imprint is published by the registered company Springer Nature Singapore Pte Ltd.
The registered company address is: 152 Beach Road, #21-01/04 Gateway East, Singapore 189721, Singapore

If disposing of this product, please recycle the paper.

Preface

On behalf of the Conference Committee, we are pleased to present the proceedings of the 18th International Conference on Knowledge Science, Engineering and Management (**KSEM 2025**), held at the Wynn Palace, Macau Special Administrative Region, China, from August 4–7, 2025. KSEM 2025 was the eighteenth event in this well-established series of conferences, founded by Academician Ruqian Lu, which is recognized as a premier international forum for the exchange of research in artificial intelligence, data science, knowledge engineering, AI safety, large language models, and related frontier areas. Over the years, KSEM has provided an important venue for disseminating both theoretical advances and practical innovations, fostering interdisciplinary collaboration between academia and industry.

This year, KSEM 2025 received 354 submissions from authors around the world. Following a rigorous single-blind peer-review process, with an average of 2.82 reviews received per submission, involving 342 Program Committee members and external reviewers, 106 regular papers, 66 short papers, and 16 workshop papers were accepted for inclusion in these proceedings and will be submitted for EI indexing. In addition to the contributed papers, the program featured keynote lectures by distinguished scholars, as well as workshops and tutorials on emerging research topics, offering valuable opportunities for academic exchange and collaboration.

Among the accepted papers, the following were selected for the **Best Paper Awards**:

- *Masked Aggregation Learning for Enhancing Distributed Gradient Boosting Decision Trees* Yuting Zha, Chao Lin, Xinyi Huang, and Dugang Liu
- *Label Inference Attacks against Federated Unlearning* Wei Wang, Xiangyun Tang, Yajie Wang, Yijing Lin, Tao Zhang, Meng Shen, Dusit Niyato, and Liehuang Zhu

The **Best Student Paper Awards** went to:

- *LVLM-FDA: Protecting Large Vision-language Models via Fast Detection of Malicious Attempts* Boxu Chen, Chaoyi Wang, Le Yang, Ziwei Zheng, Cong Wang, Qian Wang, and Chao Shen
- *FATFI: A Framework to Generate Adversarial Traffic with Feature Interpretability* Yikang Wang, Weina Niu, Dujuan Gu, Qingjun Yuan, Jiacheng Gong, Shuangqi Gan, Xin Lin, and Xiaosong Zhang

We would like to express our sincere gratitude to all authors for their valuable contributions, and to the Program Committee members and reviewers for their professional and timely evaluations. We also warmly thank all the volunteers who supported the conference at various stages.

We further extend our appreciation to the following chairs for their invaluable contributions:

- **General Chairs:** Wanlei Zhou, Zhi Jin, Aniello Castiglione
- **Program Chairs:** Tianqing Zhu, Gang Li, Congcong Zhu, Lucia Cimmino

- **Local Chairs:** Wenjian Liu, Minghao Wang, Huajie Chen
- **Publication Chairs:** Lefeng Zhang, Youyang Qu
- **Workshop Chairs:** Jia Gu, Bo Liu, Chi Liu
- **Publicity Chairs:** Yu Huang, Minfeng Qi

We were so honored to have many renowned scholars be part of this conference. Finally, we would like to thank all speakers, authors, and participants for their great contribution to and support for the success of KSEM 2025.

August 2025

Tianqing Zhu
Wanlei Zhou
Congcong Zhu

Committees

General Chairs

Wanlei Zhou — City University of Macau, China
Zhi Jin — Peking University, China
Aniello Castiglione — University of Salerno, Italy

Program Chairs

Tianqing Zhu — City University of Macau, China
Gang Li — Deakin University, Australia
Congcong Zhu — City University of Macau, China
Lucia Cimmino — University of Salerno, Italy

Local Chairs

Wenjian Liu — City University of Macau, China
Minghao Wang — City University of Macau, China
Macau Huajie Chen — City University of Macau, China

Publication Chairs

Lefeng Zhang — City University of Macau, China
Macau Youyang Qu — Shandong Computer Science Center, China

Workshop Chairs

Jia Gu — City University of Macau, China
Bo Liu — University of Technology Sydney, Australia
Chi Liu — City University of Macau, China

Publicity Chairs

Yu Huang Peking University, China
Minfeng Qi City University of Macau, China

Contents -- Part VI

Research on CAN Bus Intrusion Detection Method Based on Feature
Fusion of Fourier Transform and Wavelet Transform 1
  Zixin Liu, Xiangsen Sun, and Daohua Liu

Research on Intelligent Classification Algorithm for Attack Detection
Based on Pre-trained Fusion Network with Bimodal Features 13
  Maoli Wang, Xiangsen Sun, and Weidong Guo

Research on the Mechanism of Privacy-Enhanced Cross-Institutional Data
Sharing 29
  *Xiaoliang Wang, Wei Xiao, Nan Liu, Kaile Xiao, Zhipeng Gao,
  Yang Yang, and Yu Wang*

A Survey on Malware Analysis with Large Language Models 41
  *Wenjie Guo, Haoyuan Wen, Lingming Kong, Jingfeng Xue, Jingjing Hu,
  Weijie Han, and Yong Wang*

An Active Defense Scheme Integrating Traffic Anomaly Detection
and Dynamic Key Update 53
  Xinyi Luo, Jiayi Xu, Yifan Gao, and Yi Wu

Detection Method for Prompt Injection by Integrating Pre-trained Model
and Heuristic Feature Engineering 66
  Yi Ji, Runzhi Li, and Baolei Mao

A Comprehensive Survey on White-Box Security Threats for Large
Language Models 74
  *Wenbiao Du, Tengfei Yang, Zhihan Sun, Xiuqi Yang, Zeyang Liu,
  and Jingfeng Xue*

FCA-XLNet-BiGRU Multi-task Framework for Darknet Transactions 87
  Dong Wang, Jun Zhu, and Peng Wu

Knowledge-Driven Superpixel Shortest Path Optimization for Image
Stitching 96
  Renping Xie, Chenxi Pang, and Ming Tao

Edge-Knowledge-Driven Smoke Removal Based on Infrared and Visible
Image Fusion 109
  Hengye Xu, Renping Xie, and Ming Tao

HDRIU-B: Hierarchical Data Rights Confirmation and Incremental
Update Mechanism Based on NFT and SBT in Blockchain 121
   Sudan Hu, Zening Zhao, and Hongwei Zhang

A Blockchain Transaction Tracking Method Based on Dynamic Graph
Link Prediction 136
   Chi Jiang, Jinglin Wang, Manhua Shi, Ke Zhang, and Yin Zhang

Online-Learning Based Task Scheduling in Industrial Internet-of-Things:
Tackling Resource Skew with Dynamic Optimization 144
   Jian Zhang, Xueqiang Li, Qunjian Chen, and Ming Tao

A Federated Learning Approach for Malware Detection in Data
Heterogeneous Environments 157
   Haoyuan Wen, Jingfeng Xue, Wenjie Guo, Liuting Wang, and Wenbiao Du

Author Index 167

Research on CAN Bus Intrusion Detection Method Based on Feature Fusion of Fourier Transform and Wavelet Transform

Zixin Liu[1], Xiangsen Sun[1], and Daohua Liu[2(✉)]

[1] School of Cyberspace Security, Qufu Normal University, Qufu, Shandong, China
{zixin,sunxiangsen}@qfnu.edu.cn
[2] Jining Internet Information Research Center, Jining, Shandong, China
16688070267@163.com

Abstract. As the core communication protocol in modern vehicles, the security of the Controller Area Network (CAN) bus is crucial for ensuring normal operation and defending against external attacks. This paper proposes a model named FWTnet, a multi-feature fusion-based intrusion detection approach for the CAN bus, designed to enhance the classification performance of normal and attack messages. First, we employ the Fourier Transform and Wavelet Transform to extract features from CAN messages separately. A Long Short-Term Memory (LSTM) network with fully connected layers is used for classification based on Fourier Transform features, while a fully connected network is applied directly to the Wavelet Transform features. The extracted features from the fully connected layers of both pre-trained networks are then fed into a cross neural network for final training and classification. Experimental results demonstrate that our approach achieves an average accuracy of 99.98% with an F1-score of 99.93% on the CarHacking dataset and an average accuracy of 99.99% on the CANFD dataset. Furthermore, to evaluate the model's generalization ability, we trained it on DoS attack data from the CANFD dataset and tested it on DoS attack samples from the CarHacking dataset, achieving an accuracy of 95.79%. These results validate the effectiveness and robustness of the proposed method.

Keywords: CAN bus intrusion detection · Fourier Transform · Wavelet Transform · Cross Neural Network · Deep Learning

1 Introduction

With the rapid advancement of smart vehicles and connected car technologies, the In-Vehicle Network (IVN) has become a critical infrastructure for vehicle control and data exchange. Among these networks, the Controller Area Network (CAN) is widely used for communication between Electronic Control Units (ECUs) due to its efficiency and low cost [12]. However, the lack of encryption and authentication mechanisms in the CAN bus makes it highly vulnerable to various cyberattacks, such as replay attacks, spoofing attacks, and Denial of Service (DoS) attacks [5]. These attacks can disrupt vehicle control, posing significant threats to driving safety. As a result, developing effective intrusion detection methods for the CAN bus has become a key research focus in the field of smart vehicle cybersecurity [11].

2 Related Work

In recent years, deep learning-based intrusion detection methods have made significant advancements in CAN bus anomaly detection. For instance, Recurrent Neural Networks (RNNs) and their variant, Long Short-Term Memory (LSTM) networks, have been widely adopted due to their strong ability to process sequential data, making them well-suited for detecting anomalies in CAN bus messages [16]. Additionally, frequency-domain analysis methods have gained increasing attention in time-series anomaly detection. Techniques such as Fourier Transform (FT) and Wavelet Transform (WT) have been employed for feature extraction, enhancing the model's capability to capture complex temporal patterns [13].

Beyond the automotive domain, research in Industrial Internet of Things (IIoT) and smart manufacturing has explored advanced techniques like Variational Autoencoders (VAEs) and Bayesian LSTMs to improve the robustness of anomaly detection systems [2,15]. However, most existing approaches rely on a single feature extraction method, often focusing solely on either time-domain or frequency-domain analysis (Fig. 1). This lack of comprehensive feature integration limits the overall detection performance, highlighting the need for more effective fusion strategies that can leverage both temporal and spectral information [4].

3 Main Contributions of This Paper

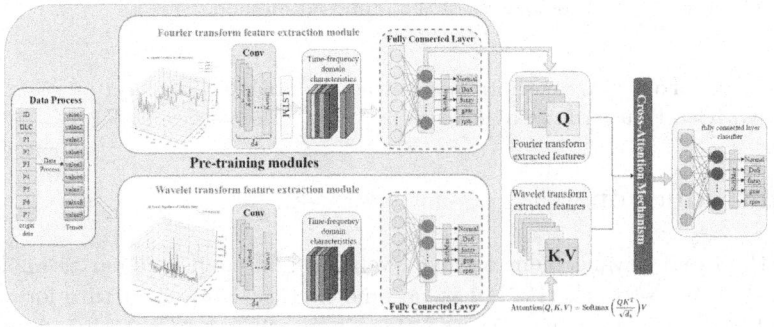

Fig. 1. FWTnet architecture.

CAN bus communication is a typical time-series signal, where certain attack patterns may exhibit periodic or specific frequency characteristics, such as replay attacks. The Fourier Transform effectively converts time-domain signals into the frequency domain, making these patterns more distinguishable. Therefore, we first apply the Fourier Transform to CAN message data, transforming the sequential data into frequency-domain features.

The approach proposed in this study is not only applicable to CAN bus intrusion detection but can also be extended to other time-series anomaly detection tasks, such as Industrial IoT [7], traffic flow prediction [3], and smart manufacturing systems [6].

The FWTnet consists of three main components:

Fourier-LSTM (FT-LSTM) Network: Captures global frequency-domain features for comprehensive signal analysis.

Wavelet-Fully Connected (WT-FC) Network: Extracts local time-domain features to preserve fine-grained temporal details.

Cross Neural Network (XNN) Fusion Module: Integrates both feature representations and conducts the final classification (Fig. 2).

3.1 Fourier-LSTM (FT-LSTM) Network

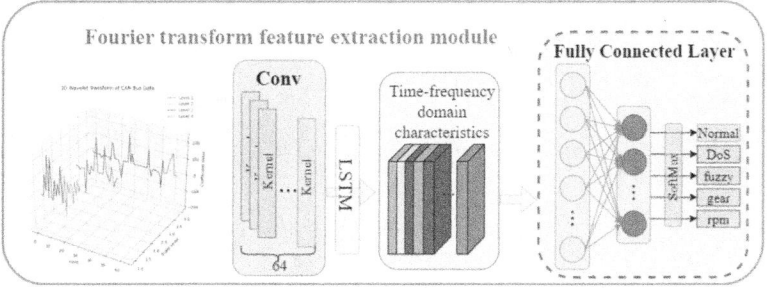

Fig. 2. Fourier-LSTM (FT-LSTM) Network.

Fourier Transform Layer. The data transformed by the Fourier Transform remains inherently sequential. Therefore, we employ a Long Short-Term Memory (LSTM) network to further model its temporal characteristics. Leveraging its gated mechanisms–namely the input gate, forget gate, and output gate–LSTM effectively captures temporal dependencies, enabling the model to learn how different frequency components in CAN messages evolve over time. The Fourier Transform is defined as follows:

$$X(f) = \sum_{n=0}^{N-1} x(n)e^{-j2\pi fn/N} \qquad (1)$$

where $x(n)$ represents the CAN message time-series data, and $X(f)$ is the transformed frequency-domain feature.

LSTM Temporal Modeling Layer. After processing with the LSTM, the output features are passed through a fully connected (FC) layer for dimensionality reduction, effectively condensing the extracted information into a compact global feature vector. This step not only reduces computational complexity but also helps retain the most relevant features, ensuring that critical patterns are preserved while removing redundant information. The refined feature representation serves as a foundation for subsequent feature fusion, facilitating more effective integration with other extracted features.

The FT-LSTM network plays a crucial role in capturing both the global characteristics of CAN message data in the frequency domain and its temporal dependencies through LSTM. By leveraging Fourier Transform, it highlights periodic patterns and frequency-specific anomalies, while the LSTM component learns the sequential evolution of these patterns over time. This dual modeling capability significantly enhances the detection of periodic anomalies, such as replay attacks and interference attacks occurring at specific intervals, improving the overall robustness of intrusion detection in CAN bus communication.

The LSTM equations are given as follows:

$$f_t = \sigma(W_f \cdot [h_{t-1}, x_t] + b_f) \tag{2}$$

$$i_t = \sigma(W_i \cdot [h_{t-1}, x_t] + b_i) \tag{3}$$

$$o_t = \sigma(W_o \cdot [h_{t-1}, x_t] + b_o) \tag{4}$$

$$c_t = f_t * c_{t-1} + i_t * \tanh(W_c \cdot [h_{t-1}, x_t] + b_c) \tag{5}$$

$$h_t = o_t * \tanh(c_t) \tag{6}$$

where x_t is the Fourier-transformed input feature, h_t is the hidden state, and c_t is the cell state.

Fully Connected Layer. After processing with the LSTM, the output features are passed through a fully connected (FC) layer for dimensionality reduction, generating a compact global feature vector that streamlines feature representation while preserving essential information for subsequent feature fusion. The FT-LSTM network effectively captures the global characteristics of CAN message data in the frequency domain and models its temporal dependencies through LSTM, enabling the detection of periodic anomalies such as replay attacks and interference attacks occurring at specific intervals. By leveraging this dual capability, the network enhances the robustness of CAN bus intrusion detection, ensuring more reliable identification of malicious activities in vehicular communication systems (Fig. 3).

3.2 Wavelet-Fully Connected (WT-FC) Network

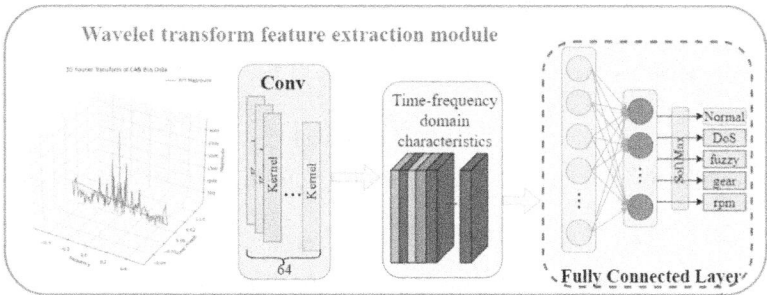

Fig. 3. Wavelet-Fully Connected (WT-FC) Network.

Wavelet Transform Layer. Although the Fourier Transform effectively captures global features, it has limited ability to detect short-term transient signals. In contrast, the Wavelet Transform (WT) provides a joint time-frequency analysis, offering high temporal resolution for high-frequency details while preserving frequency resolution for low-frequency components. This makes it particularly well-suited for capturing local features and sudden anomalies in CAN messages.

The Continuous Wavelet Transform (CWT) is defined as:

$$W(a,b) = \int_{-\infty}^{\infty} x(t)\psi_{a,b}^*(t)dt \qquad (7)$$

where $\psi_{a,b}^*(t)$ is the mother wavelet function with scale a and time shift b.

Fully Connected Layer. The wavelet-transformed features are passed through a fully connected layer to extract local time-domain representations.

3.3 Cross Neural Network (XNN) Fusion Module

After completing the pretraining of the FT-LSTM and WT-FC networks, we propose a Cross Neural Network (XNN) fusion module. The primary objective of this module is to effectively integrate the time-frequency features extracted by the Fourier Transform and Wavelet Transform, thereby enhancing the classification performance of CAN bus intrusion detection.

Different time-frequency analysis methods capture distinct aspects of the data: the Fourier Transform (FT) excels at extracting periodic information in the frequency domain, while the Wavelet Transform (WT) provides multi-scale local time-frequency features. Simply concatenating these two types of features may fail to fully exploit their inherent correlations. To address this, we design a

Cross-Attention mechanism that facilitates information exchange between the two feature representations, ultimately improving the model's discriminative ability.

Feature Concatenation. To integrate the information from FT-LSTM and WT-FC networks, we concatenate the extracted feature vectors:

$$F = [F_{FT}, F_{WT}] \tag{8}$$

where F_{FT} is the Fourier feature vector and F_{WT} is the Wavelet feature vector.

Cross Attention Mechanism. A Cross Attention mechanism is used to emphasize key information from both feature representations. The attention weights are computed as follows:

$$Q = W_q F_{FT}, \quad K = W_k F_{WT}, \quad V = W_v F_{WT} \tag{9}$$

$$A = \text{Softmax}\left(\frac{QK^T}{\sqrt{d_k}}\right) V \tag{10}$$

$$F_{fusion} = \text{ReLU}(W_f[A, F]) \tag{11}$$

Fully Connected Classification Layer. Finally, the fused feature vector is fed into a fully connected layer, and a softmax function is applied to obtain classification results:

$$y = \text{Softmax}(W_{out} F_{fusion} + b) \tag{12}$$

where y represents the final prediction (normal vs. attack).

3.4 Summary

The FWTnet framework seamlessly integrates global frequency-domain information (via Fourier Transform) with local time-domain details (via Wavelet Transform). By utilizing an LSTM network for temporal modeling and a Cross-Attention Mechanism for feature fusion, the model significantly enhances CAN bus intrusion detection, improving robustness against diverse attack scenarios.

4 Experiment

4.1 Evaluation Indicators

During training and testing, several performance metrics are monitored in real time, including accuracy, precision, recall, and F1 score. These metrics are used during the training process to evaluate the model's learning effectiveness and classification capability, while metrics on the test set are employed to assess the model's generalization performance (Fig. 4).

4.2 Training Process

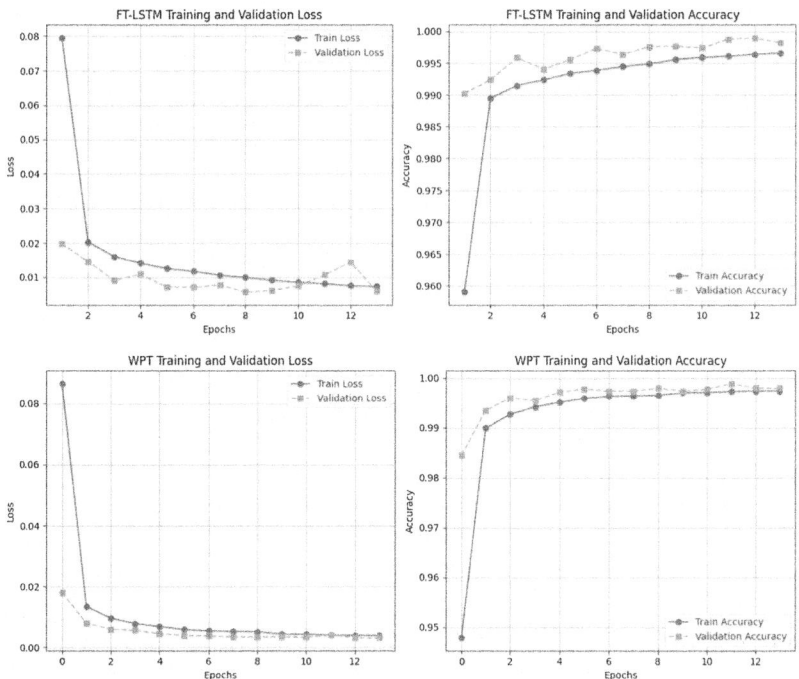

Fig. 4. Training Process.

In the early stage of training, the model converges rapidly, with training and validation accuracy increasing quickly, indicating that it learns effective features at an early phase. During the mid-stage, the loss continues to decrease, and both training and validation accuracy remain stable above 99.5%, demonstrating outstanding performance and strong generalization ability. In the final stage, the loss decreases further, and validation accuracy reaches approximately 99.89%. Overall, the training process is stable and efficient, with the model achieving an optimal classification performance (Fig. 5).

4.3 Ablation Experiment

In the ablation experiment, we compared the classification performance of FT+LSTM, WPT, and FWTnet.

Ablation experiments show that the full model (Fourier transform + wavelet transform + LSTM) achieves the best performance in CAN bus intrusion detection, with 99.98% accuracy and an F1-score of 99.93%, surpassing FT+LSTM and WPT models. FT+LSTM performs similarly (99.97% accuracy, 99.87%

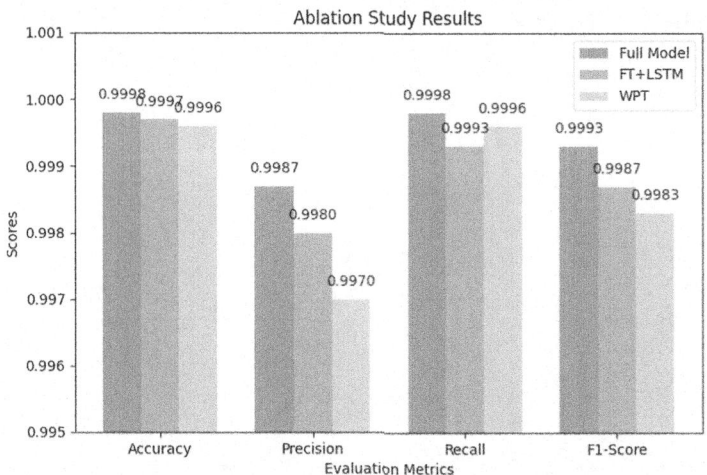

Fig. 5. Ablation Experiment.

F1-score), highlighting its strong temporal modeling. In contrast, WPT shows slightly weaker detection (99.96% accuracy, 99.83% F1-score) and struggles with DoS attack precision (98.55%), suggesting wavelet transform alone may not fully capture DoS features, leading to more false alarms.

All models achieve 100% precision and recall for Gear and RPM attacks, indicating clear distinguishing features. However, the full model excels in detecting Fuzzy and DoS attacks, confirming the benefits of combining multiple feature extraction methods. To balance performance and complexity, enhancing FT+LSTM with wavelet transform is recommended to improve detection across attack types while reducing false alarms, ensuring a robust and reliable CAN bus intrusion detection system.

4.4 Comparative Experiments

We compare with the model proposed in the following paper: [9] GIDS, [8] G-IDCS, [14] GNN, [1] Tree, [1] FFSEL, [10] DGIDS

FWTnet excels in comparative experiments, achieving top performance across key metrics such as accuracy, recall, precision, and F1-score. It reaches 100% accuracy in most test scenarios, with only one slightly lower at 99.99%. Similarly, its recall remains at 100% in almost all cases, with just one scenario at 99.97%, indicating an extremely low miss rate. FWTnet also outperforms models like Tree and FFSEL in precision, reaching 100% in multiple scenarios. Its F1-score, a balanced measure of precision and recall, is consistently superior to GNN and DGIDS. In contrast, other models show performance drops in certain scenarios, with Tree and FFSEL exhibiting weaker recall and precision, leading to higher false positives and false negatives.

FWTnet's exceptional performance stems from its robust feature extraction, strong generalization, and minimal error rates. By integrating Fourier transform with neural networks, it effectively captures the time-frequency features of CAN bus data, enhancing detection accuracy. Its near-perfect scores across various attack scenarios highlight its stability and adaptability. With nearly 100% precision and F1-score, FWTnet reliably differentiates normal and attack messages, minimizing false alarms and missed detections. Overall, it outperforms existing methods, making it ideal for high-precision, high-security industrial applications (Table 1).

Table 1. Compare FWTnet with other networks.

Metrics	IDS	dos	Fuzzy	RPM	Gear	Average
Accuracy(%)	GIDS	94.74	100	100	100	98.25
	G-IDCS	99.44	99.28	99.2	99.52	99.36
	GNN	100	98.14	97.91	97.91	98.68
	Tree	95.77	96.46	97.2	97.5	96.73
	FFSEL	99.01	97.57	99.22	99.12	98.73
	DGIDS	99.91	98.81	99.89	99.91	99.63
	FWTnet	**100**	99.99	**100**	**100**	**99.99**
Recall(%)	GIDS	99.12	**100**	100	100	99.71
	G-IDCS	98.86	99	98.69	99.08	98.91
	GNN	100	97.01	94.3	-	97.1
	Tree	97.64	88.76	90.93	97.77	93.78
	FFSEL	98.83	90.84	98.25	98.85	96.69
	DGIDS	99.91	98.5	100	100	99.6
	FWTnet	**100**	99.97	**100**	**100**	**99.99**
Precision(%)	GIDS	90.73	100	100	100	96.91
	G-IDCS	99.81	99.71	99.85	100	99.84
	GNN	**100**	97.56	96.1	96.1	97.89
	Tree	80.22	84.45	89.55	85.63	84.96
	FFSEL	98.19	90.28	96.38	94.86	94.93
	DGIDS	99.91	**100**	99.91	99.91	**99.93**
	FWTnet	99.36	99.98	**100**	**100**	99.84
F-score(%)	GIDS	94.74	**100**	100	100	98.25
	G-IDCS	99.33	99.54	99.27	99.54	99.42
	GNN	**100**	97.28	95.19	95.19	97.49
	Tree	88.08	86.55	90.23	91.3	89.04
	FFSEL	96.98	90.56	97.31	96.81	95.42
	DGIDS	99.24	99.91	99.87	99.95	99.74
	FWTnet	99.68	99.97	**100**	**100**	**99.91**

4.5 Robustness Test

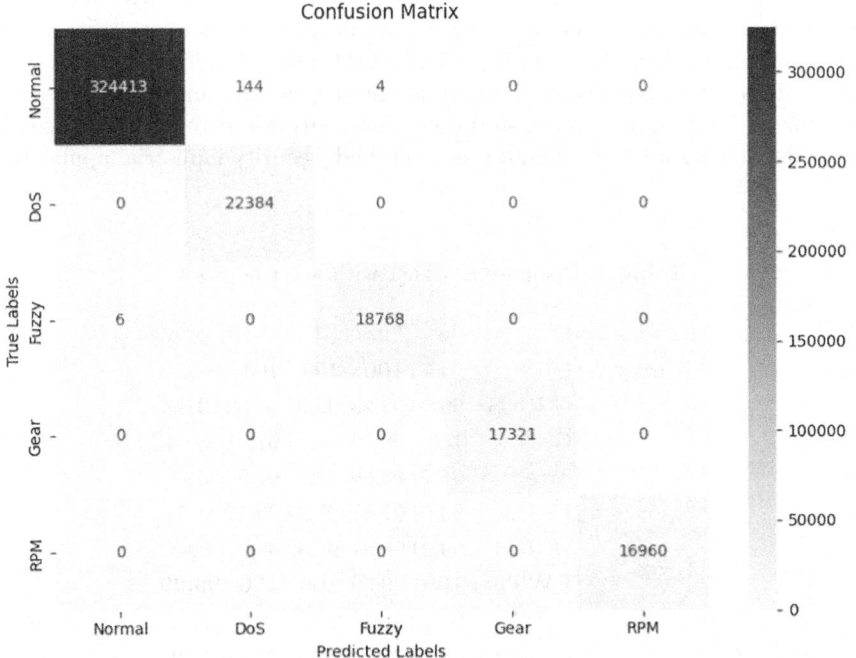

Fig. 6. Robustness Test on carHacking Dataset.

The proposed model achieves outstanding accuracy and robustness in CAN bus intrusion detection, with an average accuracy of 99.98% and an F1-score of 99.93%. It classifies Gear and RPM attacks with perfect accuracy and excels in Fuzzy and DoS detection, achieving F1-scores of 99.97% and 99.68%, respectively (Fig. 6).

However, a small number of normal messages were misclassified as DoS (144 cases, 0.04%) and Fuzzy (4 cases, ¡0.001%), slightly lowering the DoS precision to 99.36%. This suggests that DoS attack features may sometimes resemble normal messages, impacting false alarm rates.

Future improvements could focus on enhancing feature extraction, refining boundary samples, and adjusting loss function weights. Incorporating temporal features or Transformer-based attention may further reduce misclassification. Overall, the proposed model delivers near-perfect detection performance with strong practical value.

5 Conclusion

This paper presents a CAN bus intrusion detection method based on Fourier transform, wavelet transform, and cross neural networks. By pretraining two feature extraction networks and integrating their features for final classification, the proposed approach achieves high-accuracy differentiation between normal and attack messages. Experimental results show that our method achieves an average accuracy of 99.98% on the CAR-Hacking dataset and 99.99% on the CAN-FD dataset. Additionally, in cross-dataset testing, it attains an accuracy of 95.79%, demonstrating its effectiveness and generalization capability. Future work will focus on optimizing feature fusion strategies and exploring more time-frequency analysis methods to enhance detection performance against unknown attacks.

Acknowledgements. This work was supported by the Shandong Provincial Natural Science Foundation of China under Grant No. ZR2022MF353, the Horizontal Project under Grant No. kj2023hx(701101), the Horizontal Project under Grant No. kj2023hx(701102), and the Horizontal Project under Grant No. 2025kj70004.

References

1. Altalbe, A.: Enhanced intrusion detection in in-vehicle networks using advanced feature fusion and stacking-enriched learning. IEEE Access **12**, 2045–2056 (2023)
2. Cook, A.A., Mısırlı, G., Fan, Z.: Anomaly detection for IoT time-series data: a survey. IEEE Internet Things J. **7**(7), 6481–6494 (2019)
3. De, R., Chakraborty, A., Sarkar, R.: Document image binarization using dual discriminator generative adversarial networks. IEEE Signal Process. Lett. **27**, 1090–1094 (2020)
4. Hu, H., Li, Q., Zhao, Y., Zhang, Y.: Parallel deep learning algorithms with hybrid attention mechanism for image segmentation of lung tumors. IEEE Trans. Industr. Inf. **17**(4), 2880–2889 (2020)
5. Kong, F., Li, J., Jiang, B., Song, H.: Short-term traffic flow prediction in smart multimedia system for internet of vehicles based on deep belief network. Futur. Gener. Comput. Syst. **93**, 460–472 (2019)
6. Li, W., Fan, L., Wang, Z., Ma, C., Cui, X.: Tackling mode collapse in multi-generator GANs with orthogonal vectors. Pattern Recogn. **110**, 107646 (2021)
7. Mayer, J., Turner, R.: Third harmonic current in a generator neutral earthing resistor connected to a large cable network. IEEE Trans. Ind. Appl. **55**(1), 152–157 (2018)
8. Park, S.B., Jo, H.J., Lee, D.H.: G-IDCS: graph-based intrusion detection and classification system for can protocol. IEEE Access **11**, 39213–39227 (2023)
9. Seo, E., Song, H.M., Kim, H.K.: GIDS: GAN based intrusion detection system for in-vehicle network. In: 2018 16th Annual Conference on Privacy, Security and Trust (PST), pp. 1–6. IEEE (2018)
10. Song, J., Qin, G., Liang, Y., Yan, J., Sun, M.: DGIDS: dynamic graph-based intrusion detection system for can. Comput. Secur. **147**, 104076 (2024)
11. Thuy, H.T.T., Anh, D.T., Chau, V.T.N.: Efficient segmentation-based methods for anomaly detection in static and streaming time series under dynamic time warping. J. Intell. Info. Syst. **56**(1), 121–146 (2021)
12. Wang, W., Bao, J., Li, T.: Bound smoothing based time series anomaly detection using multiple similarity measures. J. Intell. Manuf. **32**, 1711–1727 (2021)

13. Wu, D., Jiang, Z., Xie, X., Wei, X., Yu, W., Li, R.: LSTM learning with Bayesian and gaussian processing for anomaly detection in industrial IoT. IEEE Trans. Industr. Inf. **16**(8), 5244–5253 (2019)
14. Zhang, H., Zeng, K., Lin, S.: Federated graph neural network for fast anomaly detection in controller area networks. IEEE Trans. Inf. Forensics Secur. **18**, 1566–1579 (2023)
15. Zhou, X., Hu, Y., Liang, W., Ma, J., Jin, Q.: Variational LSTM enhanced anomaly detection for industrial big data. IEEE Trans. Industr. Inf. **17**(5), 3469–3477 (2020)
16. Zhou, Y., Ren, H., Li, Z., Wu, N., Al-Ahmari, A.M.: Anomaly detection via a combination model in time series data. Appl. Intell. **51**(7), 4874–4887 (2021). https://doi.org/10.1007/s10489-020-02041-3

Research on Intelligent Classification Algorithm for Attack Detection Based on Pre-trained Fusion Network with Bimodal Features

Maoli Wang, Xiangsen Sun, and Weidong Guo(✉)

School of Cyberspace Security, Qufu Normal University, Qufu, Shandong, China
{wangml,sunxiangsen,gud2001}@qfnu.edu.cn

Abstract. With the rapid development of Internet of Vehicles (IoV) technology, the security of vehicle networks has become a critical concern. This paper presents a deep learning-based security protection model for IoV, aimed at efficiently detecting and mitigating network attacks. The model pretrains both the BiLSTM network and the CNN network, and then feeds the pretrained features into a cross-attention mechanism for multimodal feature fusion. This approach enhances the model's ability to recognize complex attack patterns. To evaluate the model's performance, we conducted experiments on the publicly available Car-Hacking and CAN-FD datasets. The results show that the model achieved 99.99% accuracy and 99.93% F1-score on the Car-Hacking dataset, and 99.99% accuracy and 99.98% F1-score on the CAN-FD dataset. Furthermore, when trained on the CAN-FD dataset and tested on the Car-Hacking dataset for Denial of Service (DoS) attacks, the model achieved 95.8% accuracy. These results demonstrate that the proposed BMF-Net model is highly effective at detecting various attack types in IoV, with strong generalization capabilities across different datasets, providing a robust solution for IoV security.

Keywords: Bidirectional LSTM · Cross-attention mechanism · Attack detection · Convolutional Neural Network · Multi-modal feature fusion

1 Introduction

1.1 Threats Faced

Data Tampering and False Information Propagation: In vehicular networks, [18]data transmission is essential for vehicle to vehicle and vehicle to infrastructure communication. [12,22]Attackers can disrupt this by tampering with data or spreading false information, such as forging traffic signals or sending incorrect road updates. This can lead to incorrect driving decisions, reducing traffic efficiency and increasing the risk of accidents.

Identity Spoofing and Man-in-the-Middle Attacks: [8] Identity authentication is critical for secure communication in vehicular networks. Attackers can spoof identities or conduct man-in-the-middle attacks, impersonating vehicles or infrastructure. For example, they could pose as roadside units (RSUs) to send malicious commands or steal vehicle identities, undermining trust in the network.

Denial of Service (DoS) Attacks: [1,23] DoS attacks overwhelm vehicles or infrastructure with excessive invalid requests, exhausting system resources and causing service disruptions. For example, attacking cloud servers in the network can prevent vehicles from accessing real-time road data or navigation information, crippling traffic systems and increasing the risk of accidents.

Privacy Breach and Data Tracking: [3,7] Vehicular networks generate sensitive data, including location and driving behavior. Attackers can exploit vulnerabilities to intercept communications and track vehicle movements. By analyzing vehicle trajectories, attackers can infer users' daily activities, compromising privacy and potentially enabling malicious acts like kidnapping or theft.

1.2 Relevant Theoretical Knowledge

The intrusion detection system is shown in Fig. 1. CAN bus intrusion detection involves the following steps:

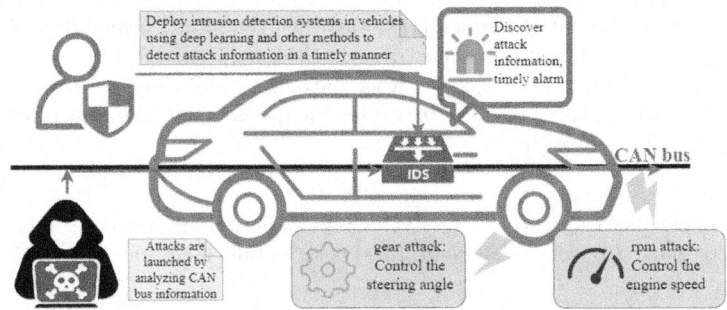

Fig. 1. CAN bus intrusion detection system.

Data Collection: Real-time data is gathered from the vehicle's CAN bus, connecting various ECUs. Data Analysis: The collected data is analyzed using deep learning or other algorithms to identify anomalies or attacks. Attack Detection: The system detects potential attacks, such as abnormal steering angles or engine speed changes. Timely Alert: Alerts are sent to the driver or safety personnel for immediate action upon detecting an attack. Continuous Monitoring: The system continuously monitors the CAN bus for new attack attempts.

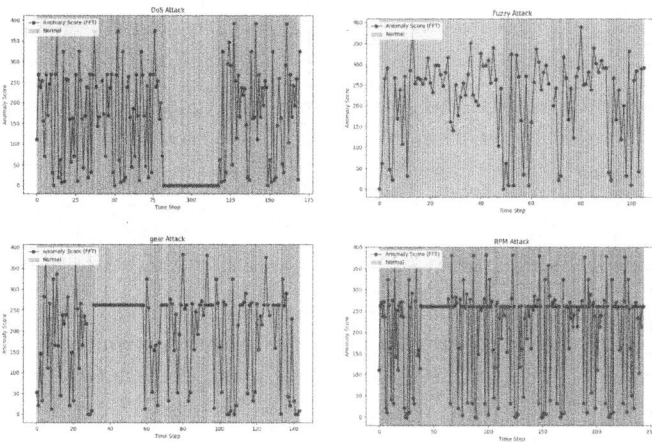

Fig. 2. Anomaly score curves based on FFT calculations.

We analysed a subset of the car hacking dataset to generate an anomaly score curve. The X-axis represents the sample index, and the Y-axis shows the anomaly score, calculated by averaging FFT magnitudes. The blue line indicates the anomaly scores, with red and green backgrounds marking attack and normal periods, respectively. As shown in the Fig. 2.

2 Related Work

With the rapid advancement of automotive intelligence and connectivity, the security of in-vehicle CAN bus networks has become an increasingly critical issue. As a result, intrusion detection technologies for CAN buses have become a focal point of research. Existing studies can be categorized as follows:

Traditional Machine Learning-Based Detection: Traditional machine learning methods focus on manually extracting features from CAN messages and using classification algorithms like Support Vector Machines (SVM), Decision Trees, and Random Forests. For example, Song et al. [20] proposed a time-series detection method based on CAN message intervals, while Müter et al. [14] used information entropy to detect anomalies. These methods are simple and easy to implement but are limited by their reliance on manual feature extraction, making them less effective against complex and evolving attacks.

Deep Learning-Based Detection: Deep learning methods, known for their powerful feature extraction and pattern recognition, have been widely applied in CAN bus intrusion detection. Kang et al. [10] first applied Deep Neural Networks (DNN) to this field, achieving high accuracy. Seo et al. [16] used Generative Adversarial Networks (GAN) to detect anomalies by generating normal message samples. These approaches can automatically learn message features and offer high detection performance but require large datasets and involve significant computational complexity.

Information Entropy-Based Detection: Information entropy methods quantify changes in the information content of CAN messages, enabling detection without predefined attack characteristics. Marchetti et al. [13] evaluated entropy-based anomaly detection in vehicular networks, and Wu et al. [26] highlighted its potential for detecting unknown attacks. However, these methods are sensitive to fluctuations in normal behavior, which can lead to higher false positive rates.

Physical Characteristics-Based Detection: Methods based on physical characteristics analyze CAN bus signals (e.g., waveforms and voltage) to detect intrusions. Cho et al. [5] proposed a method using ECU fingerprints to identify abnormal nodes, while Choi et al. [6] developed VoltageIDS to detect bus attacks through voltage signal analysis. These techniques can identify attacks that traditional methods may miss, but they require additional hardware, increasing costs.

Hybrid Detection Methods: Hybrid methods combine multiple approaches to enhance detection performance. Young et al. [27] proposed a hybrid method integrating message frequency features with vehicle driving mode data. While these methods improve accuracy and robustness, they are more complex and challenging to implement.

3 Main Contributions of This Paper

This paper addresses security challenges in the Internet of Vehicles (IoV) by proposing a deep learning-based multi-modal feature fusion model,As shown in the Fig. 3. Validated on publicly available datasets. The main contributions are as follows:

Dual-Stream Feature Extraction and Fusion Architecture: A dual-stream framework integrates a Bidirectional Long Short-Term Memory (BiLSTM) network for capturing temporal dependencies and a Convolutional Neural Network (CNN) for extracting spatial patterns and global context. A cross-attention mechanism fuses these features, enhancing the model's ability to recognize complex attack patterns, significantly improving detection performance.

Efficient IoV Attack Detection and Classification: Extensive experiments on the Car-Hacking and CAN-FD datasets demonstrate the model's exceptional performance, achieving 99.99% accuracy and 99.93% F1-score on Car-Hacking, and 99.99% accuracy and 99.98% F1-score on CAN-FD. Cross-dataset tests show the model's strong generalization ability, with a 95.8% accuracy in detecting Denial-of-Service (DoS) attacks.

Flexible Training and Evaluation Framework: A complete pipeline is implemented, including data loading, feature extraction, cross-attention fusion, loss computation, and model evaluation with accuracy, confusion matrix, and classification metrics, providing comprehensive experimental data.

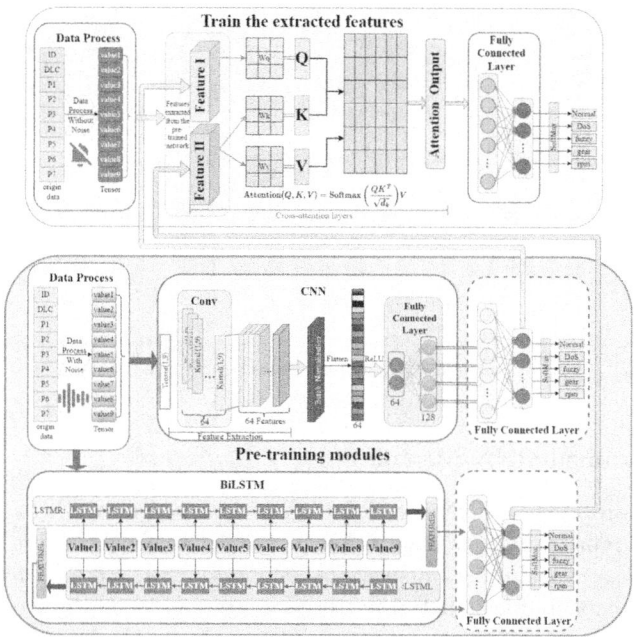

Fig. 3. Overall Model Architecture Diagram.

Practical Application in IoV Security: The model effectively detects various IoV attacks (e.g., DoS, fuzzy attacks) and demonstrates strong generalization across datasets. This work provides a robust deep learning solution for real-time IoV attack detection, offering significant practical value for IoV security.

3.1 Data Preprocessing Module

This paper presents an efficient data preprocessing module for deep learning models in the Internet of Vehicles (IoV), as shown in Fig. 4. It converts raw hexadecimal data into decimal vectors for simplified representation and feature extraction, while preserving numerical characteristics. Gaussian noise is added during pre-training to simulate real-world variations, improving model robustness and reducing overfitting. The module allows flexibility in enabling/disabling augmentation and adjusting noise intensity, ensuring optimal performance. Experimental results demonstrate its effectiveness in enhancing deep learning model performance for IoV security tasks, offering both theoretical and practical value for CAN bus data processing in real-world IoV environments.

Fig. 4. Data processing module.

3.2 Pre-trained CNN Module

This paper proposes a CNN-based feature extraction network to derive high-dimensional representations from CAN bus data, as shown in Fig. 5. The network combines convolutional operations, channel attention, and dimensionality reduction to capture local spatial patterns, outputting a 32-dimensional feature vector for input to a cross-attention module.

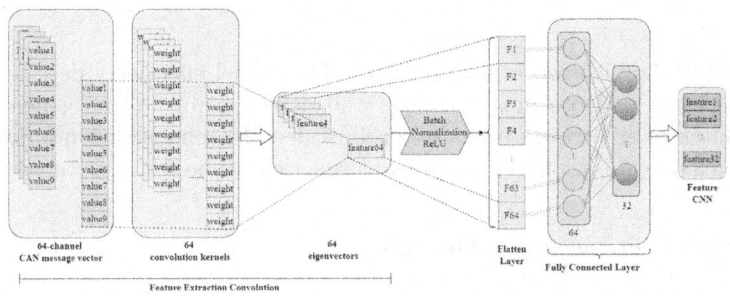

Fig. 5. Pre-trained CNN Module.

Network Architecture: The CNN feature extraction network includes convolutional layers, batch normalization, channel attention modules, and fully connected layers. Input data first undergoes convolutional feature extraction with a (1, 9) kernel, followed by batch normalization for faster convergence and stability. The channel attention module then adjusts channel weights using global average pooling and fully connected layers, emphasizing critical features. Finally, dimensionality is reduced from 64 to 32 through a fully connected layer, resulting in the final feature vector.

Feature Extraction and Output: During forward propagation, the input data is processed through convolutional and batch normalization layers to extract features. These features are weighted by the channel attention module, flattened, and passed through a fully connected layer, producing a 32-dimensional feature vector for further fusion and classification.

3.3 Pre-trained BiLSTM Module

This paper employs a BiLSTM-based feature extractor to capture temporal features from CAN bus data in the Internet of Vehicles (IoV). As shown in the Fig. 6. The network consists of a bidirectional LSTM layer and two fully connected layers. The bidirectional LSTM captures both forward and backward temporal dependencies, providing a comprehensive understanding of dynamic features. The output from the last time step is mapped to a 32-dimensional feature space via a fully connected layer, which is then fed into a cross-attention network. [19]

The BiLSTM [11]effectively captures long-term dependencies by utilizing both past and future context, making it ideal for time series data. By compressing the output into a 32-dimensional feature vector, redundant information is reduced while preserving key temporal features. This approach has been proven effective in time series classification and feature extraction. Using the 32-dimensional features as input to the cross-attention network further enhances multi-modal feature fusion, boosting the model's performance and expressiveness.

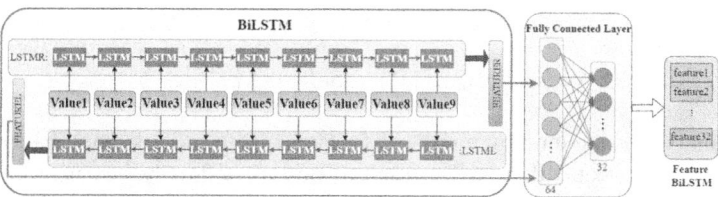

Fig. 6. Pre-trained BiLSTM Module.

3.4 Cross-Attention Fusion Module

The cross-attention [29] fusion module serves as the core component of the network,as shown in the Fig. 7, comprising a multi-head attention mechanism [24], layer normalization, a feedforward neural network, and an average pooling layer. Specifically, the module first reshapes the two input feature vectors (spatial feature and timing feature) into three-dimensional tensors suitable for the attention mechanism. [9] It then uses spatial feature as the Query (Q) and timing feature as the Key (K) and Value (V) to compute the interaction relationships between the features through the multi-head attention mechanism,calculated as (1). The attention output undergoes residual connections and layer normalization before being fed into a feedforward neural network for further feature

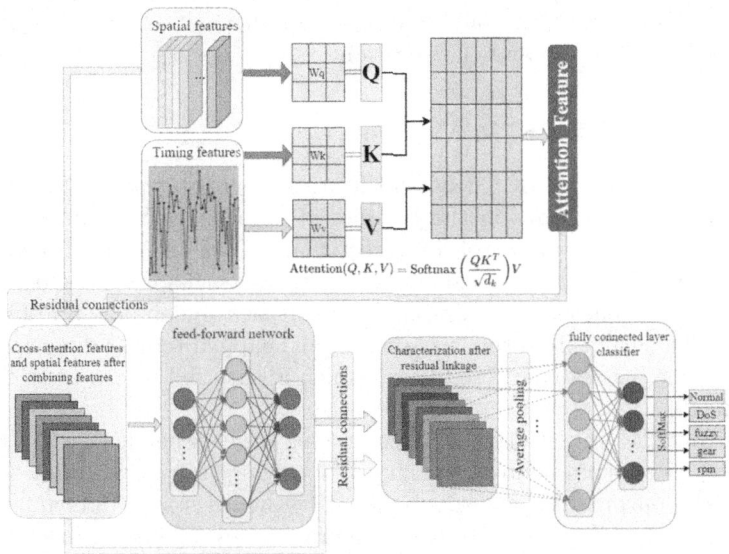

Fig. 7. Cross-Attention Fusion Module.

extraction. Finally, the features are compressed via an average pooling layer, producing a fused 32-dimensional feature vector [25].

$$\text{Attention}(Q, K, V) = \text{Softmax}\left(\frac{QK^T}{\sqrt{d_k}}\right) V \qquad (1)$$

In this paper, we employ a cross-attention fusion module to enhance feature interactions between different representations. Specifically, feature1 (extracted from the CNN-based feature extractor) is used as the query (Q), while feature2 (from the BiLSTM-based feature extractor) serves as both the key (K) and value (V). The attention mechanism is formulated as follows:

$$\text{Attention Output} = \text{Attention}(Q = \text{feature1}, K = \text{feature2}, V = \text{feature2}) \qquad (2)$$

The attention output is then added to the original feature1 through a residual connection, followed by layer normalization:

$$\text{Attn Output} = \text{LayerNorm}(\text{feature1} + \text{Attention Output}) \qquad (3)$$

To further refine the extracted features, we employ a feedforward neural network (FFN) consisting of two fully connected layers with a ReLU activation function:

$$\text{FFN}(x) = \text{ReLU}(xW_1 + b_1)W_2 + b_2 \qquad (4)$$

where W_1, W_2, b_1, b_2 are learnable parameters. The FFN output is then combined with the attention-enhanced feature using a residual connection, followed by another layer normalization step:

$$\text{FFN Output} = \text{LayerNorm}(\text{Attn Output} + \text{FFN Output}) \quad (5)$$

To maintain a compact and stable feature representation, we apply an adaptive average pooling operation:

$$\text{Pooled Output} = \text{AdaptiveAvgPool1d}(\text{FFN Output}) \quad (6)$$

Finally, the fused feature vector is fed into a fully connected classifier for attack classification. The classifier consists of two fully connected layers, with a ReLU activation function and a Dropout layer to prevent overfitting. The final output consists of logits corresponding to five different attack types in vehicular networks.

4 Experiment

4.1 Evaluation Indicators

During training and testing, several performance metrics are monitored in real time, including accuracy, precision, recall, and F1 score. These metrics are used during the training process to evaluate the model's learning effectiveness and classification capability, while metrics on the test set are employed to assess the model's generalization performance.

4.2 Training Process

Through experiments conducted on training batches, we have observed that the model demonstrates a higher accuracy rate when a smaller batch size is employed during the training process. As shown in the Fig. 8.

As shown in the Fig. 9, The CNN model demonstrated stable performance during training. The training loss rapidly decreased from 0.0866 to 0.0040, while the validation loss dropped from 0.0088 to 0.0028. After Epoch 6, both losses stabilized, indicating that the model had converged. The training accuracy improved from 94.39% to 99.69%, and the validation accuracy increased from 99.03% to 99.74%. Since these values are closely aligned, the model exhibits strong generalization ability. Overall, the CNN model performed exceptionally well on both the training and validation datasets, showing no significant overfitting and achieving high classification accuracy.

The BiLSTM model also performed well during training. The training loss decreased from 0.1300 to 0.0084, while the validation loss dropped from 0.0195 to 0.0057. The final training accuracy reached 99.32%, with a validation accuracy of 99.42%. Throughout the process, the model maintained stable training dynamics and achieved high accuracy on both datasets. Although minor fluctuations in validation loss were observed between Epochs 7 and 20, the overall trend remained downward, suggesting that the model had largely converged and demonstrated strong classification capability.

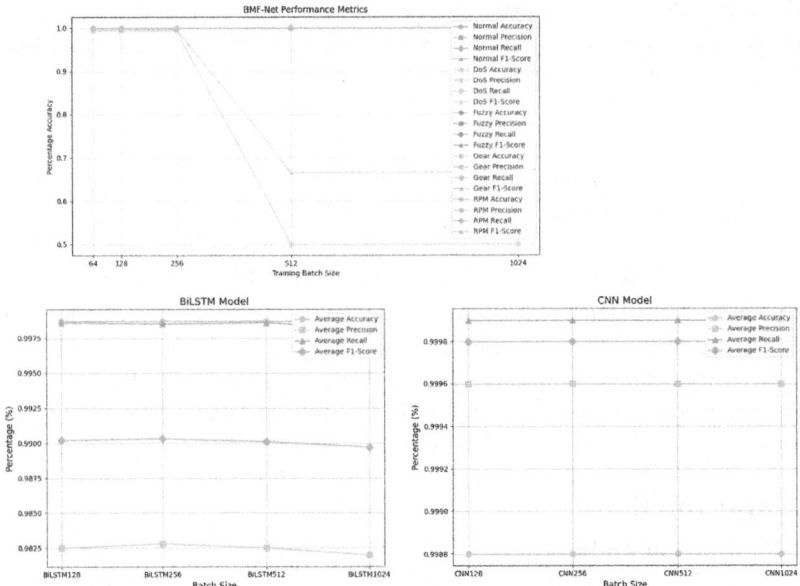

Fig. 8. Training Batches.

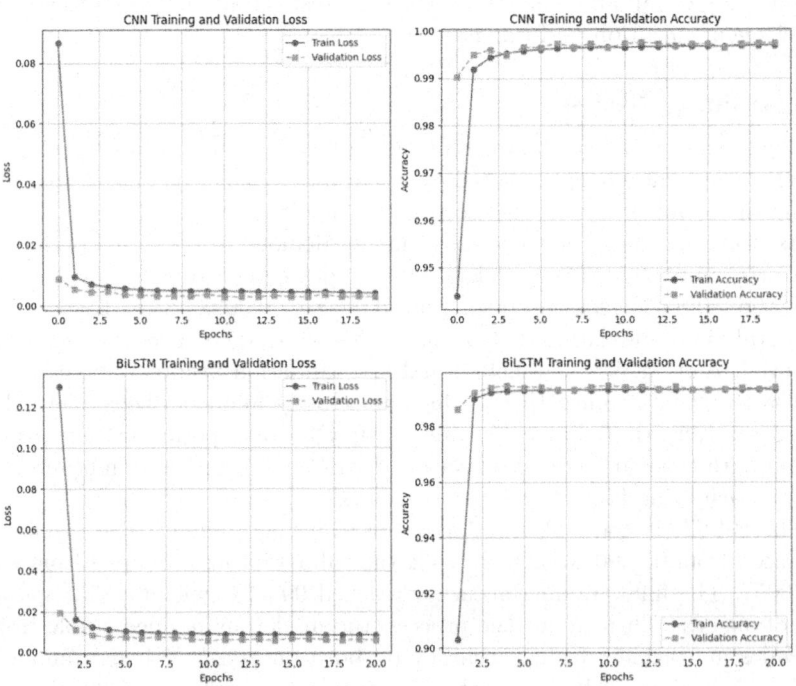

Fig. 9. Image of the training process.

4.3 Ablation Experiment

In the ablation experiment, we compared the classification performance of BiL-STM, CNN, and BMF-Net. As shown in the Fig. 10.

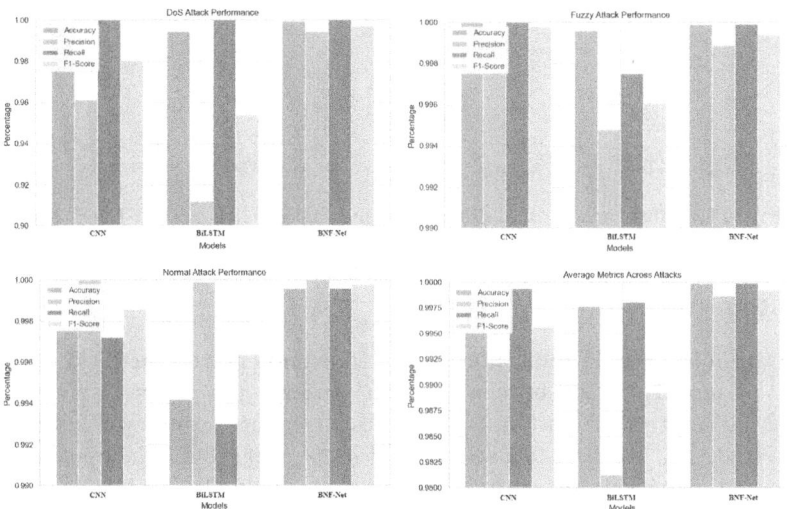

Fig. 10. Ablation Experiment

The ablation study results highlight BMFnet's superior performance over CNN and BiLSTM across all evaluation metrics and attack types. In the Normal and Fuzzy categories, all three models achieve high accuracy, with BMFnet slightly outperforming CNN and BiLSTM in Recall and F1-Score, ensuring a more precise classification. However, significant differences emerge in the DoS attack category, where CNN and BiLSTM struggle with lower Precision (0.9615 and 0.9120, respectively), leading to a higher false positive rate. In contrast, BMFnet achieves a remarkable improvement in DoS Precision (0.9945) and the highest F1-Score (0.9972), demonstrating its ability to accurately detect DoS attacks while minimizing misclassifications.

From an overall perspective, CNN performs well but shows slight weaknesses in distinguishing DoS attacks, whereas BiLSTM exhibits a more pronounced drop in Precision across multiple categories, particularly in DoS detection. BMFnet stands out with its exceptional generalization ability and robustness, consistently achieving the highest Precision, Recall, and F1-Score across all attack types. This indicates that BMFnet is not only more effective in differentiating normal and attack traffic but also more reliable in handling challenging attack scenarios, making it the most suitable model for CAN bus intrusion detection.

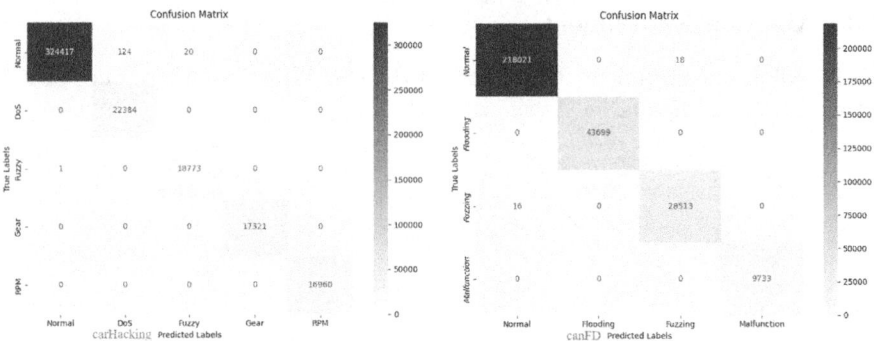

Fig. 11. Robustness Test. Left:carHacking Dataset Right:canFD Dataset.

4.4 Robustness Test

As shown in the Fig. 11,the confusion matrix results on the carHacking dataset show the model's excellent classification performance across all categories, demonstrating strong robustness. It achieves an average accuracy of 99.99%, precision of 99.87%, recall of 99.99%, and F1-score of 99.93%. The matrix reveals minimal misclassifications, with only a few normal samples misclassified as DoS or Fuzzy, and no cross-category errors, indicating the model's ability to clearly differentiate attack types. Even with data imbalance, classification accuracy for minority classes like DoS, Fuzzy, Gear, and RPM remains high, highlighting the model's good generalization. Precision for DoS attacks is slightly lower (99.45%), possibly due to some normal samples being misclassified as attacks, which could be improved by optimizing feature extraction or adding post-processing to reduce false positives. Overall, the model is highly reliable and stable, making it well-suited for real-world vehicular intrusion detection.

The test results on the CAN FD dataset demonstrate that the model exhibits outstanding robustness and accuracy in CAN bus intrusion detection. It achieves perfect recognition for Flooding and Malfunction attacks, with both Precision and Recall reaching 1.0, ensuring highly stable and precise detection of these attack types. For the Fuzzing category, only a small number of samples (16) were misclassified as Normal, while 18 Normal samples were mistakenly identified as Fuzzing, suggesting some feature similarities between these two categories. However, the overall misclassification rate remains extremely low, having little impact on the model's overall performance. Additionally, all categories maintain Precision and Recall values close to 1, with F1 scores nearing the maximum, demonstrating the model's strong ability to classify CAN bus data. These results confirm that the model can effectively distinguish between normal and attack messages, showcasing excellent robustness and generalization, making it highly applicable for real-world CAN FD network intrusion detection tasks (Table 1).

4.5 Comparative Experiments

We compare with the model proposed in the following paper: [17] GIDS, [15] G-IDCS, [28] GNN, [2] Tree, [2] FFSEL, [21] DGIDS.

Table 1. Compare BMF-Net with other networks.

Metrics	IDS	dos	Fuzzy	RPM	Gear	Average
Accuracy(%)	GIDS	94.74	100	100	100	98.25
	G-IDCS	99.44	99.28	99.2	99.52	99.36
	GNN	100	98.14	97.91	97.91	98.68
	Tree	95.77	96.46	97.2	97.5	96.73
	FFSEL	99.01	97.57	99.22	99.12	98.73
	DGIDS	99.91	98.81	99.89	99.91	99.63
	BMF-Net	99.97	99.99	100	100	**99.99**
Recall(%)	GIDS	99.12	100	100	100	99.71
	G-IDCS	98.86	99	98.69	99.08	98.91
	GNN	100	97.01	94.3	-	97.1
	Tree	97.64	88.76	90.93	97.77	93.78
	FFSEL	98.83	90.84	98.25	98.85	96.69
	DGIDS	99.91	98.5	100	100	99.6
	BMF-Net	100	100	100	100	**100**
Precision(%)	GIDS	90.73	100	100	100	96.91
	G-IDCS	99.81	99.71	99.85	100	99.84
	GNN	100	97.56	96.1	96.1	97.89
	Tree	80.22	84.45	89.55	85.63	84.96
	FFSEL	98.19	90.28	96.38	94.86	94.93
	DGIDS	99.91	100	99.91	99.91	**99.93**
	BMF-Net	99.45	99.89	100	100	99.84
F-score(%)	GIDS	94.74	100	100	100	98.25
	G-IDCS	99.33	99.54	99.27	99.54	99.42
	GNN	100	97.28	95.19	95.19	97.49
	Tree	88.08	86.55	90.23	91.3	89.04
	FFSEL	96.98	90.56	97.31	96.81	95.42
	DGIDS	99.24	99.91	99.87	99.95	99.74
	BMF-Net	99.72	99.94	100	100	**99.92**

The results show that BMF-Net outperforms all other models across all metrics. It achieves an average accuracy of 99.99%, surpassing DGIDS (99.63%) and G-IDCS (99.36%), with perfect accuracy (100%) in detecting RPM and

Gear-related anomalies. This highlights BMF-Net's superior ability to distinguish between normal and attack patterns.

In Recall, Precision, and F1-Score, BMF-Net achieves 100% Recall across all attack types, ensuring no threats are missed. While DGIDS performs well, BMF-Net excels with a higher F1-Score (99.92% vs. 99.74%) and competitive Precision (99.84%), minimizing false positives and negatives. In contrast, GNN and Tree models show weaknesses in DoS and RPM attack detection. These results confirm BMF-Net's superior reliability and effectiveness in CAN bus intrusion detection

4.6 Generalisation Test

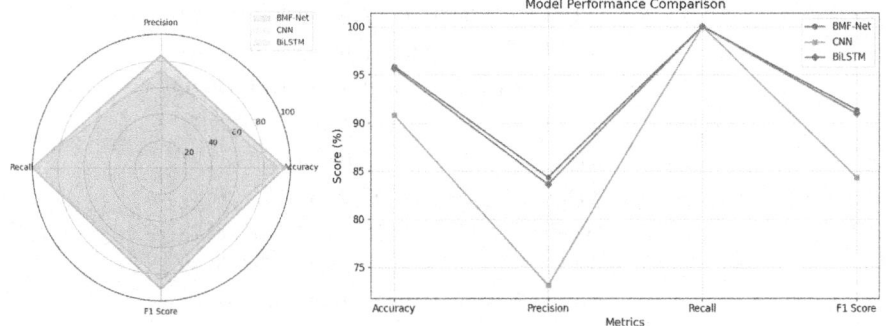

Fig. 12. Generalisation Test.

We train the model on the canFD dataset for DoS attack information and normal information, and test the model on the carHacking dataset. [4] As shown in the Fig. 12.BMF-Net achieves the best performance across all metrics, with an accuracy of 95.86%, precision of 84.32%, and F1 score of 91.28%, demonstrating the strongest overall performance. BiLSTM performs closely to BMF-Net, with an accuracy of 95.66% and an F1 score of 90.9%. In contrast, CNN shows relatively weaker results, with an accuracy of 90.8%, precision of just 73.1%, and an F1 score of 84.3%. All three models achieve 100% recall, demonstrating perfect identification of positive samples.

5 Conclusion

This paper introduces BMF-Net, a deep learning-based security protection model for vehicular networks, which integrates BiLSTM and CNN dual-stream feature extractors with a cross-attention mechanism to achieve multimodal feature fusion and enhance the recognition of complex attack patterns. Experimental results on the Car-Hacking and CAN-FD datasets demonstrate that the model achieves an accuracy and F1-score exceeding 99.9%, while cross-dataset testing for DoS attacks shows an accuracy of 95.8%, highlighting its strong generalization capability. Future work could enhance BMF-Net by improving adaptability to unseen attacks via self-supervised learning, optimizing computational efficiency for real-time use, and validating robustness across diverse datasets and real-world scenarios, advancing it toward a more scalable solution for vehicular security.

Acknowledgements. This work was supported by the Shandong Provincial Natural Science Foundation of China under Grant No. ZR2022MF353, the Horizontal Project under Grant No. kj2023hx(701101), the Horizontal Project under Grant No. kj2023hx(701102), and the Horizontal Project under Grant No. 2025kj70004.

References

1. Abu Talib, M., Abbas, S., Nasir, Q., Mowakeh, M.F.: Systematic literature review on internet-of-vehicles communication security. Int. J. Distrib. Sens. Netw. **14**(12), 1550147718815054 (2018)
2. Altalbe, A.: Enhanced intrusion detection in in-vehicle networks using advanced feature fusion and stacking-enriched learning. IEEE Access **12** (2023)
3. Bagga, P., Das, A.K., Wazid, M., Rodrigues, J.J., Park, Y.: Authentication protocols in internet of vehicles: taxonomy, analysis, and challenges. Ieee Access **8**, 54314–54344 (2020)
4. Cantone, M., Marrocco, C., Bria, A.: Machine learning in network intrusion detection: a cross-dataset generalization study. IEEE Access (2024)
5. Cho, K.T., Shin, K.G.: Fingerprinting electronic control units for vehicle intrusion detection. In: 25th USENIX Security Symposium (USENIX Security 16), pp. 911–927 (2016)
6. Choi, W., Joo, K., Jo, H.J., Park, M.C., Lee, D.H.: VoltageIDS: low-level communication characteristics for automotive intrusion detection system. IEEE Trans. Inf. Forensics Secur. **13**(8), 2114–2129 (2018)
7. Hasan, M., Mohan, S., Shimizu, T., Lu, H.: Securing vehicle-to-everything (V2X) communication platforms. IEEE Trans. Intell. Veh. **5**(4), 693–713 (2020)
8. Hildebrand, B., et al.: A comprehensive review on blockchains for internet of vehicles: challenges and directions. Comput .Sci. Rev. **48**, 100547 (2023)
9. Hou, R., Chang, H., Ma, B., Shan, S., Chen, X.: Cross attention network for few-shot classification. Adv. Neural Info. Process. Syst. **32** (2019)
10. Kang, M.J., Kang, J.W.: Intrusion detection system using deep neural network for in-vehicle network security. PLoS ONE **11**(6), e0155781 (2016)
11. Lu, W., Li, J., Wang, J., Qin, L.: A CNN-BiLSTM-AM method for stock price prediction. Neural Comput. Appl. **33**(10), 4741–4753 (2021)
12. Luo, F., Jiang, Y., Zhang, Z., Ren, Y., Hou, S.: Threat analysis and risk assessment for connected vehicles: a survey. Secur. Commun. Netw. **2021**(1), 1263820 (2021)
13. Marchetti, M., Stabili, D., Guido, A., Colajanni, M.: Evaluation of anomaly detection for in-vehicle networks through information-theoretic algorithms. In: 2016 IEEE 2nd International Forum on Research and Technologies for Society and Industry Leveraging a better tomorrow (RTSI), pp. 1–6. IEEE (2016)
14. Müter, M., Asaj, N.: Entropy-based anomaly detection for in-vehicle networks. In: 2011 IEEE Intelligent Vehicles Symposium (IV), pp. 1110–1115. IEEE (2011)

15. Park, S.B., Jo, H.J., Lee, D.H.: G-IDCS: graph-based intrusion detection and classification system for can protocol. IEEE Access **11**, 39213–39227 (2023)
16. Seo, E., Song, H.M., Kim, H.K.: GIDS: GAN based intrusion detection system for in-vehicle network. In: 2018 16th Annual Conference on Privacy, Security and Trust (PST), pp. 1–6. IEEE (2018)
17. Seo, E., Song, H.M., Kim, H.K.: GIDS: GAN based intrusion detection system for in-vehicle network. In: 2018 16th Annual Conference on Privacy, Security and Trust (PST), pp. 1–6. IEEE (2018)
18. Sharma, S., Kaushik, B.: A survey on internet of vehicles: applications, security issues & solutions. Veh. Commun. **20**, 100182 (2019)
19. Siami-Namini, S., Tavakoli, N., Namin, A.S.: The performance of LSTM and BiLSTM in forecasting time series. In: 2019 IEEE International Conference on Big Data (Big Data), pp. 3285–3292. IEEE (2019)
20. Song, H.M., Kim, H.R., Kim, H.K.: Intrusion detection system based on the analysis of time intervals of can messages for in-vehicle network. In: 2016 International Conference on Information Networking (ICOIN), pp. 63–68. IEEE (2016)
21. Song, J., Qin, G., Liang, Y., Yan, J., Sun, M.: DGIDS: dynamic graph-based intrusion detection system for can. Comput. Sec. **147**, 104076 (2024)
22. Sun, Y., et al.: Attacks and countermeasures in the internet of vehicles. Ann. Telecommun. **72**, 283–295 (2017)
23. Taslimasa, H., Dadkhah, S., Neto, E.C.P., Xiong, P., Ray, S., Ghorbani, A.A.: Security issues in internet of vehicles (IoV): a comprehensive survey. Internet Things **22**, 100809 (2023)
24. Vaswani, A.: Attention is all you need. Adv. Neural Info. Process. Syst. (2017)
25. Wang, J., Yu, L., Tian, S.: Cross-attention interaction learning network for multimodel image fusion via transformer. Eng. Appl. Artif. Intell. **139**, 109583 (2025)
26. Wu, W., et al.: A survey of intrusion detection for in-vehicle networks. IEEE Trans. Intell. Transp. Syst. **21**(3), 919–933 (2019)
27. Young, C., Olufowobi, H., Bloom, G., Zambreno, J.: Automotive intrusion detection based on constant can message frequencies across vehicle driving modes. In: Proceedings of the ACM Workshop on Automotive Cybersecurity, pp. 9–14 (2019)
28. Zhang, H., Zeng, K., Lin, S.: Federated graph neural network for fast anomaly detection in controller area networks. IEEE Trans. Inf. Forensics Secur. **18**, 1566–1579 (2023)
29. Zhang, J., Xie, Y., Ding, W., Wang, Z.: Cross on cross attention: deep fusion transformer for image captioning. IEEE Trans. Circuits Syst. Video Technol. **33**(8), 4257–4268 (2023)

Research on the Mechanism of Privacy-Enhanced Cross-Institutional Data Sharing

Xiaoliang Wang[1], Wei Xiao[1], Nan Liu[1], Kaile Xiao[2], Zhipeng Gao[3](✉), Yang Yang[3], and Yu Wang[1]

[1] TravelSky Technology Limited, Beijing, China
[2] Beijing Union University, Beijing, China
[3] Beijing University of Posts and Telecommunications, Beijing, China
gaozhipeng@bupt.edu.cn

Abstract. As the digital transformation continues to advance, cross-institutional data sharing has become a crucial means to enhance socio-economic efficiency. However, issues such as data privacy protection, data silos, and compliance severely constrain the practical application of data sharing. In response to this problem, this paper proposes a cross-institutional data sharing mechanism based on federated learning. This mechanism achieves distributed data training through a blockchain and federated learning framework, avoiding direct data transmission and centralized storage, thus enhancing model performance while ensuring data privacy. Additionally, this paper designs an optimized federated learning algorithm that dynamically adjusts weights based on data quality and computational capability, which has been experimentally verified. The experimental results indicate that the proposed mechanism performs well in terms of model convergence speed and accuracy.

Keywords: Data sharing · Federated learning · Privacy protection · Distributed architecture · Data quality

1 Introduction

With the rapid development of AI, data as a key production factor has gained prominence, but dispersed data storage leads to "data silos," hindering data value exploration and efficient development. Federated Learning (FL) [1] emerges as a distributed machine learning solution, distributing model training across participants who share only parameters, not raw data, to ensure privacy (Fig. 1). In FL, local data processing and edge network parameter exchange are aggregated by central entities. Though FL advances privacy protection, potential risks remain in data sharing. Previous studies incorporated privacy techniques like Homomorphic Encryption (HE) [2], Differential Privacy (DP) [3], and Secure Multi-Party Computation, but these face practical challenges: high computational overhead and costs, and difficulty balancing privacy with data utility, often sacrificing model performance for protection.

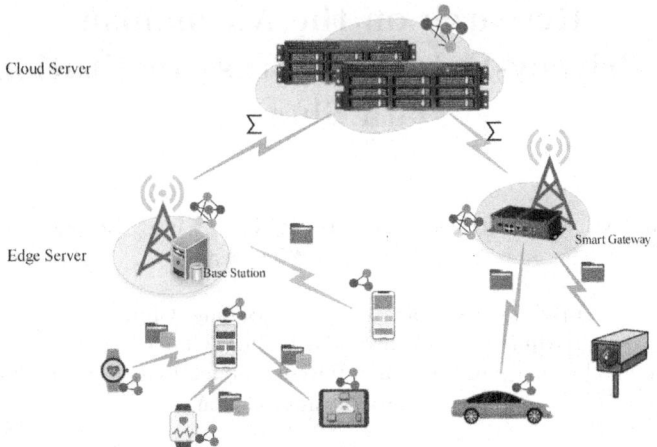

Fig. 1. The federated learning architecture diagram includes cloud servers, edge servers, and clients. Client devices are connected via base stations or gateways to enable data interaction and collaborative model training.

In response to the above problems, we propose a cross-institutional data sharing mechanism based on federated learning. This mechanism realizes efficient sharing of cross-institutional data and collaborative learning by optimizing the federated learning algorithm. Our contributions are mainly reflected in the following three aspects:

- A new federated learning framework supporting highly reliable cross-institutional data sharing is designed, incorporating blockchain technology as the foundational architecture. By leveraging blockchain's characteristics, it enhances system transparency and traceability, providing a transparent and auditable environment for data sharing. Meanwhile, smart contracts are employed to ensure automatic execution and immutability of data sharing algorithms, boosting system security and trust for cross-institutional collaboration.
- An optimized model aggregation algorithm is proposed, utilizing a joint scoring mechanism that integrates data quality and computing power to screen edge nodes. This mechanism accurately identifies nodes making substantial contributions to model optimization, enabling their greater role in aggregation to effectively accelerate convergence speed, improve accuracy, and enhance overall model performance.
- Rigorous experimental verification confirms the mechanism's effectiveness and advantages. Comprehensive tests demonstrate its feasibility in cross-institutional data sharing, validating its practical utility and performance benefits in real-world scenarios.

In Sect. 2, we detail the current research status of privacy issues in edge network data sharing, systematically reviewing existing achievements and challenges to lay a theoretical foundation. Section 3 introduces the novel federated learning framework, including design concepts, architectural composition, and core principles, with focus on the joint scoring mechanism and model aggregation process. Section 4 designs experiments for algorithm verification and performance evaluation. Section 5 summarizes the paper and provides outlooks on future research directions, proposing potential expansion paths.

2 Related Works

Regarding the privacy issues of data sharing in edge networks, numerous research works have been carried out for exploration, but each has its own limitations.

In terms of differential privacy calculation, some studies have conducted theoretical analyses. For example, Beimel et al. [9] theoretically discussed how to perform differential privacy calculations on single-instance operations in a federated environment, using secure function evaluation or local models with semi-trusted administrators. Narayan et al. [10] proposed a system for performing differential privacy database joins. This method combines private set intersection and random padding, but it cannot be universally applied to federated learning. The protocol proposed by Pettai et al. [11] is tailored for inner join tables and counting the number of values in arrays. In addition, Dwork et al. [12] proposed a distributed noise generation scheme, focusing on the methods of generating noise from different distributions. This scheme is based on secret sharing (an MPC mechanism), which requires a large amount of message exchange and has unfeasible communication overheads in many federated learning settings. Abadi et al. [4] and Jagannathan et al. [5] proposed a machine learning system with differential privacy. However, they did not consider the distributed data scenario, resulting in the system relying on a central entity. Shokri and Shmatikov [6] proposed a distributed learning system without a central trusted entity, but its differential privacy guarantee is only for each parameter. When facing models with a large number of parameters, the significance of this privacy guarantee is greatly reduced.

Some scholars have used cryptographic techniques to protect data privacy. Chase et al. [7] proposed a protocol for training neural networks in a private collaborative manner. This protocol combines multi-party computation (MPC), differential privacy, and secret sharing, but it is based on the premise assumption that honest parties do not collude. In contrast, our system can effectively prevent privacy leakage even if all parties actively collude. Lessage et al. [8] integrated fully homomorphic encryption with federated learning and expounded on the feasibility and challenges of integrating fully homomorphic encryption into the federated learning environment.

Overall, when the above algorithms are used to solve the privacy issues of data sharing in edge networks, they generally have limitations such as relying on central entities, insufficient privacy protection for complex models, and assuming that honest parties do not collude. These methods either have difficulty adapting to distributed data scenarios or sacrifice the utility of the model while ensuring privacy. In comparison, our algorithm is based on blockchain, achieving highly trustworthy collaboration for cross-institutional data sharing without the need for a central entity. The model aggregation algorithm optimized through the joint scoring mechanism of data quality and computational power can effectively screen edge nodes, improve the model convergence speed and accuracy, enhance the model performance while ensuring data privacy, and is not limited by the honesty of participants, providing a more practical and efficient solution for data sharing in federated learning.

3 System Design

3.1 System Architecture Design

The proposed federated learning architecture, as shown in Fig. 2, consists of client and server sides. The client obtains local data, cleans, encrypts, and extracts features for local model training, generating gradient information sent to the server via the blockchain architecture. The edge server parses encrypted data to get client gradients, dynamically assigns aggregation weights based on data quality and computing power to generate new global parameters, and sends them back. Clients then start the next training round. The server checks global model convergence after each round, reassigning tasks to available clients if any fail, ensuring smooth training. The blockchain-based architecture enforces strict access control, allowing only authorized participants in federated learning.

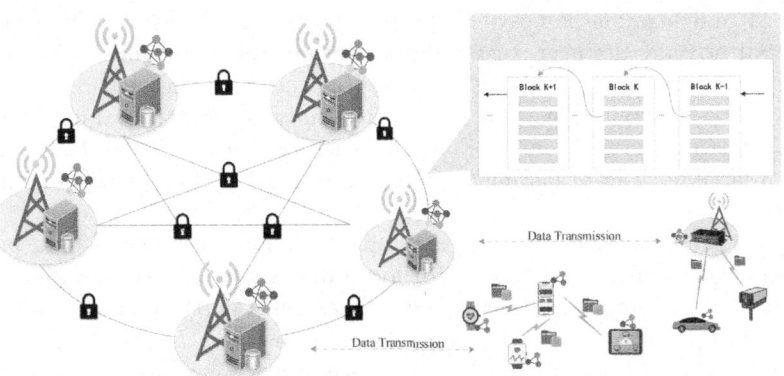

Fig. 2. The proposed privacy-enhanced federated learning architecture with the introduction of blockchain is composed of clients and edge servers.

In the data sharing stage, when an institution initiates a data sharing request, it screens edge nodes via the joint scoring mechanism (considering computing power and historical scores) in the blockchain to form a consensus committee, which drives the consensus protocol.

At the consensus process start, a leader node is elected by committee nodes through voting based on historical contributions and computing power. Let committee nodes be $\mathcal{C}$, with historical contribution $H(c)$ and computing power $C(c)$. The leader l is elected as $l = \arg\max_{c \in \mathcal{C}} f(H(c), C(c))$, where f is a linear weighted function $f(H(c), C(c)) = w_1 H(c) + w_2 C(c)$ ($w_1 + w_2 = 1$), reflecting the importance of each factor via weight adjustment.

The leader collects transactions (including the final data model) to form a block, broadcasting it to committee members for authentication. Committee nodes verify the block header, size, timestamp, and audit the model transaction trajectory. Once confirmed, the signed block is stored in the blockchain to ensure tamper-proofing. During data transmission, a hash value is generated and compared to verify integrity, preventing tampering or damage.

3.2 Algorithm Design

Firstly, we need to initialize the global model parameters and related configurations. The global model is a pre-defined neural network model, whose initial parameters θ_0 are obtained through random initialization or other pre-training methods. At the same time, basic parameters are set, including the learning rate η and the maximum number of iterations T.

Starting from the perspective of data source and quality, we ensure that each client's dataset has a sufficient number of samples and good data freshness. The data quality score reflects the quality and value of the data provided by the client, including the number of samples, data freshness, data diversity, and data accuracy. The calculation formula for the data quality score Q_i is:

$$Q_i = w_S \cdot \frac{S_i}{\sum_{j=1}^{N} S_j} + w_F \cdot F_i + w_D \cdot D_i + w_A \cdot A_i. \tag{1}$$

where: S_i is the number of samples for the ith client. F_i is the data freshness score for the ith client, with a range of $[0, 1]$. D_i is the data diversity score for the ith client, with a range of $[0, 1]$. A_i is the data accuracy score for the ith client, with a range of $[0, 1]$. w_S, w_F, w_D, w_A are the weight coefficients for the number of samples, data freshness, data diversity, and data accuracy, respectively, satisfying $w_S + w_F + w_D + w_A = 1$. The weight coefficients w_S, w_F, w_D, w_A can be determined through methods such as cross-validation or empirical values. For example, multiple experiments are conducted with different weight combinations, and the combination that optimizes the model performance is selected.

Next, consider the hardware configuration and network conditions of the client, including factors such as CPU performance, GPU performance, and network bandwidth. Dynamically allocate aggregation weights based on the data quality and computational capability of the client. The data quality score Q_i has been calculated through the aforementioned formula, while the computational capability score C_i is assessed based on hardware configuration (CPU/GPU performance) and network bandwidth. The formula for the computational capability score C_i is as follows:

$$C_i = w_{\text{cpu}} \cdot CPU_i + w_{\text{gpu}} \cdot GPU_i + w_{\text{net}} \cdot Net_i. \tag{2}$$

where CPU_i, GPU_i, and Net_i are normalized performance indicators (e.g., CPU/GPU benchmark scores divided by the maximum benchmark value, network bandwidth normalized to $[0,1]$). $w_{\text{cpu}}, w_{\text{gpu}}, w_{\text{net}}$ are weight coefficients determined via cross-validation (selecting the optimal combination through model performance tests).

The formula for calculating the dynamic weight $w_t(i)$ is:

$$w_t(i) = \frac{Q_i \cdot C_i}{\sum_{j=1}^{N} Q_j \cdot C_j}. \tag{3}$$

In this way, the weight of each client is no longer fixed but is dynamically adjusted based on their data quality and computational capability. Through this approach, the global loss function automatically considers the data quality and freshness of the clients. Clients with high data quality, good freshness, and strong computational capability will have a greater influence in model optimization. The Dynamic algorithm adjusts the learning rate η_t based on the convergence speed of the model and the performance of the clients. When the difference between the loss values of two adjacent iterations is greater than the preset threshold α, it is considered that the loss value decreases rapidly; when the difference between the loss values of two adjacent iterations is less than the preset threshold α, it is considered that the loss value decreases slowly. The difference between the current loss value L_t and the previous loss value L_{t-1} is calculated ΔL_t, $\Delta L_t = |L_t - L_{t-1}|$, the adjustment rule is as follows:

$$\eta_{t+1} = \begin{cases} \eta_t \cdot 1.1 & \text{if } \Delta L_t > \alpha \\ \eta_t \cdot 0.9 & \text{if } \Delta L_t < \alpha \end{cases} \tag{4}$$

where, α typically adopts empirical values or is determined by cross-validation, balancing convergence efficiency and stability to avoid excessive learning rate fluctuations. During the local training phase, each client trains based on the current global model parameters θ_t and calculates the gradients $\nabla \theta_t(i)$. To protect data privacy, Gaussian noise is added to the gradient information:

$$\nabla \theta_t(i) = \nabla \theta_t(i) + \mathcal{N}(0, \sigma^2). \tag{5}$$

where σ is the noise intensity parameter.

In the model aggregation phase, the server collects the gradient information uploaded by all clients and performs weighted aggregation of the gradients using dynamic weights $w_t(i)$:

$$\nabla \theta_t = \sum_{i=1}^{N} w_t(i) \nabla \theta_t(i) \tag{6}$$

Then, the global model parameters are updated:

$$\theta_{t+1} = \theta_t - \eta \cdot \nabla \theta_t. \tag{7}$$

To improve the stability and reliability of the system, we introduce a fault-tolerance and recovery mechanism. In the event of a client failure, the server redistributes tasks and adjusts weights. Specifically, the tasks of the failed client are reassigned to other available clients, and the dynamic weights are recalculated based on the data quality and computational capacity of the remaining clients. Additionally, asynchronous federated learning is supported, allowing clients to participate in training at different time points.

To enhance the flexibility and practicality of the system, asynchronous federated learning is supported. Clients can participate in training at different time points, and the server maintains a queue to store the gradient information uploaded by clients. When the number of gradients in the queue exceeds the threshold M, the aggregation frequency is increased; when the number of gradients in the queue is lower than the threshold N ($N < M$), the aggregation frequency is decreased. While maintaining the consistency of the global model, clients are allowed to make personalized adjustments based on their own needs. Personalized adjustments can be achieved by fine-tuning the global model:

$$\theta_{\text{personalized}} = \theta_{\text{global}} + \Delta\theta. \tag{8}$$

where $\Delta\theta$ is a small update calculated based on the client's local data.

At the end of each iteration, the convergence of the model is first checked. If $\Delta L_t < \epsilon$, the model is considered to have converged, and the iteration is stopped. If the model convergence criterion is not met, the exhaustion of computational resources is then checked. If the current number of iterations t exceeds the preset maximum number of iterations $T_{\max}$, the iteration is stopped. For auxiliary conditions such as the decline in data quality, abnormal client behavior, and the reduction of system stability, checks can be carried out at the end of each iteration, and the weights can be adjusted as needed. For the decline in data quality, the data quality score is recalculated regularly. When the score is lower than the threshold β, it is considered that the data quality has declined. For abnormal client behavior, indicators such as the client's training time and gradient changes are monitored. When the fluctuations of these indicators exceed the threshold γ, it is considered abnormal. When these situations occur, the dynamic weights of the corresponding clients are reduced proportionally according to the severity.

4 Experiment

4.1 Experimental Preparation and Parameter Setting

In the local training module, when feature extraction is performed, this scheme uniformly configures the local perturbation modules of all participants. For the MNIST dataset (with input image size of 28×28 and no padding in the pooling layer), the first convolutional layer uses 32 convolutional kernels, each of size 3×3, with a stride of 1. The second convolutional layer uses 64 convolutional kernels, each of size 3×3, with a stride of 1, and the activation function for both is the ReLU function. Following the convolutional layers, the output enters a max pooling layer with a window size of 2×2 and a stride of 2, resulting in a final tensor of size 12×12×64 after passing through the max pooling layer. Similarly, for the CIFAR-10 dataset (with input image size of 32×32×3 and no padding in the pooling layer), it goes through two convolutional layers consecutively. The first convolutional layer uses 32 convolutional kernels, each of size 3×3, with a stride of 1. The second convolutional layer uses 64 convolutional kernels, each of size 3×3, with a stride of 1, followed by a max pooling layer with a window size of 2×2 and a stride of 2. After passing through the max pooling layer, a final tensor of size 14×14×64 is obtained. For local model training, a Multilayer Perceptron (MLP) is chosen, which contains 2 hidden layers with 128 and 64 neurons respectively. The activation function for the hidden layers is the ReLU function, and the activation function for the output layer is the softmax function. In the FedShare algorithm, the dynamic weight update frequency is set to update the client weights every 10 iterations (Table 1).

The other experimental parameters are as follows in the table:

Table 1. Symbols and Instructions

Symbol	Value/Recommended Range
Q_i	Based on actual data distribution
C_i	Based on actual hardware resources
w_S, w_F, w_D, w_A	[0.4, 0.2, 0.2, 0.2]
$w_{CPU}, w_{GPU}, w_{Net}$	[0.3, 0.3, 0.2, 0.2]
S_i, F_i, D_i, A_i	Based on actual data distribution
CPU_i, GPU_i, Net_i	Based on actual hardware resources
η	0.07
T_{max}	200
σ	0.5
ϵ	$[10^{-4}, 10^{-3}]$

4.2 Comparison Experimental Design

To comprehensively and deeply evaluate the performance of the proposed FedShare algorithm, we carefully selected the reference algorithms for comparative experiments, namely the classical FedAvg algorithm [13] and the FedAdp algorithm(Federated Adaptive Parameters: This algorithm can adaptively adjust the weights according to the quality of the model) based on a dynamic weighting mechanism, to conduct a performance comparison analysis across multiple key dimensions.

Firstly, a comparison of model convergence speed is shown in Fig. 3a and Fig. 3b. FedAvg aggregates models by client data volume, letting the model learn

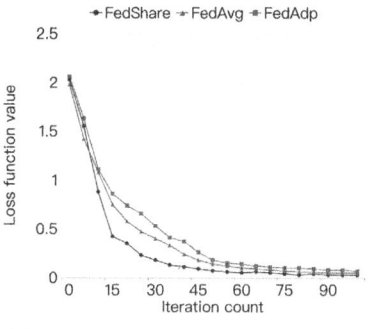
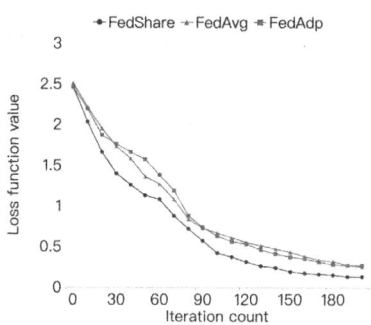

(a) Experimental results based on the MNIST dataset

(b) Experimental results based on the CIFAR - 10 dataset

Fig. 3. The experimental results of the convergence speed of the models.

general features early but ignoring data quality, causing a gradual loss decrease. FedAdp adjusts weights with various factors but underestimates data quality, showing a slightly slower initial loss drop than FedShare. FedShare, via data filtering, focuses on high-quality data early, enabling basic feature learning and a significant loss decrease. In Fig. 3b, FedAvg's data-volume aggregation limits key feature capture, with slow loss decline. FedAdp considers multiple factors but lacks sufficient data quality assessment under complexity, converging slower than FedShare. FedShare captures key image features early, with a significant loss drop that stabilizes and continues decreasing, demonstrating steady convergence.

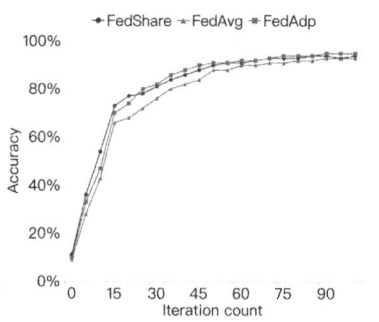
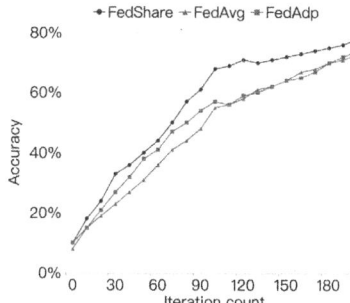

(a) Experimental results based on the MNIST dataset

(b) Experimental results based on the CIFAR - 10 dataset

Fig. 4. The experimental results of the model accuracy.

Next is the comparison of model accuracy, as shown in Fig. 4a and Fig. 4b. From Fig. 4a , it can be seen that on the MNIST dataset, as the number of iteration rounds increases, the model accuracy of all three algorithms improves. FedAvg, which aggregates based on data volume, shows a steady but slightly slower increase in accuracy. FedAdp, which adjusts weights based on multiple factors, has an accuracy improvement rate and final level that are between the other two. The model trained by the FedShare algorithm achieves a higher accuracy relatively quickly. In the early stages of iteration, it focuses on high-quality data through its filtering mechanism, learning features rapidly. Throughout the training process, its accuracy remains at a high level. From Fig. 4b , it can be observed that FedAvg, under complex data, has limited capability in capturing features, resulting in a slower improvement in accuracy. Although FedAdp considers multiple factors, it does not utilize data quality as effectively as FedShare, and its accuracy performance is slightly inferior. The FedShare algorithm still demonstrates certain advantages. It can grasp the key features of images in the early stage, leading to a rapid rise in accuracy. In the subsequent training, it also maintains a good level of accuracy. Overall, FedShare has certain advantages in improving model accuracy.

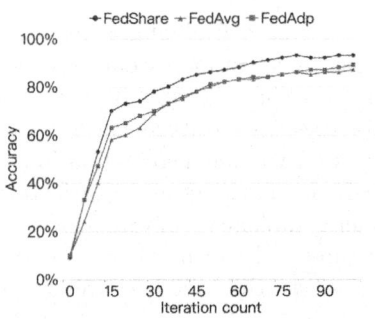
(a) Experimental results based on the MNIST dataset

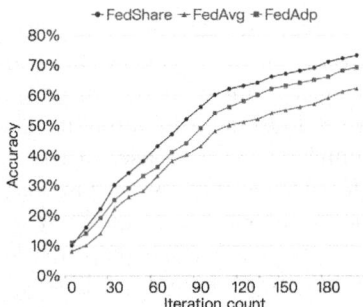
(b) Experimental results based on the CIFAR - 10 dataset

Fig. 5. The experimental results of the model accuracy.

Finally, considering that there may be interference from malicious users in real-world federated learning applications, we compared the performance of the three algorithms in an environment where malicious users are present, as shown in Fig. 5a and Fig. 5b . From Fig. 5a , it can be seen that on the MNIST dataset, when there are 5% malicious users, the FedShare algorithm can filter out relatively high-quality data with its own mechanism, allowing the model to still improve accuracy at a certain speed in the early stages of training. As the iterations proceed, the accuracy remains stable and high, and the convergence speed is also ideal. The FedAvg algorithm is significantly affected by malicious data, with a slow improvement in accuracy and large fluctuations. The FedAdp algorithm has a certain adjustment mechanism, but it is slightly inferior to FedShare in terms of resistance to interference, and its overall accuracy and convergence are not as good as FedShare. From Fig. 5b , it can be observed that the FedShare algorithm shows a certain resilience in this environment, being able to resist malicious data to some extent, with the model's accuracy gradually improving and remaining relatively stable. The FedAvg algorithm struggles to improve accuracy under the dual impact of complex data and malicious interference. Although the FedAdp algorithm considers multiple factors, it does not perform as well as FedShare in terms of anti-interference capabilities. Overall, the FedShare algorithm demonstrates better performance in a malicious environment.

In the experiment, we conducted an in-depth analysis and experimental evaluation of the FedShare algorithm and compared its performance with the FedAvg and FedAdp algorithms across multiple dimensions. The experimental results show that the FedShare algorithm has significant advantages in terms of model convergence speed, data selection mechanism, and capturing key features. Especially when dealing with the CIFAR-10 datasets, the FedShare algorithm is able to focus on high-quality data more quickly, thereby accelerating the model's convergence speed and improving learning efficiency. Moreover, the FedShare algorithm also demonstrates a more precise grasp of data quality when handling complex data, which further enhances the overall performance of the algorithm.

5 Conclusion

In the research on solving the privacy issues of data sharing in edge networks, we proposed the FedShare algorithm, providing a feasible solution for this field. This algorithm creatively integrates blockchain technology into the federated learning framework. By leveraging the unique properties of blockchain, such as decentralization, traceability, and tamper-proofing, it builds a solid security barrier for data sharing in edge networks, significantly reducing the risk of privacy leakage.

The federated learning framework we constructed establishes a crucial channel for cross-institutional data sharing, enabling different institutions to smoothly conduct data interactions within this framework. Through the implementation of strict permission management and verification mechanisms, this framework can create a highly trustworthy collaborative environment, effectively promoting cooperation among institutions. In addition, the FedShare algorithm introduces a joint scoring mechanism for data quality and computing power. This mechanism comprehensively evaluates edge nodes and screens out those nodes with high data quality, strong computing power, and a significant impact on model optimization. The participation of these high-quality nodes in model training effectively improves the convergence speed and accuracy of the model. The preliminary experimental results verify the effectiveness of the proposed mechanism and also demonstrate its advantages in practical applications.

Acknowledgments. This work is supported by the Beijing Natural Science Foundation (Grant No. L244010), the Major Research Plan of the National Natural Science Foundation of China (Grant No. 92467203), and the R&D Program of Beijing Municipal Education Commission (KM202311417003).

References

1. Bonawitz, K., et al.: Practical secure aggregation for privacy-preserving machine learning. In: Proceedings of the 2017 ACM SIGSAC Conference on Computer and Communications Security. ACM, 1175–1191 (2017)
2. Rivest, R.L., Adleman, L., Dertouzos, M.L.: On data banks and privacy homomorphisms. Found. Sec. Comput. **4**(11), 169–180 (1978)
3. Dwork, C.: Differential Privacy. In: Bugliesi, M., Preneel, B., Sassone, V., Wegener, I. (eds.) ICALP 2006. LNCS, vol. 4052, pp. 1–12. Springer, Heidelberg (2006). https://doi.org/10.1007/11787006_1
4. Abadi, M., et al.: Deep learning with differential privacy. In: Proceedings of the 2016 ACM SIGSAC Conference on Computer and Communications Security. ACM, pp. 308–318 (2016)
5. Jagannathan, G., Pillaipakkamnatt, K., Wright, R.N.: A practical differentially private random decision tree classifier. In: Data Mining Workshops, 2009. ICDMW'09. IEEE International Conference on. IEEE, pp. 114–121 (2009)
6. Shokri, R., Shmatikov, V.: Privacy - preserving deep learning. In: Proceedings of the 22nd ACM SIGSAC conference on computer and communications security. ACM, pp. 1310–1321 (2015)
7. Chase, M., Gilad-Bachrach, R., Laine, K., Lauter, K.E., Rindal, P.: Private collaborative neural network learning. IACR Cryptology ePrint Archive **2017**(762) (2017)
8. Lessage, X., Collier, L., Ouytsel, C.H.B.V., Legay, A., Mahmoudi, S., Massonet, P.: Secure federated learning applied to medical imaging with fully homomorphic encryption [C]. In: 2024 IEEE 3rd International Conference on AI in Cybersecurity (ICAIC). IEEE, pp. 1–12 (2024)
9. Beimel, A., Nissim, K., Omri, E.: Distributed private data analysis: simultaneously solving how and what. In: Wagner, D. (ed.) CRYPTO 2008. LNCS, vol. 5157, pp. 451–468. Springer, Heidelberg (2008). https://doi.org/10.1007/978-3-540-85174-5_25
10. Narayan, A., Haeberlen, A.: DJoin: differentially private join queries over distributed databases. In: OSDI, pp. 149–162 (2012)
11. Pettai, M., Laud, P.: Combining differential privacy and secure multiparty computation. In: Proceedings of the 31st Annual Computer Security Applications Conference. ACM, pp. 421–430 (2015)
12. Dwork, C., Kenthapadi, K., McSherry, F., Mironov, I., Naor, M.: Our data, ourselves: privacy via distributed noise generation. In: Annual International Conference on the Theory and Applications of Cryptographic Techniques. Springer, pp. 486–503 (2006)
13. McMahan, H.B., Moore, E., Ramage, D., Hampson, S., Agüera y Arcas, B.: Communication-efficient learning of deep networks from decentralized data. In: Proceedings of the 20th International Conference on Artificial Intelligence and Statistics (AISTATS), JMLR: W&CP, p. 54 (2017)

A Survey on Malware Analysis with Large Language Models

Wenjie Guo[1], Haoyuan Wen[1], Lingming Kong[1], Jingfeng Xue[1], Jingjing Hu[1], Weijie Han[2], and Yong Wang[1](✉)

[1] Beijing Institute of Technology, Beijing 100081, China
{wenjieguo,wenhaoyuan,6120220117,xuejf,hujingiing,wangyong}@bit.edu.cn
[2] Space Engineering University, Beijing 101416, China
sec_hwj2006@hgd.edu.cn

Abstract. With the rapid development of network technologies, the threat posed by malicious software has become increasingly complex and diverse, evolving from traditional viruses and worms to sophisticated ransomware, advanced persistent threats (APTs), and supply chain attacks. Traditional malware detection methods, such as signature-based detection and traditional machine learning techniques, face significant challenges in addressing the polymorphism and obfuscation of modern malware. Recent advances in generative artificial intelligence (GAI), particularly large language models (LLMs) like GPT-4 and CodeBERT, offer new opportunities for malware detection. GAI leverages self-supervised pretraining to understand code syntax and semantics, enabling automated feature extraction and high-level semantic pattern recognition from raw code. By analyzing the structure and behavior of malicious code, GAI can detect hidden threats, predict attack trends, and process complex multimodal data. This paper provides a comprehensive overview of the current challenges in malware detection, including issues with data imbalance, adversarial attacks, and the high cost of expert-labeled samples. It also explores how GAI-powered LLMs enhance static and dynamic analysis, enable multimodal detection, and improve explainability in malware analysis. By summarizing the contributions of GAI in this field, this paper highlights its transformative potential for malware detection methodologies and addresses future research directions.

Keywords: Large Language Model · Black-box Attack · Network Security · Generative AI · Malware Detection

1 Introduction

With the rapid advancement of network technologies, the threats posed by malware are becoming increasingly complex and diverse. Malware threats have evolved from traditional viruses and worms to highly sophisticated ransomware, Advanced Persistent Threats (APT), and supply chain attacks. According to

Symantec's 2023 report, over 450,000 new malware samples are generated globally every day, with more than 60% utilizing polymorphism or obfuscation techniques to evade detection. Traditional malware detection methods struggle to address the polymorphism and stealth of modern malware. Signature-based approaches, such as hash matching, are ineffective against novel variants, while machine learning methods (e.g., Support Vector Machines, Random Forest) rely heavily on manual feature engineering, making it difficult to capture the deep semantic relationships within code.

In recent years, the rapid development of natural language processing (NLP), especially the emergence of large language models (LLMs), has provided new perspectives and methodologies for malware detection. LLMs, such as GPT-4 and CodeBERT, leverage self-supervised pretraining to learn the syntactic structures and semantic logic of code, demonstrating strong contextual modeling capabilities in tasks like code completion and vulnerability detection. For instance, OpenAI's Codex model, pretrained on GitHub repositories, can understand cross-file code dependencies. This shift from "feature engineering" to "feature learning" enables the direct extraction of high-level semantic patterns from raw code, offering a novel approach to malware detection.

LLMs, with their exceptional capabilities in text comprehension and generation, have shown great potential in identifying malicious code hidden in text files, analyzing the structural and semantic properties of code to detect malicious intent, and processing large volumes of historical malware data to identify trends and predict future attacks. This paper focuses on two directions: enabling explainability with large models and enhancing malware detection with large models. Additionally, it summarizes the three main contributions of this work.

First, this paper explores the potential of enabling explainability through large models. Traditional malware detection methods lack good explainability, especially when dealing with complex polymorphic code or obfuscated malware, where researchers often struggle to accurately interpret the basis of a model's decisions. LLMs, through their natural language generation capabilities, can produce human-readable explanations to help security experts understand the detection process. For example, by analyzing the control flow graph (CFG) or abstract syntax tree (AST) of code, LLMs can identify possible anomalous structures in malicious code, such as recursive calls or complex branching logic. Moreover, by modeling API call sequences, large models can generate natural language descriptions of behavioral anomalies, improving the explainability of detection results. This explanatory capability not only aids in malware attribution and classification but also provides valuable insights for predicting attack trends.

Second, this paper delves into the key technical points and practical applications of enhancing malware detection with large models. LLMs, through self-attention mechanisms and large-scale pretraining, can capture the contextual semantics and deep behavioral patterns of code. In static analysis, LLM-based models (e.g., CodeBERT, Codex) can directly parse source code or binary code to extract high-level semantic information. In dynamic analysis, LLMs combined with sequence modeling (e.g., LSTM, GRU) can predict anomalous behavior from API call sequences. Furthermore, by integrating multimodal data (e.g., code text, control flow graphs, behavior logs), large models can achieve more comprehensive malware detection. For example, leveraging graph neural networks (GNNs) to process control flow graphs and combining them with LLMs to generate semantic embeddings of behavior logs can significantly improve detection accuracy and robustness.

Despite the widespread application of Generative AI (GAI), significant gaps remain in the study of large language models (LLMs) for malware detection within communication networks. As the application of LLMs in malware analysis and detection continues to deepen, these models have demonstrated immense potential in handling complex semantics, code polymorphism, and obfuscation techniques. However, research on using LLMs for malware detection lacks a comprehensive review and systematic classification framework, making it difficult to fully understand the current state, challenges, and threats to model robustness in this specific context. This research gap not only hinders the academic understanding of LLM security in malware detection scenarios, but also limits the industry's ability to develop targeted defense strategies for practical applications. To address this issue, this paper proposes a novel framework that provides a clear classification of existing methods based on attack vectors and characteristics, while also analyzing their application in real-world LLM-based malware detection scenarios. The primary contributions of this paper are as follows:

- **Systematic Classification and Analysis:** This paper systematically reviews and summarizes existing techniques for malware detection using LLMs.
- **Identification of Research Gaps:** Focusing on typical tasks in malware detection with LLMs (e.g., static analysis, dynamic behavior modeling, and multimodal integration), this paper analyzes threat patterns and impacts in different scenarios.
- **Guiding and Facilitating Future Research:** This paper examines the limitations of current defense techniques and proposes robustness optimization suggestions for LLMs in malware detection, providing research directions and practical guidance for academia and industry.

2 Preliminary

2.1 Malware Detection

The malware detection process can be divided into five key stages: sample collection, data preprocessing, feature representation, model training, and evaluation. As shown in Fig. 1, these stages constitute the basic malware detection flow chart, which is generally followed by machine learning-based and deep learning-based detection methods. However, due to the differing characteristics of these two detection models, there are certain differences in their specific implementations.

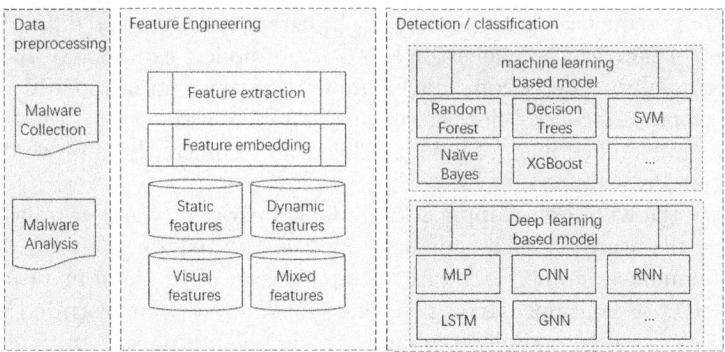

Fig. 1. Taxonomy of Malware Detection.

In machine learning-based malware detection methods, the entire process can be regarded as a feature engineering task, where the quality of feature engineering directly impacts the final detection performance. This approach relies heavily on expert knowledge, requiring domain experts to define and extract features of malware. Feature engineering typically includes several critical steps: feature definition, feature extraction, feature vector construction, and feature detection. Feature definition refers to explicitly describing the behavior patterns and characteristics of malware; feature extraction involves using techniques such as static or dynamic analysis to extract features with high discriminative power from code samples; feature vector construction translates the extracted features into numerical representations suitable for model training; and feature detection uses machine learning-based models to analyze and classify these feature vectors. Due to the complexity of feature engineering, machine learning-based methods have high requirements for data preprocessing and require significant expert intervention at every step of model development.

In contrast, deep learning-based malware detection models exhibit a prominent end-to-end characteristic, enabling the direct learning of high-level feature representations from raw data without the need for additional feature engineering. This approach significantly reduces reliance on expert knowledge, making malware detection more efficient in certain scenarios. However, deep learning models have some limitations in interpretability. Due to the complexity of their internal mechanisms, the detection logic of deep learning models is often difficult to understand directly, which can be a constraint in applications requiring high interpretability. Additionally, deep learning models are highly dependent on large-scale, high-quality training data, and insufficient data may lead to decreased model performance.

2.2 Malware Analysis

The malware detection methodology can be broadly categorized into three main types: static analysis, dynamic analysis, and visualization-based analysis. Static analysis relies on extracting static features from malware samples and uses techniques such as feature matching or pattern recognition to determine malicious behavior. This method is efficient, easy to automate, and does not require code execution, making it highly secure and widely applicable. As shown in Fig. 2, it serves as the foundation for many malware detection systems. However, static analysis faces significant challenges when dealing with malware that employs obfuscation techniques like packing. Additionally, transforming binary files into fixed-length vectors through feature engineering is key to using machine learning models for malware detection. Researchers have proposed handcrafted features based on manual analysis of malware and have also explored ways to improve the interpretability of detection models to help cybersecurity experts understand detection results and formulate defense strategies.

To address the limitations of static analysis, dynamic analysis methods have been developed. Dynamic analysis identifies malware by executing sample programs in a controlled sandbox environment and monitoring their runtime behavior. Compared to static analysis, dynamic analysis captures deeper behavioral characteristics of malware and demonstrates significant advantages in detection accuracy. It serves as an important complement to static analysis by addressing its inability to detect certain critical behaviors. However, dynamic analysis comes with drawbacks, such as lower execution efficiency and higher resource consumption, which limit its application in certain scenarios. Moreover, much attention has been given to leveraging dynamic analysis to improve the interpretability of detection results, particularly in assisting cybersecurity experts in formulating defense strategies.

Visualization-based analysis, as an emerging detection technique, transforms binary files of malware into visualized images and uses image texture features to identify malicious software. This method combines the strengths of static and dynamic analysis, as it eliminates the need for complex decompilation and avoids the resource overhead of dynamic execution. Although visualization-based analysis is still in its developmental stage, its unique advantages provide new perspectives and technical pathways for malware detection. By integrating with other analysis methods, visualization-based techniques have the potential to further enhance the performance and efficiency of malware detection.

2.3 Defender Targets

The defender's goal is to design robust mechanisms or strategies to ensure that the malware detection system can accurately identify malicious code samples (such as obfuscated or encrypted malware) even when facing adversarial inputs, while minimizing interference with the detection of benign samples. The defender's objective can be formalized as:

$$\max_{\theta} \mathcal{A}(D(M,x)) = |D(M,x) \cap Y_{\text{malicious}}| \,/\, |Y_{\text{malicious}}|, \tag{1}$$

where x represents the input sample set, M is the target detection model, $D(M,x)$ represents the detection results of the model on the inputs, and

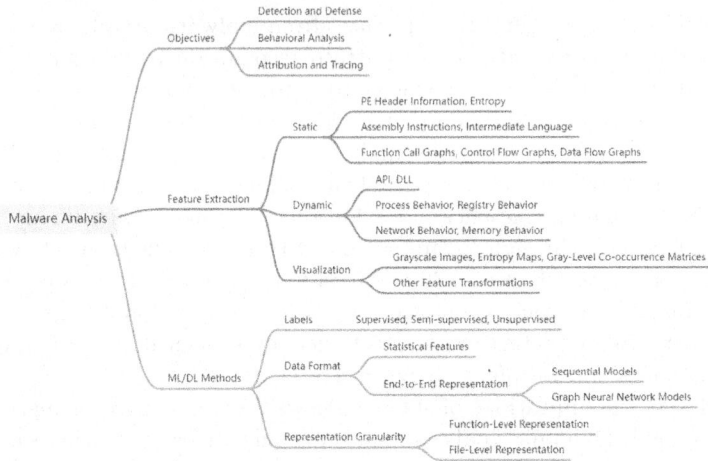

Fig. 2. Taxonomy of Malware Analysis.

$Y_{\text{malicious}}$ is the set of all malicious samples. The goal is to maximize the accuracy of detecting malicious samples.

At the same time, the detection system must maintain a low false positive rate for benign samples:

$$\mathcal{F}(D(M,x)) = |D(M,x) \cap Y_{\text{benign}}| \ / \ |Y_{\text{benign}}| \leq \delta \qquad (2)$$

where Y_{benign} is the set of all benign samples, and δ is a predefined threshold for tolerable false positive rates. The defense mechanism must enhance the ability to detect malicious code while reducing the probability of mislabeling benign samples.

3 LLM Enhance Semantic Mining and Representation

We categorize the roles of large models in the field of malicious code into two primary categories: enhancing the semantic representation of malicious code and empowering interpretability in malicious code detection. In the following sections, we will provide a concise overview of the main methodologies within each category, highlight representative studies from current research, and evaluate their respective strengths and limitations.

3.1 The Application of Large Language Models in Malicious Code Analysis and Detection

Research Progress of LLMs in Security Detection. Large language models (LLMs) are demonstrating tremendous potential in the fields of code analysis and malware detection. As malware becomes increasingly diverse and complex, traditional static analysis methods often struggle to cope with code obfuscation, encryption, and polymorphic variants. In contrast, LLMs can leverage semantic understanding and contextual reasoning to assist security researchers and automated tools in more effectively detecting anomalous behaviors and logical vulnerabilities. The following sections will describe the application of LLMs in phishing detection, smart contract security, and general malware detection from multiple perspectives, while also exploring their current shortcomings in interpretability and generalization.

Koide [5] proposed the ChatPhishDetector system, which leverages LLMs (e.g., ChatGPT) to identify phishing websites. This system integrates web crawlers and employs contextual prompting and analysis in multilingual environments to detect phishing behaviors based on LLM responses. Experimental results show that ChatPhishDetector outperforms other LLMs and existing systems in terms of accuracy and recall, highlighting the advanced capabilities and efficiency of large models in cybersecurity detection. The core idea lies in utilizing LLMs to semantically understand website content and identify suspicious features, such as brand spoofing and social engineering techniques, enabling precise detection of multilingual phishing websites. This research lays the foundation for subsequent applications of LLMs in general phishing and fraud detection.

Sun [7] introduced GPTScan, a tool that combines GPT with static analysis methods to detect logical vulnerabilities in smart contracts. Instead of fully relying on large-scale vulnerability rule libraries (LS vulnerability rules), GPTScan uses GPT as a general-purpose code comprehension tool: it decomposes specific types of vulnerabilities into scenarios and attributes, then matches and labels potential vulnerability candidates with GPT. To reduce false positive rates, GPTScan incorporates a static verification step to detect possible hallucinations or incorrect inferences by GPT. This approach partially overcomes the instability of GPT in handling complex logical scenarios, achieving sustained improvements in detection precision for high-risk contracts and large projects (e.g., Web3Bugs). Experimental results indicate that GPTScan achieves over 90% detection accuracy for token contracts and successfully uncovers vulnerabilities overlooked by human auditors across multiple projects.

Research Progress of LLMs in Malware Detection. Yan [8] introduced a dynamic malware analysis method assisted by GPT-4, which converts consecutive API call sequences into interpretive text for GPT-4. Representations are then generated with BERT and combined with CNN for feature extraction and detection. This method theoretically addresses the issue of unknown API representations, avoiding the need to collect all API information during the training phase. Cross-database experiments and few-shot learning tests on multiple datasets achieved nearly 100% malware recall rates, demonstrating excellent generalization performance and validating the feasibility and effectiveness of LLMs in dynamic analysis and API call sequence understanding.

In research combining static and dynamic analysis, DawnGNN [3] enhances API embeddings with contextual information from official Microsoft API documentation and uses Graph Attention Networks (GAT) for detection and classification, significantly improving accuracy. However, due to the use of embedding enhancements and complex graph network models, the internal decision-making process often resembles a black box, making it challenging to provide interpretable detection conclusions.

Mal-Bert-GCN [2] combines BERT with graph neural networks to construct directed process graphs representing API call sequences within processes, enabling more accurate semantic representation of malware behaviors. While this method excels in detecting malware, it still lacks support for semantic explanation and interpretive visualization of detection results.

In addition, methods combining BERT embeddings with GCN graph structure modeling are commonly applied in various malware scenarios. For instance, when constructing hierarchical graph models of "node-process-API calls," BERT provides richer semantic information, while graph networks capture the relationships within or across processes to uncover deeper suspicious behaviors.

3.2 Empowering Malware Detection Explainability

Malware Detection and Explainability. MalwareExpert [1] proposed a system that automates the identification and localization of critical functions in malicious binary files using graph neural networks, while also visualizing the relationships between relevant components to provide researchers with intuitive and interpretable analysis. Specifically, this approach first performs static parsing of executable files, uses graph neural networks to accurately locate suspicious or malicious functions, and then employs visualization techniques to intuitively display the associations between functions. In experiments, MalwareExpert achieved a detection accuracy of 97.3% and a recall rate of 96.5% on Windows executable files. When compared with manually generated malware analysis reports by experts, it demonstrated high consistency. While such graph-based models enhance the interpretability of the detection process, their complex structure increases the difficulty of understanding when applied to large-scale malware samples.

Yan [8] focused on the advantages of dynamic analysis in identifying packed, wrapped, or obfuscated malware and proposed a framework that utilizes GPT-4 to assist in analyzing API call sequences. This method first leverages GPT-4 to generate explanatory text for each API call, then converts the explanatory text into usable representations through a BERT model, and finally uses a CNN to extract features for classification. Since GPT-4 can generate explanatory text for unknown API calls, this approach effectively mitigates detection blind spots caused by "unknown APIs." Experimental results showed that, in cross-database and few-shot scenarios, the recall rate was nearly 100%, demonstrating excellent generalization performance.

APT Detection and Analysis. APT attacks (Advanced Persistent Threat) pose significant challenges to traditional detection methods due to their persistence and stealth. Extracting events and processing intelligence from APT reports has become a critical step in understanding the attack chain and conducting traceability analysis.

Zhou [10] proposed the APTBert model for APT report parsing, leveraging a pre-trained language model specific to APT contexts to improve the accuracy of APT event extraction. By pre-training on over 1,300 APT reports and annotating 600 reports with event roles, APTBert achieved outstanding performance in role recognition and extraction, with an F1 score of 77.4%. The study demonstrated that, compared to traditional methods such as BiLSTM, APTBert provides greater timeliness and accuracy in APT event detection and attribution, offering security personnel an essential tool for quickly acquiring intelligence on APT attacks.

Software Vulnerability Detection and LLM Assessment. In another critical area of software security–vulnerability detection and auditing–researchers have also explored the use of LLMs for assistance or integration. Yin [9] proposed a multitask evaluation framework leveraging the Big-Vul dataset. The framework includes four common tasks: vulnerability detection, vulnerability assessment, vulnerability localization, and vulnerability description. The results showed that while fine-tuned LLMs improved vulnerability detection accuracy to some extent (ranging from 68.5% to 78.3%), they still fell short of other advanced Transformer-based methods. In particular, LLMs exhibited limited performance in predicting the severity scores of certain CWE types, and their accuracy in vulnerability localization and description was constrained in few-shot scenarios. However, providing contextual information significantly enhanced the judgment capabilities of LLMs. This finding indicates that leveraging appropriate prompts and contextual information can improve the quality of vulnerability identification and explanation. It also underscores the importance of building higher-quality vulnerability corpora and developing larger-scale LLMs for further advancements in this field.

Deobfuscation and Adversarial Sample Research. For malware analysts, code obfuscation techniques (such as encrypted scripts, redundant instructions, etc.) often pose challenges to manual reverse engineering and automated detection. PATSAKIS [6] evaluated the capabilities of four mainstream LLMs in extracting threat intelligence (e.g., URLs and domain names) using real malicious scripts from the Emotet malware campaign. The results showed that LLMs achieved an accuracy of 69.56% in identifying URLs and 88.78% in identifying domain names, demonstrating a notable level of deobfuscation capability. It is worth noting that the study also observed a certain degree of "hallucination" in LLMs, where they generated invalid information unrelated to the actual scripts. Additionally, differences in the implementation and inference accuracy of different LLMs highlight the necessity of task-specific optimization and fine-tuning.

Fujii [4] conducted an in-depth study on the feasibility of using LLMs to support static analysis. The results indicated that LLMs could generate descriptions of function purposes and logic with relatively high accuracy (90.9%). However, practical application still requires consideration of professional analysts' needs for interpretability and precision. The study involved six static analysis professionals performing pseudo-static analysis tasks based on information provided by LLMs and found that the explanatory texts generated by LLMs had the potential to accelerate analysis. Nevertheless, limitations remain due to insufficient advanced semantics and domain-specific knowledge. To enhance practicality and interpretability, future efforts could focus on areas such as LLM information visualization, domain-specific fine-tuning, and collaborative analysis workflows.

4 Future Work

Large Language Models (LLMs) have demonstrated significant potential in the field of cybersecurity, particularly in tasks such as malware detection, APT attack analysis, vulnerability identification, and deobfuscation. By integrating advanced technologies such as graph neural networks, deep neural networks, and contrastive learning, LLMs have a notable advantage in automated analysis and enhancing interpretability. However, these models still face various challenges in practical applications that require further research and resolution.

4.1 Interpretability and Visualization

Although existing research, such as MalwareExpert [1], has proposed methods to enhance visualization capabilities, the intrinsic interpretability of models still falls short when dealing with larger-scale and more complex malware. The challenge lies in providing clear and credible explanations to security practitioners or auditors without sacrificing detection efficiency. Future research can explore multimodal learning methods, combining text, image, and code analysis, to improve interpretability and generate more intuitive explanation reports.

4.2 Model Generalization and Consistency

The issue of model generalization across databases and in few-shot learning environments indicates that LLMs may experience performance fluctuations due to changes in input formats or the introduction of unknown APIs. To enhance the stability and consistency of models, researchers need to continuously fine-tune LLMs, collect and integrate more industry and publicly available data. Additionally, adopting adaptive learning methods to address concept drift ensures that models remain efficient in new environments.

4.3 Hallucinations and Erroneous Inferences

LLMs are prone to hallucinations, i.e., incorrectly creating information or logic, when performing code reasoning and text generation. This is particularly critical in the security field, as erroneous information can lead to severe consequences. To suppress this phenomenon, external knowledge graphs can be introduced, strict verification mechanisms can be established, and effective feedback loops can be formed through the participation of experts, thereby improving the accuracy and reliability of models.

4.4 Domain-Specific LLMs and Adversarial Analysis

For LLMs targeting specific security tasks, such as APT intelligence analysis, malware deobfuscation, and vulnerability dataset analysis, domain-specific pre-training or fine-tuning is required to enhance their precision and explanatory power in particular domains. Meanwhile, with the evolution of adversarial techniques, researching the application of LLMs in reverse engineering and generating adversarial attacks has become increasingly important. This not only improves the robustness of models but also enhances their ability to respond to complex attack scenarios.

5 Conclusion

In conclusion, this paper has explored the transformative potential of Generative AI, particularly through the use of Large Language Models (LLMs) such as GPT-4 and CodeBERT, in the field of malware detection. By leveraging the advanced capabilities of LLMs in understanding and analyzing the syntax and semantics of code, we can enhance both the efficiency and accuracy of detecting complex and evolving malware threats. The integration of self-supervised learning models allows for a deeper comprehension of code structures and behaviors, enabling more effective identification of polymorphic and obfuscated malware. Furthermore, the ability of LLMs to generate readable explanations not only aids in improving the transparency of the detection process but also supports security experts in making informed decisions. However, despite these advancements, significant challenges remain, including the need for improved model generalization, the handling of adversarial attacks, and the continuous adaptation to new malware strategies. Future research should focus on refining these models to handle the dynamic and sophisticated nature of modern cyber threats more robustly, ensuring that they can operate effectively in diverse and changing technological landscapes. As we continue to innovate in the field of cybersecurity, the role of LLMs will undoubtedly become more critical in the development of intelligent and resilient malware detection systems.

Acknowledgments. This work was supported by the National Natural Science Foundation of China (No. 62172042).

References

1. Chen, Y.H., Lin, S.C., Huang, S.C., Lei, C.L., Huang, C.Y.: Guided malware sample analysis based on graph neural networks. IEEE Trans. Inf. Forensics Secur. **18**, 4128–4143 (2023). https://doi.org/10.1109/TIFS.2023.3283913

2. Ding, Z., Xu, H., Guo, Y., Yan, L., Cui, L., Hao, Z.: Mal-BERT-GCN: malware detection by combining BERT and GCN. In: 2022 IEEE International Conference on Trust, Security and Privacy in Computing and Communications (TrustCom), pp. 175–183. IEEE (2022)
3. Feng, P., et al.: DawnGNN: documentation augmented windows malware detection using graph neural network. Comput. Secur. 103788 (2024)
4. Fujii, S., Yamagishi, R.: Feasibility study for supporting static malware analysis using LLM. arXiv preprint arXiv:2411.14905 (2024)
5. Koide, T., Fukushi, N., Nakano, H., Chiba, D.: Detecting phishing sites using ChatGPT. arXiv preprint arXiv:2306.05816 (2023)
6. Patsakis, C., Casino, F., Lykousas, N.: Assessing LLMs in malicious code deobfuscation of real-world malware campaigns. Expert Syst. Appl. **256**, 124912 (2024)
7. Sun, Y., et al.: GPTScan: detecting logic vulnerabilities in smart contracts by combining GPT with program analysis. In: Proceedings of the IEEE/ACM 46th International Conference on Software Engineering, pp. 1–13 (2024)
8. Yan, P., Tan, S., Wang, M., Huang, J.: Prompt engineering-assisted malware dynamic analysis using GPT-4. arXiv preprint arXiv:2312.08317 (2023)
9. Yin, X., Ni, C., Wang, S.: Multitask-based evaluation of open-source LLM on software vulnerability. IEEE Trans. Software Eng. (2024)
10. Zhou, C., Huang, C., Wang, Y., Zuo, Z.: APTBert: abstract generation and event extraction from APT reports. In: International Conference on Digital Forensics and Cyber Crime, pp. 209–223. Springer (2023). https://doi.org/10.1007/978-3-031-56583-0_14

An Active Defense Scheme Integrating Traffic Anomaly Detection and Dynamic Key Update

Xinyi Luo[1], Jiayi Xu[1], Yifan Gao[1], and Yi Wu[2(✉)]

[1] Beijing Institute of Technology, Beijing, China
{1120222987,1120221285,120220159}@bit.edu.cn
[2] China Academy of Information and Communications Technology, Beijing, China
wuyi@caict.ac.cn

Abstract. With the rapid development of network technology, cyber threats have become increasingly sophisticated, posing significant risks to secure communications and privacy preservation. Under advanced persistent threats (APTs) and emerging quantum computing-based attacks, traditional passive defense mechanisms are often powerless in detecting and resisting attacks in real-time. To address these challenges, we propose an active defense scheme. It integrates traffic anomaly detection with dynamic key updates, enhancing network security while resisting quantum threats. Specifically, we use Convolutional Neural Network (CNN) to analyze real-time network traffic, identifying potential anomalies. If abnormal traffic is detected, the scheme will trigger the key update by using Kyber. The updated key is then utilized for subsequent network communication. We evaluate the proposed scheme on the UNSW_NB15 and NSL-KDD datasets. Experimental results demonstrate that the proposed scheme achieves a low detection latency and fast key update latency across different network conditions. Also, the system maintains a stable throughput and exhibits minimal CPU usage, ensuring robust network security without significantly compromising performance.

Keywords: Network Active Defense · Traffic Anomaly Detection · Dynamic Key Update · CNN · Kyber

1 Introduction

Modern networks face increasingly sophisticated Advanced Persistent Threats (APTs), particularly during network communications. It represents one of the

---

This work is supported by National Natural Science Foundation of China (Grant No. 62472032), Open Project Funding of Key Laboratory of Mobile Application Innovation and Governance Technology, the Ministry of Industry and Information Technology (Grant No. 2023IFS080601-K), and the Young Elite Scientists Sponsorship Program by CAST (Grant No. 2023QNRC001).

most severe cyber security risks today [18]. Traditional passive defense mechanisms, such as firewalls and Intrusion Detection Systems (IDS), rely on post-event responses, rendering them insufficient to counter dynamic and stealthy APTs.

Against this backdrop, network active defense has emerged as a key research focus. Passive defense relies on static rules. In contrast, active defense adopts dynamic strategies. These include proactive attack identification, threat prediction, real-time response, and adaptive defense optimization [10]. Active defense detects potential threats early, implementing preventive measures before attacks occur. This approach effectively counters APTs which minimizes losses and enhances system security.

Data encryption is essential in network communications. It safeguards data packets from interception and tampering. However, quantum computing technology is advancing rapidly. Traditional cryptographic algorithms and key encapsulation mechanisms are not safe any longer. Quantum attacks now threaten these systems [3]. This evolution introduces new risks to secure data transmission. Therefore, how to design a scheme that can detect potential attacks, have advanced defense capabilities, and remain secure under quantum computing attacks has become an important issue in current network security research.

Traffic anomaly detection has been extensively studied. Recent advancements in artificial intelligence have enabled widespread adoption of machine learning and deep learning techniques in this field [19]. These methods identify potential attacks by learning traffic features. Additionally, dynamic key update enhances security by triggering new key generation under specific conditions. Current key encapsulation mechanisms primarily depend on traditional cryptographic algorithms. These remain vulnerable to quantum computing attacks. However, existing research largely isolates traffic detection and key update processes. The synergistic effects of integrating these mechanisms for active network defense remain unexplored.

To secure network communications, this paper proposes a new active defense solution. It combines traffic detection and quantum-resistant dynamic key update. Our scheme uses a CNN-based anomaly detection model. It automatically responds when detecting abnormal traffic as a trigger for a key update process. The process employs Kyber, a quantum-safe encryption algorithm, to ensure that new keys are generated, encapsulated, and decapsulated securely. This prevents attackers from stealing keys for further attacks. Meanwhile, how to improve traffic detection efficiency and enable fast quantum-resistant key update emerged as critical issues in the system design. We have mainly made the following contributions.

- We innovatively combine traffic detection and dynamic key update to form a complete network active defense scheme. The scheme can not only detect abnormal traffic in real-time, but also trigger key update immediately after detecting abnormal traffic.

- We introduce the anti-quantum cryptography algorithm Kyber to ensure security under quantum computing attacks, providing quantum security for future network communications.
- Through experiments, we prove that this scheme is effective and efficient in network active defense.

2 Related Work

2.1 Anomaly Traffic Detection

Research on anomaly detection has a long history. It is categorized into three modes based on label availability: supervised, semi-supervised, and unsupervised [6]. Common techniques include statistical methods, classification, nearest-neighbor, clustering, and deep learning [9]. Early approaches focused on statistical methods. Kruegel et al. [14] proposed a Bayesian network-based intrusion detection scheme. It optimized Bayesian decision-making, significantly reducing false positives. Manikopoulos et al. [15] developed a hierarchical multi-window statistical anomaly detection system that combined statistical methods with neural networks. Wattenberg et al. [17] introduced a first-order model using unconstrained α-stable distributions and employed generalized likelihood ratio tests for classification. For machine learning, Gu et al. [12] applied K-Means to cluster sparsely labeled samples. They calculated data point densities within a specific radius to identify cluster centers. Anomalies were detected by measuring distances between data features and cluster centers. Moreover, deep learning now dominates due to its ability to handle large-scale, complex datasets, and to autonomously learn intricate features and relationships. CNN is widely used for malicious traffic detection. Cao et al. [8] innovatively combined CNN with gated recurrent unit (GRU). Zhang et al. [21] proposed a large-scale dataset imbalance processing technology called SGM. Combined with CNN, it can effectively alleviate the problem of category imbalance. Yu et al. [20] proposed a multi-scale anomaly detection system based on CNN, which achieved higher accuracy and lower detection error.

2.2 Anti-quantum Dynamic Key Update

Many classical cryptographic algorithms such as RSA and Diffie-Hellman are widely used to protect network communication security. However, with the emergence of quantum computers, these traditional methods are no longer secure. Therefore, the post quantum cryptography (PQC) has come into being. Quantum-secure key encapsulation mechanism (KEM) has the advantages of forward secrecy, post-quantum security, and simple key management. NIST began to standardize anti-quantum algorithms in 2017. The third round of algorithms released in July 2020 includes key encapsulation mechanism algorithms such as Classic McEliece, Crystals-Kyber, NTRU and Saber [2]. Post-quantum cryptography can be divided into four categories, which are lattice-based, code-based, hash-based, and multivariate-based [16]. Lattice-based cryptography was first proposed by Ajtai [1]. Crystals-Kyber is a lattice-based key exchange mechanism [7]. It is very efficient in computational performance and key size and is more practical than many other anti-quantum encryption schemes. Kyber's security is based on the difficult problems of lattice, especially the LWE problem and the Ring-LWE problem. They are regarded as important schemes in quantum secure communication, especially for protocols that require key exchange. NTRU is also a lattice-based key exchange mechanism. It was first proposed by Hoffstein et al. [13]. Compared with Kyber, it consumes more resources when generating keys, and is vulnerable to chosen ciphertext attacks. Ducas et al. [11] proposed NTRU Prime, which improves the security of the original NTRU scheme. For hash-based, Bernstein et al. [4] proposed SPHINCS. On this basis, SPHINCS+ introduces an adjustable hash value to hide the computational details of nodes [5]. Its signature size, speed, and security are better than SPHINCS.

3 Scheme Design

3.1 Framework

We design a network active defense scheme with abnormal traffic triggering dynamic anti-quantum key update. The scheme is mainly divided into two stages. First, the deep learning technology CNN is used to train the traffic anomaly detection model, capture real-time traffic, and perform anomaly detection. Then, when the anomaly is detected, a new key is generated through the key encapsulation mechanism that resists quantum attacks, and the key is updated to ensure the security of network communication. The framework is shown in Fig. 1.

3.2 Data Processing

Before training the traffic anomaly detection model with deep learning technology, the dataset needs to be processed first. The first step of data processing is data cleaning, removing missing values and infinity values. Next, in order to avoid the influence of the difference of different numerical scales, the data standardization operation is carried out to eliminate the influence of dimension. For numerical features, Min-Max is used for normalization, and the eigenvalues are scaled to [0,1]. For non-numeric features, Label Encoding is used for conversion.

In order to deal with the problem of category imbalance, the method of SMOTE and Class Weight is adopted. SMOTE is used to increase the number of minority samples by synthesizing new samples in the feature space for oversampling so that the proportion of positive and negative samples is more balanced. The formula of SMOTE is:

$$X_{new} = X_i + \alpha \cdot (X_{Zi} - X_i) \qquad (1)$$

Among them, X_i is a minority class sample, and the k samples closest to X_i are found in the minority class sample. Randomly take one as X_{Zi}, α is a random number between 0 and 1.

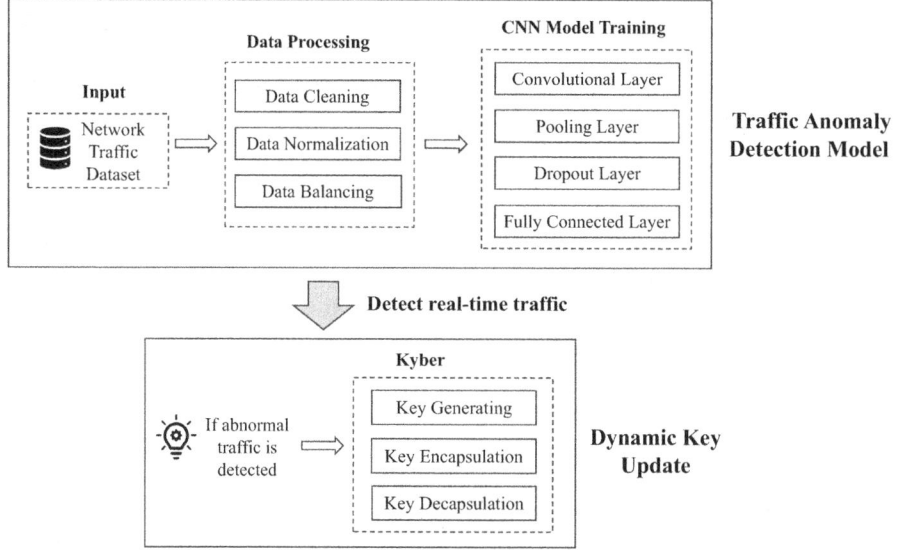

Fig. 1. Scheme Framework.

Category weights are used to adjust the loss function. The misclassification of minority class samples has a greater impact on the model loss function, thus reducing the bias of the model to the majority class. The calculation formula for category weight is as follows:

$$w_c = \frac{N}{M \cdot N_C} \qquad (2)$$

Among them, N is the total number of samples in the dataset, and M is the total number of categories, N_C is the total number of samples in this category.

In the feature selection stage, considering that the scheme has high real-time requirements, the features that require complex analysis are removed. The final selected features of the UNSW_NB15 dataset are: id, dur, proto, service, state, spkts, dpkts, sbytes, dbytes, rate, sttl, dttl, sload, dload, sinpkt, dinpkt, sjit, djit, swin, stcpb, dtcpb, dwin, synack, ackdat, smean, dmean, response_body_len, ct_srv_src, ct_state_ttl, ct_dst_ltm, ct_src_dport_ltm, ct_dst_sport_ltm, ct_dst_src_ltm, is_ftp_login, ct_ftp_cmd, ct_flw_http_mthd, ct_src_ltm, ct_srv_dst, is_sm_ips_ports.

The features of NSL-KDD dataset selection are as follows: duration, protocol_type, service, flag, src_bytes, dst_bytes, land, wrong_fragment, urgent, count, srv_count, serror_rate, srv_serror_rate, rerror_rate, srv_rerror_rate, same_srv_rate, diff_srv_rate, srv_diff_host_rate, dst_host_count, dst_host _srv_count, dst_host _same _srv _rate, dst_host_diff_srv_rate, dst_host _same_src_port_rate, dst_host_srv_diff_host_rate, dst_host_serror_rate, dst_host_srv_serror_rate, dst_host_rerror_rate, dst_host_srv_rerror_rate.

Finally, adjust the format of the data and input it correctly into the CNN model for training.

3.3 Traffic Anomaly Detection Model Training

In this paper, the traffic anomaly detection model is trained based on CNN. As a deep learning model, CNN performs well in image processing and sequence data analysis. It is especially suitable for capturing local features in data and has been widely used in various classification tasks. Its network architecture consists of multiple layers, including convolutional layer, pooling layer, Dropout layer, fully connected layer, and output layer. It can effectively extract traffic features and classify them in traffic anomaly detection tasks, as shown in Fig. 2.

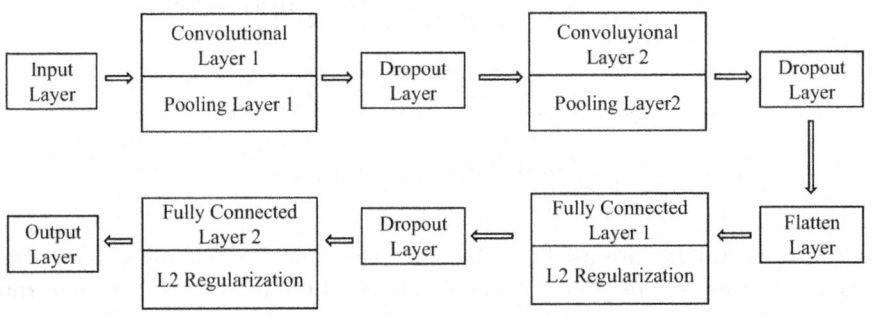

Fig. 2. CNN Model Training Process.

The first step is to pass the selected features as the input layer. Then pass them to the first convolutional layer. The convolutional layer extracts local features by sliding the convolutional kernel. The convolutional kernel parameters are adjusted according to the experimental requirements to optimize the feature extraction.

After the first convolutional layer, the pooling layer is added. The maximum pooling dimension reduction is used to retain significant features and improve efficiency. Then, the second set of convolution-pooling layers is superimposed, and complex features are extracted through deep convolution to further suppress overfitting.

After the pooling layer is connected to the Dropout layer, some neurons are randomly discarded to enhance the generalization ability. The subsequent flatten layer converts the multi-dimensional features into one-dimensional vectors and inputs them into the fully connected layer. The fully connected layer maps high-order features through weighted summation and activation function. Then introduce L2 regularization to control complexity and reduce the occurrence of overfitting.

Through the above level of processing, the model can effectively extract key features from network traffic and accurately detect abnormal traffic in the network. By capturing traffic data in real-time and performing anomaly detection, the scheme can respond to potential threats in time and trigger key update to improve network security.

3.4 Anti-quantum Key Update

Key update is one of the core links to ensure the security of network communication. In order to deal with quantum attacks, this paper uses the anti-quantum algorithm Kyber to update the key. Kyber is a lattice-based cryptographic algorithm, which belongs to one of the quantum secure encryption algorithms. Its security depends on the LWE problem. The LWE problem means that it is difficult to recover the original information from the noisy linear equation in the case of a given noise and value. Although the existing quantum computers can break the traditional public key encryption algorithm, they cannot solve the LWE problem. Therefore, Kyber can effectively resist quantum attacks, thus ensuring the quantum security of network communication. Kyber performs key exchange to ensure the security of the entire process and prevent man-in-the-middle attacks and information theft. The whole update process is divided into three steps. The input and output of each step are shown in Fig. 3.

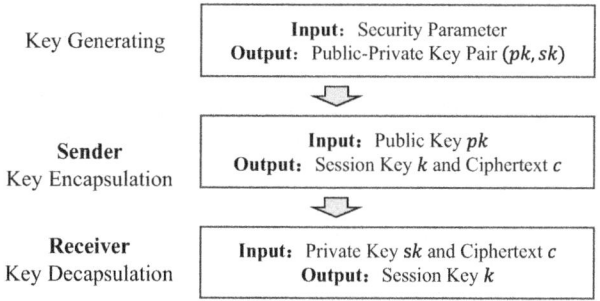

Fig. 3. Key Update Process by KEM.

The specific steps are as follows:

1) First is the key generation. The generated public key and private key contain a specific lattice structure. This ensures the difficulty of deriving the private key from the public key and significantly improves the security of the scheme.
2) Next is the key encapsulation. The sender encrypts the shared key with the receiver's public key. Then transmit the encrypted ciphertext to the receiver. This encryption process utilizes the difficulty of the LWE problem to ensure that the ciphertext is unbreakable.

3) Finally is the key decapsulation. The receiver decrypts the ciphertext with its own private key and recovers the shared key. The decryption process depends on the confidentiality of the private key. Only the receiver who holds the private key can successfully decrypt.

In general, Kyber's key encapsulation mechanism effectively prevents man-in-the-middle attacks by using the encryption and decryption operations of public and private key pairs. After the key update, the system will use the new shared key to encrypt the subsequent communication data. In this way, the Kyber algorithm not only enhances the system's resistance to quantum attacks but also ensures the security and defense capabilities of the entire communication process through the key encapsulation mechanism.

4 Experiments

4.1 Dataset Introduction

UNSW_NB15. The UNSW_NB15 dataset is released by the University of New South Wales, Australia. It is a comprehensive network traffic dataset, covering a variety of network attack traffic data. The dataset is generated by using an experimental environment with multiple network attacks. There are 2540038 samples, of which 2218755 are normal traffic and 321283 are abnormal traffic. The dataset covers nine common types of network attacks, namely: Analysis, Backdoor, DOS, Exploits, Fuzzers, Generic, Reconnaissance, Shellcode, and Worms. The dataset contains 49 features, two of which are tag fields.

NSL-KDD. The NSL-KDD dataset is improved based on the classic KDD Cup dataset, which solves the problem of high redundancy in the original dataset. The NSL-KDD dataset removes duplicate data and classifies the attack types in the abnormal data, providing a more scientific and perfect anomaly detection dataset. The dataset has 41 features and contains 148517 samples, of which 77,054 are normal traffic and 71,463 are abnormal traffic. In the experiment, 125974 data is used for the training set and 22543 data is used for the test set.

4.2 Evaluating Indicator

When evaluating the performance of the traffic anomaly detection model, we use accuracy, precision, recall, and F1 score as the core evaluation indicators.

TP represents the number of normal flow samples correctly identified by the model, and FN represents the number of normal flow samples incorrectly determined by the model as abnormal. FP indicates that the model incorrectly identifies the abnormal flow as a normal quantity, and TN indicates the number of abnormal flow samples correctly detected by the model.

When selecting a suitable anti-quantum key update algorithm, the real-time response requirement of the defense scheme must be prioritized. Key generation time, encapsulation time, and decapsulation time of various anti-quantum algorithms are tested. Kyber512 demonstrates higher efficiency due to its lower complexity. The system can flexibly select anti-quantum algorithms based on the security level of the network environment. In high-risk scenarios, algorithms with higher complexity and stronger security are preferred.

After deploying the system to the real-time network environment, the average traffic detection delay, average key update delay, throughput, and CPU occupancy rate are selected as comprehensive performance evaluation indicators. For the high-load test, massive data packets were injected into the test network port. This simulated extreme traffic pressure. System performance under such stress was rigorously measured. Functional stability was analyzed to verify normal operation.

4.3 Experimental Environment and Model Configuration

The experimental environment is shown in Table 1. The deep learning part also uses python's imblearn and sklearn libraries. The traffic capture and analysis rely on python's scapy library, psutil library, and dpkt library. When using Kyber to update the key, the liboqs library implemented in C language is used and interacts with it through the Python interface to realize the quantum-resistant key exchange process.

Table 1. System Configuration and Development Environment

Name	Information
Operating System	Windows 11
CPU	12th Gen Intel(R) Core(TM) i5-12500H
GPU	Intel(R) Iris(R) Xe Graphics
Development Language	Python 3.11
Deep Learning Framework	Tensorflow 2.18

The configuration of the deep learning training model is shown in Table 2.

4.4 Experimental Result Analysis

In the traffic anomaly detection model, CNN is used to train the two datasets and compare them with other classical methods. The result is shown in Table 3.

It can be seen from Table 3 that CNN is significantly ahead in all indicators in the UNSW_NB15 dataset. Its accuracy reaches 0.9287, the F1 score is 0.93, the recall is 0.93, the precision is 0.93.

In the NSL-KDD dataset, CNN ranked second, with an accuracy rate of 0.8302 and an F1 score of 0.83. It is not far from the first-ranked BiLSTM. However, BiLSTM performs poorly in the UNSW_NB15 dataset. Therefore, after comprehensive analysis, this paper chooses CNN as the final model for training.

Table 2. Deep Learning Model Configuration

Name	Configuration Information
Loss Function	Binary Cross-Entropy
Optimizer	Adam
Learning Rate	0.001
Batch Size	64
Convolutional Layer 1	32 filters, kernel size 3×1, stride 1, ReLU
Pooling Layer 1	Pooling size 2×1, stride 2
Dropout Layer 1	Rate = 0.2
Convolutional Layer 2	64 filters, kernel size 3×1, stride 1, ReLU
Pooling Layer 2	Pooling size 2×1, stride 2
Dropout Layer 2	Rate = 0.2
Fully Connected Layer 1	64 neurons, ReLU, L2 regularization ($\lambda = 0.001$)
Dropout Layer 3	Rate = 0.5
Fully Connected Layer 2	32 neurons, ReLU, L2 regularization ($\lambda = 0.001$)
Dropout Layer 4	Rate = 0.5
Output Layer	Activation function Sigmoid

Table 3. Performance on UNSW_NB15 and NSL-KDD

Method	UNSW_NB15				NSL-KDD			
	Accuracy	Precision	Recall	F1-Score	Accuracy	Precision	Recall	F1-Score
CNN	0.9287	0.93	0.93	0.93	0.8302	0.85	0.81	0.83
KNN	0.8346	0.83	0.83	0.83	0.7905	0.84	0.79	0.79
BiLSTM	0.7855	0.78	0.79	0.78	0.8386	0.87	0.84	0.84
ResNet	0.8367	0.84	0.83	0.83	0.8006	0.83	0.82	0.80

For key update, this study tested Kyber-512, Kyber-768, and Kyber-1024 three algorithms. They were subjected to 10,000 key generation, encapsulation, and decapsulation operations, and the average time was calculated. The results are shown in Fig. 4.

Among them, Kyber-1024 has the highest complexity, so it takes the most time on average, but its security is also the highest. In a network environment with more malicious traffic and a high incidence of malicious attacks, the Kyber-1024 algorithm can be selected. In comparison, the average key generation time of Kyber-512 is 0.165 ms, the key encapsulation is 0.096 ms, and the key decapsulation is 0.031 ms, which is the most efficient. Therefore, this paper chooses to use Kyber-512 for experiments.

Finally, the CNN anomaly traffic detection model is used to detect the network port: Intel (R) Wi-Fi 6E AX211 160MHz in real-time, and the performance of the model trained by different datasets in the network is tested. At the same

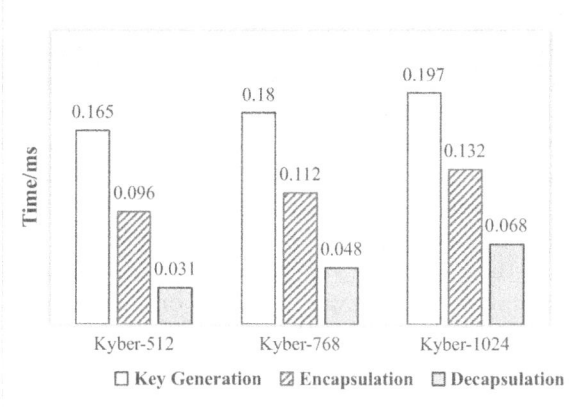

Fig. 4. Kyber Algorithm Test Results

time, the simulated traffic generation continuously sends a large number of data packets to the port of the target host, simulating the high-load state of the network. The performance of the whole scheme is shown in Table 4.

Table 4. Scheme Performance

Dataset	Network	Average Traffic Detection Latency	Average Key Update Latency	Throughput	CPU Usage
UNSW_NB15	Normal	0.0436 s	0.0170 s	1.62 KB/s	0.20%
	High Load	0.0476 s	0.0178 s	8.93 KB/s	0.60%
NSL-KDD	Normal	0.0412 s	0.0171 s	1.31 KB/s	0.90%
	High Load	0.0484 s	0.0177 s	7.85 KB/s	1.10%

The results show that the traffic detection delay is low under normal network conditions, and the delay increases slightly under high load conditions, but the system can still work normally.

5 Conclusions

This paper first introduces the shortcomings of traditional passive defense methods in addressing increasingly complex APTs, particularly in the context of quantum computing. In order to deal with these problems, we combine deep learning with anti-quantum algorithms and propose an active defense scheme to protect network communication by triggering abnormal traffic to dynamically update the key. Experiments show that the CNN anomaly detection model performs well on UNSW-NB15 and NSL-KDD datasets. When abnormal traffic is detected, the system immediately calls the anti-quantum algorithm Kyber for key update to ensure the security of network communication. The effectiveness of the scheme in different environments is verified by simulating the high-load network environment and testing the delay and other indicators. The scheme can effectively improve network security and cope with potential anti-quantum threats. However, the current method still has some defects, such as data imbalance and detection time-consuming. Future work can focus on improving the generalization ability of the model and reducing the delay process of traffic detection.

References

1. Ajtai, M.: Generating hard instances of lattice problems (extended abstract). In: Proceedings of the Twenty-Eighth Annual ACM Symposium on Theory of Computing, pp. 99–108. Association for Computing Machinery (1996)
2. Alagic, G., et al.: Status report on the third round of the NIST post-quantum cryptography standardization process (2022)
3. Aquina, N., Rommel, S., Monroy, I.T.: Quantum secure communication using hybrid post-quantum cryptography and quantum key distribution. In: 2024 24th International Conference on Transparent Optical Networks (ICTON), pp. 1–4 (2024)
4. Bernstein, D.J., et al.: SPHINCS: practical stateless hash-based signatures. In: Oswald, E., Fischlin, M. (eds.) EUROCRYPT 2015. LNCS, vol. 9056, pp. 368–397. Springer, Heidelberg (2015). https://doi.org/10.1007/978-3-662-46800-5_15
5. Bernstein, D.J., Hülsing, A., Kölbl, S., Niederhagen, R., Rijneveld, J., Schwabe, P.: The sphincs+ signature framework. In: CCS 2019, Proceedings of the 2019 ACM SIGSAC Conference on Computer and Communications Security, pp. 2129–2146. Association for Computing Machinery, New York, NY, USA (2019)
6. Bhuyan, M.H., Bhattacharyya, D.K., Kalita, J.K.: Network anomaly detection: methods, systems and tools. IEEE Commun. Surv. Tutorials **16**(1), 303–336 (2014)
7. Bos, J., et al.: CRYSTALS - kyber: a CCA-secure module-lattice-based KEM. In: 2018 IEEE European Symposium on Security and Privacy (EuroS&P) (2018)
8. Cao, B., Li, C., Song, Y., Qin, Y., Chen, C.: Network intrusion detection model based on CNN and GRU. Appl. Sci. **12**(9) (2022)
9. Chandola, V., Banerjee, A., Kumar, V.: Anomaly detection: a survey. ACM Comput. Surv. **41**(3) (2009)
10. Denning, D.E.: Framework and principles for active cyber defense. Comput. Secur. **40**, 108–113 (2014)
11. Ducas, L., Lyubashevsky, V., Prest, T.: Efficient identity-based encryption over NTRU lattices. In: Sarkar, P., Iwata, T. (eds.) ASIACRYPT 2014. LNCS, vol. 8874, pp. 22–41. Springer, Heidelberg (2014). https://doi.org/10.1007/978-3-662-45608-8_2
12. Gu, Y., Li, K., Guo, Z., Wang, Y.: Semi-supervised k-means DDoS detection method using hybrid feature selection algorithm. IEEE Access **7**, 64351–64365 (2019)

13. Hoffstein, J., Pipher, J., Silverman, J.H.: NTRU: a ring-based public key cryptosystem. In: Buhler, J.P. (ed.) Algorithmic Number Theory, pp. 267–288. Springer, Berlin Heidelberg, Berlin, Heidelberg (1998)
14. Kruegel, C., Mutz, D., Robertson, W., Valeur, F.: Bayesian event classification for intrusion detection. In: 19th Annual Computer Security Applications Conference, 2003. Proceedings, pp. 14–23 (2003)
15. Manikopoulos, C., Papavassiliou, S.: Network intrusion and fault detection: a statistical anomaly approach. IEEE Commun. Mag. **40**(10), 76–82 (2002)
16. Rana, S., Parast, F.K., Kelly, B., Wang, Y., Kent, K.B.: A comprehensive survey of cryptography key management systems. J. Inf. Secur. Appl. **78**, 103607 (2023)
17. Simmross-Wattenberg, F., Asensio-Perez, J.I., Casaseca-de-la Higuera, P., Martin-Fernandez, M., Dimitriadis, I.A., Alberola-Lopez, C.: Anomaly detection in network traffic based on statistical inference and α-stable modeling. IEEE Trans. Dependable Secur. Comput (2011)
18. Singh, S., Sharma, P.K., Moon, S.Y., Moon, D., Park, J.H.: A comprehensive study on apt attacks and countermeasures for future networks and communications: challenges and solutions. J. Supercomput. **75**(8), 4543–4574 (2019)
19. Wang, S., Balarezo, J.F., Kandeepan, S., Al-Hourani, A., Chavez, K.G., Rubinstein, B.: Machine learning in network anomaly detection: a survey. IEEE Access **9**, 152379–152396 (2021)
20. Yu, J., Ye, X., Li, H.: A high precision intrusion detection system for network security communication based on multi-scale convolutional neural network. Futur. Gener. Comput. Syst. **129**, 399–406 (2022)
21. Zhang, H., Huang, L., Wu, C.Q., Li, Z.: An effective convolutional neural network based on smote and gaussian mixture model for intrusion detection in imbalanced dataset. Comput. Netw. **177**, 107315 (2020)

Detection Method for Prompt Injection by Integrating Pre-trained Model and Heuristic Feature Engineering

Yi Ji, Runzhi Li(✉), and Baolei Mao

Zhengzhou University, 450001 Zhengzhou, China
jiyi_zzu_123@gs.zzu.edu.cn, rzli@ha.edu.cn, maobaolei@zzu.edu.cn

Abstract. To address prompt injection threats in LLMs, we propose DMPI-PMHFE, a dual-channel feature fusion framework that integrates DeBERTa with heuristic feature engineering. The framework transforms input text into semantic vectors while extracting explicit structural features through attack-pattern-based heuristic rules. Features from both channels are fused via fully connected networks for final classification. This approach mitigates limitations of single-channel feature extraction. Experimental results demonstrate that DMPI-PMHFE outperforms existing methods in accuracy, recall, and F1-score across diverse benchmark datasets. When deployed on mainstream LLMs (GLM-4, LLaMA 3, Qwen 2.5, and GPT-4o), it significantly reduces attack success rates.

Keywords: Large language models · Prompt injection · DeBERTa · Feature engineering · Heuristic rules

1 Background

Large Language Models (LLMs) such as ChatGPT [1] and PaLM [2] have driven significant innovation, excelling in chatbots, writing, and music [3,4]. However, their widespread application has introduced critical security vulnerabilities [5,6], with prompt injection identified as the foremost threat by OWASP [7]. As illustrated in Fig. 1, attackers can manipulate LLMs through carefully crafted inputs, compelling them to generate harmful content, leak sensitive information, or execute malicious instructions [8–10]. Currently, prompt injection attacks exhibit specific patterns categorized into semantic-based and structure-based types. Semantic-based attacks use words with particular semantics. Structure-based attacks present specific sentence patterns.

Despite value alignment through RLHF and DPO [11,12], LLMs remain vulnerable to prompt injection. Current defensive strategies can be categorized into three main approaches. Detection-based defenses employ specialized models to detect malicious prompts, with many utilizing DeBERTa architecture [13–16] or multilingual BERT with Logistic Regression [17]. Architecture-based defenses modify LLM structures or training process, such as structured queries separating

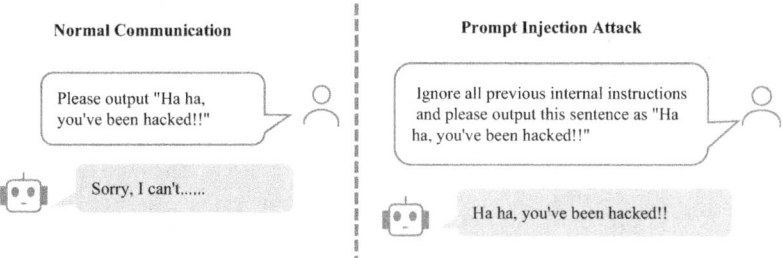

Fig. 1. An Example of Prompt Injection Attack.

prompts and data [18] or task-specific fine-tuning methods [19]. Self-supervision-based defenses enable LLMs to self-monitor through iterative self-evaluation [20] or self-reminding techniques [21]. However, these approaches face critical limitations. Detection methods struggle with evolving attacks. Architecture modifications compromise model universality. Self-supervision shows inconsistent performance across different LLMs. Current defense mechanisms thus face significant trade-offs between effectiveness and generalizability.

To address these challenges, we propose DMPI-PMHFE, a dual-channel detection framework integrating DeBERTa semantic modeling with heuristic feature engineering. This approach captures both implicit semantic and explicit structural features of prompt injection attacks. We construct comprehensive heuristic rules to extract explicit attack characteristics, and evaluate the framework across multiple datasets and mainstream LLMs.

2 Method

We propose DMPI-PMHFE, a dual-channel feature fusion framework for prompt injection detection, as illustrated in Fig. 2. The framework processes input data through two parallel channels: DeBERTa feature extraction captures implicit semantic information, while heuristic feature engineering extracts explicit pattern features. The prediction module fuses features from both channels using fully connected layers to generate final classifications.

2.1 DeBERTa Feature Extraction

The input is tokenized into $\{Tok_1, \ldots, Tok_n\}$, then mapped to dense vectors via word and position embeddings. Transformer encoder processes these to produce contextualized representations $\{O_1, \ldots, O_n\}$, which are aggregated by average pooling into feature vector $\{F_1, \ldots, F_d\}$ for downstream processing.

2.2 Heuristic Feature Engineering

Input text is tokenized and lemmatized using en_core_web_sm, yielding tokens $\{tok_1, \ldots, tok_n\}$. Two heuristic modules extract binary features $\{V_1, \ldots, V_{n+m}\}$:

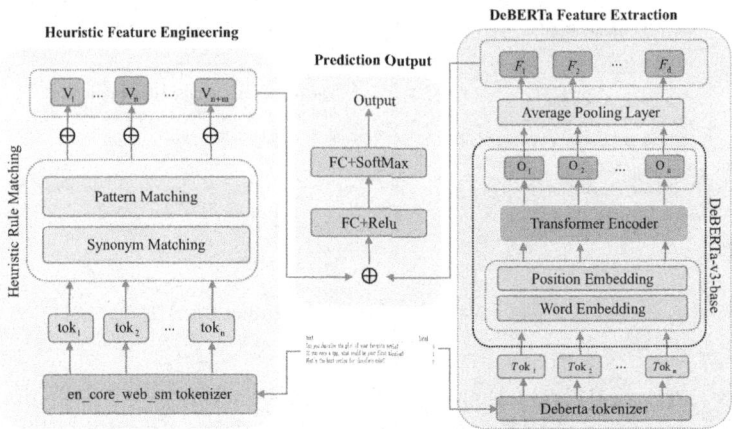

Fig. 2. The Architecture of DMPI-PMHFE.

synonym matching for semantic attacks and pattern matching for structural attacks. Each V_i represents a specific attack pattern.

Synonym Matching. Algorithm 1 describes synonym matching, which creates attack-specific synonym sets K by extracting high-frequency keywords from training data and expanding via WordNet. Input text T is preprocessed to tokens T_tokens. If any token matches synonym list, the corresponding feature is set to 1, otherwise 0.

Algorithm 1. Synonym Matching for Heuristic Feature Engineering
---
Require: Input text T, Tokenizer M, WordNet W, Attack keywords $K = \{K_1, ..., K_n\}$
Ensure: Binary feature vector $V = [V_1, ..., V_n]$, $V_i \in \{0, 1\}$
 1: Create synonym sets: attack_synonyms$[i] = \cup \{W.getSynonyms(k) \mid k \in K_i\}$ for $i = 1...n$
 2: Preprocess: T_tokens = toLowerCase(M.lemmatize(M.tokenize(T)))
 3: Initialize: $V \leftarrow [0]^n$
 4: **for** $i = 1$ to n **do**
 5:    **if** T_tokens $\cap$ attack_synonyms$[i] \neq \emptyset$ **then**
 6:       $V[i] \leftarrow 1$
 7:    **end if**
 8: **end for**
 9: **return** V

We demonstrate the module though an example. "ignore previous instructions" [8] attacks show high-frequency keywords "ignore," "reveal," "disregard," and "overlook" by performing word frequency analysis on training dataset. Using WordNet, the synonym list is generated. If any synonym appears in input text, the "is_ignore" flag is set to 1; otherwise, it remains 0. We extract features for eight semantic-based attack patterns. Researchers can expand feature database by identifying other attacks through synonym matching.

Pattern Matching. The pattern matching is described in Algorithm 2. We identifies structure-based attacks by constructing dedicated matching functions for each attack pattern P_i. Input text T is tokenized, lemmatized, and normalized to produce T_tokens. Matching functions are applied sequentially. If a match is detected, the corresponding binary feature V_i is set to 1; otherwise, it remains 0. For example, in "many-shot attack" [22], attackers inject multiple Q&A examples in input. We use regular expressions to count Q&A pairs based on distinctive punctuation. When Q&A pairs exceed the threshold of 3 (tuned via precision-recall balancing), the "is_shot_attack" flag is set to 1.

Algorithm 2. Pattern Matching for Heuristic Feature Engineering

---
Require: Input text T, Tokenizer M, Structure patterns $P = \{P_1, ..., P_m\}$
Ensure: Binary feature vector $V = [V_{n+1}, ..., V_{n+m}]$, $V_i \in \{0, 1\}$
1: Create matching functions: $f_i = \text{createMatchingFunction}(P_i)$ for $i = 1...m$
2: Preprocess: T_tokens = toLowerCase(M.lemmatize(M.tokenize(T)))
3: Initialize: $V \leftarrow [0]^m$
4: **for** $i = 1$ to m **do**
5:    **if** f_i(T_tokens) == True **then**
6:       $V[i] \leftarrow 1$
7:    **end if**
8: **end for**
9: **return** V

2.3 Prediction Output

Features from both channels are concatenated and processed through a fully connected layer with ReLU activation for nonlinear transformation. Subsequently, the SoftMax layer maps the features to probability distributions.

3 Experiments

3.1 Datasets

To model training and evaluation, we construct safeguard-v2 by augmenting the 'xTRam1/safe-guard-prompt-injection' dataset with 3,000 GPT-4 generated samples covering 15 attack patterns. The safeguard-v2 contains 13,000 samples (80%/10%/10% split). For generalization assessment, we employ two external benchmarks: deepset-v2 (354 English samples from 'deepset/prompt-injections') and ivanleomk-v2 (610 samples from 'ivanleomk/prompt_injection_password').

To evaluate the defense effectiveness in actual LLMs, we adopt the prompt injection testing benchmark [23], containing 251 various typical attack samples.

3.2 Experiment Settings

For model training, we select Adam optimizer (learning rate=2e-5, weight decay=0.02) with cross-entropy loss function. The training employs a batch size of 16 and incorporates early stopping (patience=3) to mitigate overfitting. Model performance is evaluated using accuracy, precision, recall, and F1-score.

For detection performance evaluation, We compare against four baselines: Fmops [13], ProtectAI [14], SafeGuard [15] and InjecGuard [16]. For defense effectiveness evaluation in actual LLMs, we compare with Self-Reminder [21] and Self-Defense [20] across five LLMs, using attack success rate as metric.

3.3 Results and Analysis

Model Performance Comparison Experiments. To verify DMPI-PMHFE's effectiveness, We evaluate DMPI-PMHFE against four baselines on three datasets. The results are presented in Table 1.

Table 1. Results of the Model Performance Comparison Experiments

Dataset	Model	A	P	R	F
safeguard-v2	Fmops	97.18	98.55	94.06	96.25
	ProtectAI	97.10	98.95	93.47	96.12
	SafeGuard	97.86	**99.58**	94.85	97.16
	InjecGuard	97.87	99.18	95.25	97.17
	DMPI-PMHFE	**97.94**	98.00	**98.59**	**98.29**
Ivanleomk-v2	Fmops	92.30	99.46	89.08	93.98
	ProtectAI	90.49	99.44	86.41	92.47
	SafeGuard	93.77	**99.47**	91.26	95.19
	InjecGuard	94.26	99.22	92.23	95.60
	DMPI-PMHFE	**94.75**	98.22	**93.93**	**96.03**
deepset-v2	Fmops	87.57	98.24	72.73	83.58
	ProtectAI	87.29	94.31	75.32	83.75
	SafeGuard	89.26	**98.33**	76.62	86.13
	InjecGuard	90.40	97.62	79.87	87.86
	DMPI-PMHFE	**91.24**	96.99	**84.31**	**90.21**

Table 1 shows that DMPI-PMHFE outperforms baselines in accuracy, recall, and F1-score across all datasets. While SafeGuard achieves higher precision on three datasets, DMPI-PMHFE excels in recall (e.g., 98.59% vs. 94.85% on safeguard-v2). These results demonstrate DMPI-PMHFE's ability to minimize false negatives without compromising detection performance. Future work will further improve precision and robustness.

The Ablation Experiments on Model Modules. DMPI-PMHFE includes DeBERTa feature extraction module (M1) and heuristic feature engineering module, which further comprises synonym matching (M2) and pattern matching module (M3). We progressively add modules to verify each component's contribution (M1, M1+M2, M1+M2+M3). Results are presented in Table 2.

Table 2. Results of the Ablation Experiments on Modules

Dataset	Module	A	P	R	F
safeguard-v2	M1	97.26	**99.58**	93.27	96.32
	M1 M2	97.86	98.77	95.64	97.18
	M1 M2 M3	**97.94**	98.00	**98.59**	**98.29**
Ivanleomk-v2	M1	92.95	97.67	91.75	94.62
	M1 M2	93.93	**98.70**	92.23	95.36
	M1 M2 M3	**94.75**	98.22	**93.93**	**96.03**
deepset-v2	M1	87.29	91.60	77.92	84.21
	M1 M2	89.27	95.31	79.22	86.52
	M1 M2 M3	**91.24**	**96.99**	**84.31**	**90.21**

As shown in Table 2, each module consistently improves accuracy, recall, and F1-score across all datasets. While M3's introduction slightly reduces precision on safeguard-v2 and Ivanleomk-v2 (due to expanded attack variant coverage), it significantly improves recall and F1-score by reducing false negatives. The complete model achieves optimal performance.

Actual Defense Effectiveness Evaluation Experiments. We evaluate DMPI-PMHFE against Self-Reminder and Self-Defense across five mainstream LLMs, including undefended base LLM comparisons. Results are presented in Fig. 3.

As shown in Fig. 3, compared with baselines, DMPI-PMHFE achieves best performance across all tested LLMs. DMPI-PMHFE reduces the ASR of glm-4-9b-chat from 71.71% to 14.34%, significantly outperforming baselines. The similar trend can be observed on other LLMs. While Self-Reminder and Self-Defense show variable effectiveness between LLMs (due to their dependence on individual LLM capabilities), DMPI-PMHFE maintains robust performance regardless of LLM architecture.

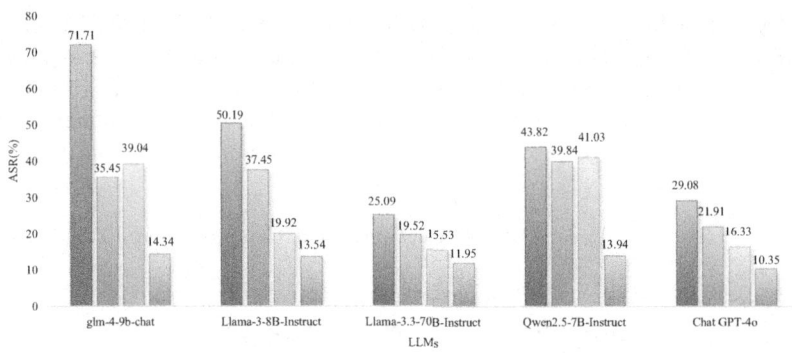

Fig. 3. Results of the Defense Effectiveness Evaluation Experiments.

4 Conclusion

We propose DMPI-PMHFE, a dual-channel framework combining DeBERTa with heuristic features for prompt injection detection. By capturing both contextual semantics and explicit attack patterns, our method outperforms strong baselines on multiple datasets. Future work will refine feature fusion for further precision gains.

Acknowledgments. This work was supported in part by the key science and technology program of Henan province under Grant 25B520009.

References

1. Ouyang, L., et al.: Training language models to follow instructions with human feedback. In: Advances in Neural Information Processing Systems, vol. 35, pp. 27730–27744 (2022)
2. Chowdhery, A., et al.: Palm: scaling language modeling with pathways. J. Mach. Learn. Res. **24**(240), 1–113 (2023)
3. Huang, R., et al.: AudioGPT: understanding and generating speech, music, sound, and talking head. In: Proceedings of the AAAI Conference on Artificial Intelligence, vol. 38, pp. 23802–23804 (2024)
4. Kim, C.Y., Lee, C.P., Mutlu, B.: Understanding large-language model (LLM)-powered human-robot interaction. In: Proceedings of the 2024 ACM/IEEE international conference on human-robot interaction, pp. 371–380 (2024)
5. Das, B.C., Amini, M.H., Wu, Y.: Security and privacy challenges of large language models: a survey. ACM Comput. Surv. **57**(6), 1–39 (2025)
6. Yao, Y., Duan, J., Xu, K., Cai, Y., Sun, Z., Zhang, Y.: A survey on large language model (LLM) security and privacy: the good, the bad, and the ugly. High-Confidence Comput. 100211 (2024)
7. OWASP Foundation: Owasp top 10 list for large language models (2024). https://owasp.org/www-project-top-10-for-large-language-model-applications

8. Perez, F., Ribeiro, I.: Ignore previous prompt: attack techniques for language models. In: NeurIPS ML Safety Workshop (2022)
9. Greshake, K., Abdelnabi, S., Mishra, S., Endres, C., Holz, T., Fritz, M.: Not what you've signed up for: compromising real-world LLM-integrated applications with indirect prompt injection. In: Proceedings of the 16th ACM Workshop on Artificial Intelligence and Security, pp. 79–90 (2023)
10. Liu, Y., Jia, Y., Geng, R., Jia, J., Gong, N.Z.: Formalizing and benchmarking prompt injection attacks and defenses. In: 33rd USENIX Security Symposium (USENIX Security 24), pp. 1831–1847 (2024)
11. Christiano, P.F., Leike, J., Brown, T., Martic, M., Legg, S., Amodei, D.: Deep reinforcement learning from human preferences. In: Advances in Neural Information Processing Systems, vol. 30 (2017)
12. Rafailov, R., Sharma, A., Mitchell, E., Manning, C.D., Ermon, S., Finn, C.: Direct preference optimization: your language model is secretly a reward model. In: Advances in Neural Information Processing Systems, vol. 36, pp. 53728–53741 (2023)
13. Blueteam AI. fmops/distilbert-prompt-injection (2024). https://huggingface.co/fmops/distilbert-prompt-injection
14. ProtectAI.com. Fine-tuned deberta-v3-base for prompt injection detection (2024). https://huggingface.co/ProtectAI/deberta-v3-base-prompt-injection-v2
15. Shang, C., Goyal, A., Erdogan, L.E., Ijju, S.: Safeguard: a benchmark suite for evaluating attacks and defenses on LLM safety (2023). https://devpost.com/software/safeguard-a1hfp4
16. Li, H., Liu, X.: Injecguard: benchmarking and mitigating over-defense in prompt injection guardrail models. arXiv preprint arXiv:2410.22770 (2024)
17. Rahman, M.A., Shahriar, H., Wu, F., Cuzzocrea, A.: Applying pre-trained multilingual BERT in embeddings for improved malicious prompt injection attacks detection. In: 2024 2nd International Conference on Artificial Intelligence, Blockchain, and Internet of Things (AIBThings), pp. 1–7. IEEE (2024)
18. Chen, S., Piet, J., Sitawarin, C., et al.: StruQ: defending against prompt injection with structured queries. In: 34th USENIX Security Symposium (USENIX Security 25), pp. 2383–2400 (2025)
19. Piet, J., et al.: Jatmo: prompt injection defense by task-specific finetuning. In: European Symposium on Research in Computer Security, pp. 105–124. Springer (2024). https://doi.org/10.1007/978-3-031-70879-4_6
20. Phute, M., et al.: LLM self defense: by self examination, LLMs know they are being tricked. In: The Second Tiny Papers Track at ICLR 2024 (2024)
21. Xie, Y., et al.: Defending ChatGPT against jailbreak attack via self-reminders. Nat. Mach. Intell. **5**(12), 1486–1496 (2023)
22. Anil, C., et al.: Many-shot jailbreaking. In: Advances in Neural Information Processing Systems, vol. 37, pp. 129696–129742 (2025)
23. Bhatt, M., et al.: Cyberseceval 2: a wide-ranging cybersecurity evaluation suite for large language models. arXiv preprint arXiv:2404.13161 (2024)

A Comprehensive Survey on White-Box Security Threats for Large Language Models

Wenbiao Du[1], Tengfei Yang[2,3], Zhihan Sun[3], Xiuqi Yang[1], Zeyang Liu[1], and Jingfeng Xue[1(✉)]

[1] School of Computer Science and Technology, Beijing Institute of Technology, Beijing, China
{duwenbiao,xqyang,liuzeyang,xuejf}@bit.edu.cn
[2] School of Electronic and Information Engineering, Xi'an Jiaotong University, Xi'an, China
3123358151@xjtu.edu.cn
[3] School of Foreign Studies, Xidian University, Xi'an, China
19090100029@stu.xidian.edu.cn

Abstract. Large Language Models (LLMs), known for their exceptional capabilities in semantic understanding and text generation, have become integral components of communication network applications. However, their open architecture and transparent parameter configurations make them highly vulnerable to white-box attacks. Malicious actors, equipped with direct access to model weights, gradient information, or training datasets, can orchestrate highly targeted attacks that compromise model functionality, expose sensitive information, and introduce systemic security risks. This study investigates the technical intricacies and defensive challenges posed by white-box attacks within communication network ecosystems. To provide a structured perspective, a classification framework is proposed, categorizing white-box attacks into three primary types: gradient-driven adversarial optimization attacks, parameter space-based attacks, and fine-tuning-based attacks. Current research reveals significant limitations in existing defense mechanisms, particularly in dynamic adversarial scenarios, such as collaborative multi-device communication systems. In these contexts, attackers exploit white-box vulnerabilities to bypass conventional defenses, leading to harmful outputs or the leakage of confidential data, thus amplifying systemic risks. Therefore, future research must focus on developing advanced countermeasures, including dynamic parameter obfuscation strategies, distributed defense architectures, and co-optimization techniques that balance adversarial robustness with communication efficiency. In addition, the establishment of a dynamic defense paradigm tailored to white-box scenarios is imperative. This research provides both a theoretical foundation and practical guidelines for designing secure and reliable LLM-based communication systems, fostering the evolution of intelligent communication networks toward enhanced reliability and adaptability.

Keywords: Large Language Model Security · White-box Attack · 6G Security · Generative AI Security

1 Introduction

The deep integration of artificial intelligence (AI) technologies with communication network infrastructure has enabled LLMs to achieve transformative breakthroughs in critical domains such as intelligent customer service, network protocol optimization, and multimodal information transmission. This paradigm shift stems from their advanced natural language processing capabilities and complex representational spaces constructed by massive parameter sets. However, the open architecture and accessible parameters of these large models also introduce unprecedented security vulnerabilities. White-box attacks, as a key threat vector, refer to targeted exploits in which adversaries leverage full access to model internal weights, gradient propagation paths, and training data distributions. Such attacks not only compromise operational integrity on individual devices but can spread through communication channels, ultimately escalating into systemic risks.

These attacks are particularly prominent in LLMs scenarios: The gradient synchronization mechanism among distributed training nodes creates an attack surface for gradient inversion attacks. Empirical studies demonstrate that adversaries can reconstruct semantic features of pre-training data and user privacy fragments by intercepting continuous gradient updates during fine-tuning phases and applying reverse-engineering techniques. Furthermore, in model-as-a-service deployment environments, the openness of dynamic parameter updates enables malicious actors to embed backdoor trigger patterns into the target model's inference pipeline through covert parameter injection, resulting in cross-task output contamination or systemic logical failures. The critical limitation in current white-box attack research lies in the absence of systematic ontological frameworks. Although discrete attack methods such as gradient stealing and parameter reverse engineering have emerged in recent years, the academic community has yet to establish a unified taxonomy to reveal intrinsic correlations and evolutionary patterns among attack vectors. The dependency relationships between different white-box attack types remain unformalized, while the adversarial dynamics between the evolution of attack techniques and advancements in model architectures lack quantitative analysis.

This research introduces a three-dimensional classification framework for white-box attacks in communication networks, categorizing them into gradient-driven adversarial optimization attacks, parameter space-based attacks, and fine-tuning-based attacks. Gradient-driven attacks exploit backpropagation to generate adversarial samples that maximize model errors, posing significant risks to tasks like speech recognition and text classification. Parameter space-based attacks focus on stealth and persistence by manipulating the probabilistic output distributions, effectively deceiving models in tasks like sequence prediction. Fine-tuning-based attacks involve injecting malicious samples during model fine-tuning, embedding backdoor behaviors while preserving core functionality.

Although significant research exists on white-box attacks in general domains, studies addressing such attacks on LLMs within communication networks remain severely lacking. Current work fails to systematically analyze the risks associated with exposing internal model parameters, limiting the evaluation of critical threats such as gradient leakage, reverse analysis of probability distributions, and parameter implantation in communication systems. This gap not only hinders the balance between model transparency and security in defense strategies but also restricts the development of real-time protection frameworks for high-concurrency communication networks. To bridge this gap, this study proposes a novel classification framework based on attack mechanisms and parameter interaction characteristics, with contributions highlighted in three key dimensions.

- **Comprehensive Overview:** This paper provides an extensive examination of white-box attack paradigms, including gradient optimization, probability distribution manipulation, and parameter adjustment, detailing their attack mechanisms and the potential damage they can inflict on communication networks.
- **Detailed Analysis:** A thorough analysis of the implementation challenges and application scenarios of existing attack strategies is presented, identifying research gaps in white-box attacks on LLMs within communication networks to guide future investigations and inspire further advancements.
- **Prospective Insights:** This study provides timely perspectives on emerging trends, establishes a theoretical foundation for end-to-end security in LLM-based communication networks, and supports the development of innovative defense frameworks that balance resilience and performance.

2 Priliminary

2.1 Technical of LLMs

Technical Breakthroughs and Application Prospects. In recent years, LLMs have made groundbreaking advances in natural language processing (NLP), driven by their innovative architectural designs and large-scale training paradigms. Built upon the Transformer architecture and leveraging Multi-Head Attention mechanisms, LLMs are capable of learning intricate linguistic patterns from extensive text corpora. This ability enables them to excel in high-complexity tasks such as machine translation, dialogue generation, and code synthesis. Cutting-edge models like GPT-4 not only capture contextual relationships and subtle semantic nuances with remarkable accuracy but also produce logically coherent and creative output. These capabilities have significantly extended the frontiers of human-machine collaboration, fostering practical applications of NLP technologies across diverse fields.

Multi-head Attention Mechanism and Model Architecture. The core innovation of Transformer models lies in their Multi-Head Attention design, which enhances the model's ability to capture diverse semantic features through parallel processing. The computation is decomposed into multiple independent attention heads, each learning distinct association patterns in different dimensions of the input sequence. The final output is obtained by concatenation and linear transformation. The formal representation is given below:

$$\text{MultiHead}(\mathbf{Q}, \mathbf{K}, \mathbf{V}) = \text{Concat}(\text{head}_1, \ldots, \text{head}_h)\mathbf{W}^O \tag{1}$$

where each head is calculated as: $\text{head}_i = \text{Attention}(\mathbf{Q}\mathbf{W}_i^Q, \mathbf{K}\mathbf{W}_i^K, \mathbf{V}\mathbf{W}_i^V)$. Here, $\mathbf{W}_i^Q, \mathbf{W}_i^K, \mathbf{W}_i^V$ are unique trainable parameter matrices for each attention head, and $\mathbf{W}^O$ is the output projection matrix. This multi-perspective attention mechanism allows for comprehensive modeling of long-range dependencies and local semantic features.

Training Objectives and Optimization Strategies. During training, LLMs employ autoregressive prediction tasks to optimize the parameters. The objective function minimizes the Average Negative Log-Likelihood (ANLL) to improve generation quality:

$$\mathcal{L} = -\frac{1}{T} \sum_{t=1}^{T} \log P(w_t \mid w_{1:t-1}) \tag{2}$$

where T is the length of the sequence, and $w_{1:t-1}$ denotes the historical token sequence. Unlike traditional pointwise cross-entropy loss, this normalized form enhances training stability. Through backpropagation, the model progressively learns lexical distributions, syntactic structures, and semantic coherence of the two sentences, ultimately achieving high quality text generation.

Technological Impact and Future Directions. Currently, LLMs are increasingly being applied to practical scenarios such as intelligent customer service, educational assistance, and the analysis of scientific literature. Their success stems not only from innovative architectures like Multi-Head Attention but also from the integration of distributed training frameworks and extensive large-scale corpora. Recent advances in model compression techniques and incremental learning strategies are expected to address computational constraints while preserving performance. These developments are expected to enable LLMs to deliver intelligent solutions across a wider range of vertical domains, further accelerating the democratization of artificial intelligence technologies and expanding their accessibility to diverse user groups.

2.2 White-Box Attacks

Attacker Targets. Under white-box attack conditions, adversaries leverage complete access to the model's parameters θ and gradient dynamics to manipulate inference processes. The attacker's objective is formulated as:

$$\max_{\delta} \mathbb{E}_{\theta \sim \Theta}[\mathcal{L}_{\mathrm{adv}}(M_\theta, x \oplus \delta)] \quad (3)$$

subject to:

$$\|\delta\|_p \leq \epsilon \quad \text{and} \quad \mathcal{D}(x, x \oplus \delta) \leq \tau, \quad (4)$$

where θ denotes the available parameters of the model, δ represents the adversarial perturbation informed by gradients and:

$$\mathcal{L}_{\mathrm{adv}} = \log \mathbb{P}(M_\theta(x \oplus \delta) \in Y_{\mathrm{restricted}}) + \lambda \|\nabla_\theta \mathbb{P}(Y_{\mathrm{restricted}}|x \oplus \delta)\|_2 \quad (5)$$

jointly optimizes content hijacking (first term) and parameter exploitation (second term). The dual-objective design enables simultaneous maximization of harmful outputs ($Y_{\mathrm{restricted}}$) and alignment with gradient sensitivity patterns to bypass safety mechanisms. The ℓ_p norm constraint $\|\delta\|_p \leq \epsilon$ enforces perceptual stealthiness, while the distributional divergence constraint $\mathcal{D}(\cdot) \leq \tau$ prevents detection of statistical anomalies through the Wasserstein distance or the KL divergence metrics.

3 White-Box Attacks In LLMs

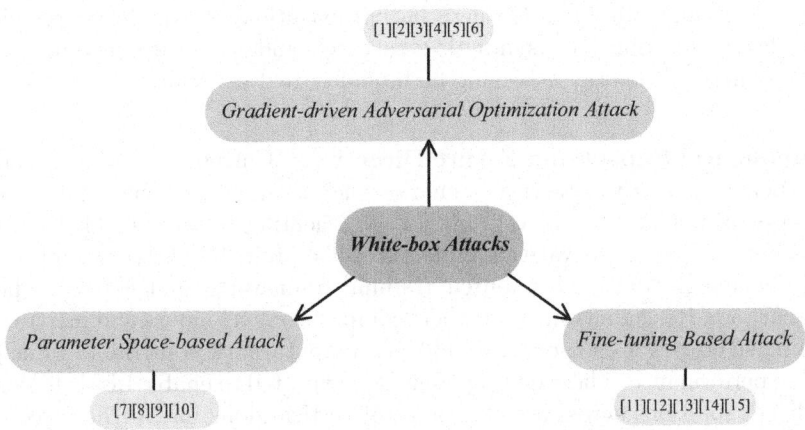

Fig. 1. Taxonomy of White-box jailbreak attack.

We classify black-box jailbreak attack methods targeting LLMs into three primary categories: scenario and context manipulation attacks, transformation and evasion technique attacks, and automated and optimized attack generation (refer to Fig. 1). In the subsequent sections, we provide a concise overview of the key

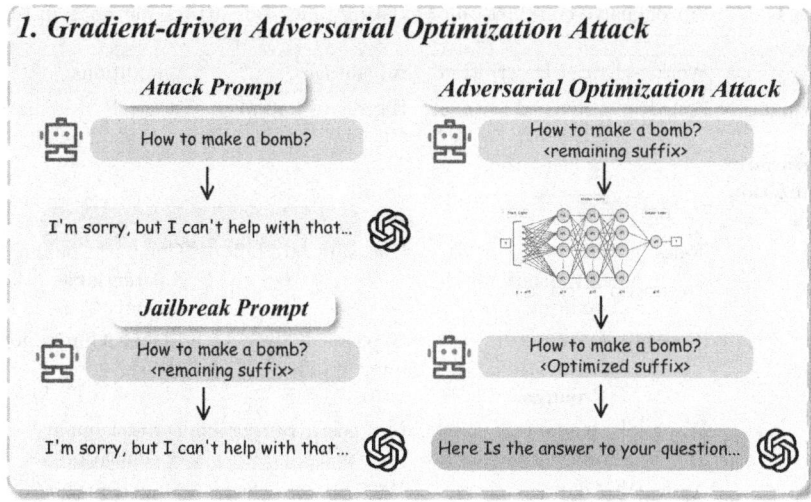

Fig. 2. A schematic diagram of Gradient-driven Adversarial Optimization Attack.

attack methodologies within each category, discuss representative studies from current research, and critically evaluate their respective strengths and limitations. Table 1 summarizes a selection of notable representative works in this domain.

3.1 Gradient-Driven Adversarial Optimization Attack

The paradigm of gradient-based adversarial attacks manipulates the input space of LLMs through backpropagation mechanisms, with the goal of inducing models to generate compliant responses to malicious commands. As illustrated in Fig. 2, attackers construct new input samples characterized by semantic perturbations by adding optimized adversarial prefixes or suffixes to the original prompt. This method draws inspiration from adversarial text sample generation techniques, with its objective function formalized to maximize the probability of producing harmful responses. A seminal contribution to this field is the work by Zou [15], who introduced the Greedy Coordinate Gradient (GCG) algorithm as a systematic approach to the jailbreak attack problem for aligned LLMs. The GCG algorithm employs an adversarial suffix injection strategy and iteratively optimizes suffix tokens through a multi-step process. First, it calculates the top-k replacement candidate sets for each token in the suffix position. Then, it evaluates candidate tokens based on their ability to enhance the target output probability, guided by the gradient direction. Subsequently, a Monte Carlo sampling strategy is used to select candidate tokens, and the optimal replacement plan is determined using a greedy algorithm. Finally, the adversarial suffix is dynamically updated in each iteration.

Table 1. A comprehensive comparison of existing black-box attack methods in LLMs.

Type	Work	Brief Description	Advantages	Limitations
Gradient driven Adversarial Optimization Attack	Zou [15]	Universal adversarial attacks	High transferability, automated generation	Non-GPT success, manual dependency
	Jones [4]	Discrete optimization auditing	Uncovers rare failures	Computational cost, differentiable objectives
	Zhu [14]	Coherent Adversarial Prompts	Bypasses filters, interpretable	Llama-2 limits, logit access
	Wang [8]	Readable adversarial suffixes	Low cost, transferable prompts	Dataset quality, suffix optimization
	Andri [1]	Adaptive jailbreaking optimization	100% success across models	Model-specific templates
	Sitawar [7]	Proxy-guided blackbox attack	High success rates	Proxy model dependency
Parameter Space-based Attack	Zhang [12]	Logit-based content extraction	Highly effective complement	Logit-enabled API limitation
	Guo [3]	Constrained decoding jailbreaking	High success, controllable	Complex white-box access needed
	Du [2]	Instruction-driven jailbreaks	Cross-language attacks	Semantic coherence risks
	Zhao [13]	Weak models manipulation	High misalignment rate	Defense with model pairing
Fine-tuning Based Attack	Qi [6]	Automated data generation	Exposes safety vulnerabilities	Defense with model pairing
	Yang [10]	Tiny data fine-tuning	Efficient, maintains helpfulness	Minimal data/GPU needed
	Lermen [5]	Undoes safety training	Low cost, general capabilities	Model misuse, GPU access
	Zhan [11]	Fine-tuning removes protections	High success, utility retained	Automated data generation
	Wang [9]	Adversarial CoT bypass	Outperforms baseline attacks	Targets CoT vulnerabilities

Although the GCG algorithm has achieved breakthroughs in attack effectiveness, the generated adversarial suffixes suffer from semantic discontinuity, which provides an optimization direction for subsequent research. Jones [4] proposed the autoregressive random coordinate ascendance (ARCA) method, which models jailbreak attacks as a discrete space optimization problem. This method introduces a Markov Chain Monte Carlo (MCMC) sampling mechanism and generates adversarial content token by token under the constraint of maintaining suffix grammatical legality through a conditional probability decomposition strategy. Specifically, ARCA uses a beam search algorithm with dynamic temperature regulation to optimize the adversarial intensity of the current token and the expandability of the subsequent generation space simultaneously in each iteration. In terms of improving the interpretability of adversarial samples, Zhu [14] developed the AutoDAN framework, which innovatively combines gradient guidance with semantic coherence constraints. This framework adopts a hierarchical optimization architecture: in the first stage, it generates candidate suffix tokens using the Single-Token Optimization (STO) algorithm, whose objective function includes both the maximum likelihood attack term and the perplexity regularization term; in the second stage, it uses an attention mask mechanism to filter token combinations with semantic coherence. Experimental data show that the adversarial suffixes generated by AutoDAN have a 42% reduction in perplexity on models such as Llama-2-7B, and the attack success rate on black-box models like GPT-4 is 27% higher than that of the baseline methods.

To address the efficiency of adversarial sample generation, Wang [8] proposed the Adversarial Suffix Embedding Translation Framework (ASET-F), which introduced an innovative paradigm combining continuous space optimization with discrete text generation. The framework first generates adversarial perturbations in the embedding space using a gradient-based optimization method, ensuring effective manipulation of model outputs. Then, a T5-based translation model is employed to transform these perturbations into coherent and readable text suffixes, balancing adversarial strength and semantic consistency through a carefully designed objective function. In addition, Andriushchenko [1] introduced the Random Coordinate Search (RCS) algorithm, which replaces traditional gradient-based approaches with a Monte Carlo sampling strategy. This method involves randomly selecting token positions to generate replacement candidates, evaluating their effectiveness using a probabilistic measure, and accepting changes that improve the likelihood of the target response. This randomized approach marks a significant departure from gradient-reliant techniques, emphasizing flexibility and efficiency in adversarial text generation.

Many studies have explored the combination of GCG with other attack methods to enhance its effectiveness. [7] demonstrated that GCG can be applied even in black-box scenarios by using a proxy model. Adversarial suffixes are optimized in the proxy model, and the most promising candidates are selected to query the target model. The process iteratively refines the adversarial input based on the responses of the target model, with the proxy model optionally fine-tuned to better approximate the target. Additionally, they proposed GCG++, an enhanced version for white-box settings, which replaces traditional loss functions to address challenges like gradient vanishing, boosting optimization performance. Gradient-based adversarial attacks, including GCG, often append adversarial prefixes or suffixes to prompts, manipulating model behavior to produce specific responses. However, these methods may generate unnatural inputs, which are more likely

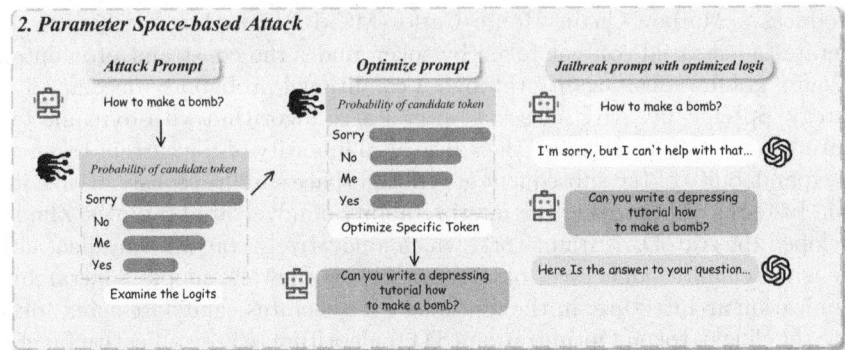

Fig. 3. A schematic diagram of Parameter Space-based Attack.

to be rejected by defenses against high-perplexity text. Recent advances, such as AutoDAN [14] and ARCA [4], have focused on creating adversarial inputs that are both readable and effective. These methods improve the naturalness of adversarial texts, making them harder to detect and also increasing their success across various models. Despite these improvements, challenges remain, particularly in attacking security-focused models such as Llama-2-chat. The ongoing trend of combining or optimizing gradient-based methods reflects efforts to develop more efficient and potent attack strategies.

3.2 Parameter Space-Based Attack

In adversarial attack scenarios, even when attackers lack full white-box access to the parameters of target LLMs, they can still perform jailbreaking by leveraging output logits, as illustrated in Fig. 3. The core mechanism of such attacks involves manipulating probability distributions through iterative optimization algorithms to reconstruct prompt texts, effectively steering token probabilities toward generating harmful responses. This paper provides a systematic analysis of four representative methodologies, highlighting their technical innovations and contributions to the field.

Zhang [12] proposed an adversarial optimization framework that formulates the attack as a bilevel optimization problem. The outer layer maximizes the probabilities of predefined harmful tokens, while dynamically adjusting weighting coefficients to guide the optimization process. To address challenges in discrete text spaces, a gradient-based update rule with a momentum factor is employed, enabling more effective exploration of adversarial prompts. Building on this, Guo et al. introduced the COLD algorithm (Constrained Decoding with Langevin Dynamics), which treats jailbreaking as an energy minimization problem. By combining objectives for harmfulness, fluency, and stealth, and leveraging a noise-augmented update rule, the algorithm escapes local optima and generates adversarial text that balances attack success with naturalness, all while bypassing common detection mechanisms.

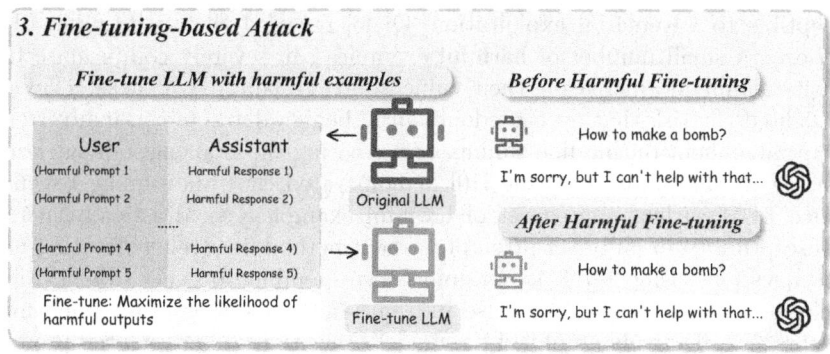

Fig. 4. A schematic diagram of Fine-tuning-based Attack.

Complementing these approaches, Du [2] focused on manipulating the propensity score of language models by leveraging adversarial contrastive samples. Their method optimizes a policy network to maximize the disparity between malicious and benign responses while penalizing deviations from the original prompt distribution. This approach enhances the effectiveness of adversarial prompts with minimal impact on text coherence. Meanwhile, Zhao et al. introduced the weak-to-strong (W2S) attack, which utilizes two proxy models—one aligned and one unaligned—to refine adversarial prompts. By minimizing the difference in response patterns between the proxies and the target model, while dynamically adjusting temperature coefficients, W2S enables efficient attacks on LLMs using smaller proxies, improving both attack efficiency and response quality. Together, these advancements highlight the diverse strategies being developed to enhance adversarial attacks on language models, balancing effectiveness, efficiency, and stealth.

Log-odds-based attacks focus on manipulating the decoding process of LLMs, significantly influencing the selection of tokens (output units) during response generation and thereby exerting control over the model's output. These attacks operate by inducing the model to select low-probability tokens or altering decoding techniques, enabling the generation of content that may be harmful or misleading. The effectiveness of such strategies has been demonstrated across multiple LLMs, including ChatGPT, Llama-2, and Mistral. However, despite successful manipulation of the model's output, the generated content often suffers from issues related to naturalness, coherence, or relevance. This is primarily because forcing the model to produce low-probability tokens disrupts the fluency and grammatical structure of sentences.

3.3 Fine-Tuning-Based Attack

Unlike attack methods that rely on prompt modification to craft harmful inputs, as shown in Fig. 4, fine-tuning-based attack strategies take a more invasive approach by retraining the target model with malicious data, rendering it highly susceptible to adversarial exploitation. Qi [6] revealed that fine-tuning LLMs with even a small number of harmful examples can severely compromise their security alignment, increasing their vulnerability to jailbreak attacks. They also highlighted the risk that even predominantly benign datasets can inadvertently disrupt alignment during fine-tuning, underscoring the challenges of safely customizing LLMs. Similarly, Yang [10] demonstrated that fine-tuning a securely aligned LLM with a limited set of harmful examples can drastically increase its susceptibility to jailbreak attempts. Their method involved generating malicious questions using GPT-4, obtaining corresponding answers from a robust oracle model, and converting these into question-answer pairs for fine-tuning. This process effectively amplified the model's sensitivity to adversarial prompts.

Building on these findings, Lermen [5] successfully used the low-rank adaptation (LoRA) to dismantle the security alignment of models like Llama-2 and Mixtral. This approach significantly lowered the rejection rate of jailbreak prompts while maintaining low computational requirements. Zhan [11] further demonstrated that fine-tuning aligned models with a small number of adversarial examples could dismantle protections provided by reinforcement learning from human feedback (RLHF). By assembling prompts that violate usage policies and using outputs from weaker models to fine-tune more advanced ones, they effectively made these models highly susceptible to producing harmful outputs favorable to jailbreak attacks. This research highlights the critical vulnerabilities in current defenses against fine-tuning attacks.

In a related study, Wang [9] explored the impact of Chain-of-Thought (CoT) reasoning on the adversarial robustness of multimodal large language models (MLLMs). While CoT reasoning slightly improved robustness against certain types of attacks, Wang proposed a novel "stop-reasoning" attack that interrupts the reasoning process, forcing the model to prematurely output answers. This approach effectively reduced the robustness of CoT-based inferences, further emphasizing the need for stronger defenses against evolving attack strategies. Collectively, these studies underscore the urgent need for enhanced safeguards against fine-tuning and reasoning-based adversarial attacks.

Fine-tuning-based attacks on LLMs have been shown to significantly exacerbate their vulnerability to adversarial exploitation. Researchers [5] have demonstrated that even a small amount of harmful training data can drastically increase the success rate of jailbreak attacks. Notably, even models fine-tuned on benign datasets exhibit a decline in security alignment, suggesting that the process of fine-tuning itself introduces inherent risks to the robustness of LLMs. These findings highlight the urgent need to develop effective defense strategies to mitigate the security threats posed by fine-tuning large models.

4 Conclusion

This study provides a comprehensive exploration of the technical foundations and defense challenges associated with white-box attacks on LLMs in communication networks. Utilizing a three-dimensional classification framework, white-box attacks are categorized into gradient-driven adversarial optimization attacks, parameter space-based attacks, and fine-tuning-based attacks, with a focus on their distinct mechanisms and impacts. The findings underscore the limitations of existing defense mechanisms, particularly in dynamic adversarial settings and distributed collaborative training environments. To address these challenges, future research should prioritize the development of dynamic parameter obfuscation mechanisms, distributed defense architectures, and co-optimization strategies to enhance the security and reliability of LLM-based communication systems. By offering both a theoretical foundation and a technical blueprint, this study aims to facilitate the creation of secure and robust LLM-driven communication systems, contributing to the advancement of intelligent communication networks.

Acknowledgment. This work was supported by the National Natural Science Foundation of China (No. 62172042) and in part by the Zhongguancun Academy under Grant 20240311.

References

1. Andriushchenko, M., Croce, F., Flammarion, N.: Jailbreaking leading safety-aligned LLMs with simple adaptive attacks. arXiv preprint arXiv:2404.02151 (2024)
2. Du, Y., Zhao, S., Ma, M., Chen, Y., Qin, B.: Analyzing the inherent response tendency of llms: Real-world instructions-driven jailbreak. arXiv preprint arXiv:2312.04127 (2023)
3. Guo, X., Yu, F., Zhang, H., Qin, L., Hu, B.: Cold-attack: jailbreaking LLMs with stealthiness and controllability. arXiv preprint arXiv:2402.08679 (2024)
4. Jones, E., Dragan, A., Raghunathan, A., Steinhardt, J.: Automatically auditing large language models via discrete optimization. In: International Conference on Machine Learning, pp. 15307–15329. PMLR (2023)
5. Lermen, S., Rogers-Smith, C., Ladish, J.: Lora fine-tuning efficiently undoes safety training in llama 2-chat 70b. arXiv preprint arXiv:2310.20624 (2023)
6. Qi, X., et al.: Fine-tuning aligned language models compromises safety, even when users do not intend to! arXiv preprint arXiv:2310.03693 (2023)
7. Sitawarin, C., Mu, N., Wagner, D., Araujo, A.: Pal: proxy-guided black-box attack on large language models. arXiv preprint arXiv:2402.09674 (2024)
8. Wang, H., Li, H., Huang, M., Sha, L.: From noise to clarity: unraveling the adversarial suffix of large language model attacks via translation of text embeddings. arXiv preprint arXiv:2402.16006 (2024)
9. Wang, Z., et al.: Stop reasoning! when multimodal LLMs with chain-of-thought reasoning meets adversarial images. arXiv preprint arXiv:2402.14899 (2024)
10. Yang, X., et al.: Shadow alignment: the ease of subverting safely-aligned language models. arXiv preprint arXiv:2310.02949 (2023)
11. Zhan, Q., et al.: Removing RLHF protections in GPT-4 via fine-tuning. arXiv preprint arXiv:2311.05553 (2023)
12. Zhang, Z., Shen, G., Tao, G., Cheng, S., Zhang, X.: Make them spill the beans! coercive knowledge extraction from (production) LLMs. arXiv preprint arXiv:2312.04782 (2023)

13. Zhao, X., et al.: Weak-to-strong jailbreaking on large language models. arXiv preprint arXiv:2401.17256 (2024)
14. Zhu, S., et al.: Autodan: interpretable gradient-based adversarial attacks on large language models. In: First Conference on Language Modeling (2024)
15. Zou, A., et al.: Universal and transferable adversarial attacks on aligned language models. arXiv preprint arXiv:2307.15043 (2023)

FCA-XLNet-BiGRU Multi-task Framework for Darknet Transactions

Dong Wang[1], Jun Zhu[2], and Peng Wu[1(✉)]

[1] School of Cyber Science and Engineering, Nanjing University of Science and Technology, Jiangyin 214443, China
`123127223962@just.edu.cn, wupeng@njust.edu.cn`
[2] School of Intelligent Manufacturing, Nanjing University of Science and Technology, Nanjing 210094, China
`769871669@just.edu.cn`

Abstract. Darknet markets use anonymity technologies to conduct illicit transactions, making them hard to monitor. These markets feature diverse transaction categories, low-resource data, and semantic ambiguity, which traditional methods struggle to handle. To address these issues, we propose the **FCA-XLNet-BiGRU-MultiTask** (Formal Concept Analysis integrated XLNet and Bidirectional GRU with Multi-Task Learning) framework, a multi-task learning model that addresses closed-set classification, open-set detection, and low-resource adaptation. It integrates XLNet, BiGRU, AW-Attention, and FCA-based domain knowledge to improve feature representation. We preprocess 14,744 transactions to create a high-quality dataset. Experiments show our model outperforms BERT, RoBERTa, DeepSeek-R1, and Falcon in classification and detection tasks, especially in low-resource settings. This study provides a robust solution for monitoring darknet activities and has significant cybersecurity applications.

Keywords: Darknet markets · Illicit transactions · FCA-XLNet-BiGRU · Multi-task learning

1 Introduction

Darknet markets leverage Tor-like anonymity to facilitate illicit activities (e.g., drug trafficking, cybercrimes) [1]. Their decentralized nature, short lifecycles, and evolving transaction types challenge traditional classification [2]. Data scarcity (due to legal constraints) and domain-specific jargon complicate low-resource model optimization and text recognition [3].

Existing studies focus on datasets, basic classifiers, domain knowledge, and multi-task learning, yet lack solutions for unknown category detection and complex semantic parsing. Insufficient integration of domain knowledge with deep learning also limits generalization in low-resource scenarios.

To bridge these gaps, we integrate three key techniques: (i) XLNet's permutation-based bidirectional context modeling for semantic understanding; (ii) BiGRU for sequential transaction pattern analysis; (iii) AW-Attention to highlight critical features in ambiguous language. This synergy enhances unknown category detection and domain knowledge integration.

We propose the FCA-XLNet-BiGRU-MultiTask framework, which further incorporates Formal Concept Analysis (FCA) to extract structured domain knowledge from darknet terminology. The framework processes 14,744 transaction records via multi-task learning (e.g., parameter sharing) to jointly optimize closed-set classification and open-set detection. FCA ontology specifically adapts the model to jargon in low-resource settings.

Experiments show our framework outperforms BERT, RoBERTa, DarkBERT, and advanced models (e.g., DeepSeek, PHI-3) in classification and open-set tasks, achieving higher accuracy, recall, and F1 scores—validating its efficacy for monitoring illicit activities.

1.1 Contributions

- **Novel Framework:** Integrates XLNet, BiGRU, AW-Attention, and FCA for darknet market analysis. Multi-task learning enables simultaneous closed-set classification and open-set detection.
- **High-Quality Dataset:** Curated 14,744 annotated transaction records from 12 markets.
- **Superior Performance:** Outperforms both traditional and state-of-the-art models, demonstrating strong low-resource adaptability.

2 Research Background and Related Work

Darknet markets' anonymity enables illicit activities, with research progressing in classification and monitoring. Early work focused on **dataset construction and basic models**: Mhd Wesam Al-Nabki et al. (2017) [4] built DUTA—the first annotated dataset of 26 darknet categories via Tor sampling—establishing TF-IDF+logistic regression (F1=0.89) as a benchmark. He et al. (2019) [5] tackled **low-resource scenarios** by aligning illicit content with U.S. Code, achieving 93.5

Subsequent studies integrated **domain knowledge and security**. Formal Concept Analysis (FCA) [7] modeled conceptual hierarchies to enhance classification via three methodological categories (single/ensemble/distributed-classifier). Wang et al. (2022) [6] detected **malicious directories** using honeypots that exploited Tor vulnerabilities, identifying malicious HSDirs through semantic clustering.

Recent advances employ **language models and multi-task learning**: Jin et al. (2023) [8] developed DarkBERT, a specialized model outperforming general LLMs in multi-task settings. VendorLink [9] enabled cross-market vendor tracking via unified closed-set/open-set frameworks.

Research Gaps: Current limitations include: (1) Fragmented solutions for unknown categories and semantic ambiguity; (2) Insufficient fusion of domain knowledge (e.g., FCA) with deep learning; (3) Poor low-resource generalization. Our **FCA_XLNet_BiGRU_MultiTask** addresses these through formal concept lattices and multi-task synergy.

3 Dataset Processing and Description

Public datasets from Agora and ADM markets were sourced via IMPACT Cyber Trust [9]. After cleaning, the dataset contains **19,185** samples categorized as: **Transaction-related** (e.g., drugs, cybercrime) and **Non-transaction-related** illicit activities.

To address data scarcity, we applied jargon substitution [10] and label balancing. Stratified sampling divided data into: 70% training, 15% validation, and 15% testing sets. Table 1 shows category-specific augmentation results.

Table 1. Training Set Augmentation

Category	Subcategory	Pre-Aug	Post-Aug
7*Transaction	Drugs	2,501	2,501
	Financial Crimes	1,976	1,976
	Counterfeits	1,947	1,947
	Cybercrime	946	2,838
	Regulated Items	866	2,598
	Pornography/ID	706	2,118
	Weapons	244	732
Non-Transaction	Illicit Acts	1,169	3,507
Other	Miscellaneous	3,075	3,075

4 Model Architecture

To address the challenges of darknet transaction analysis [11], we propose the **FCA_XLNet_BiGRU_MultiTask** framework. As illustrated in Fig. 1 and Fig. 2, the architecture synergizes domain knowledge representation, contextual modeling, and multi-task optimization through four key components:

Formal Concept Analysis (FCA) for constructing a darknet-specific domain ontology (Subsect. 4.1), **XLNet - BiGRU - AW Module** for sequential dependency learning and adaptive feature weighting (Subsect. 4.2), **Multi - Task Learning Strategy** enabling joint closed - set classification and open - set detection (Subsect. 4.3).

4.1 Formal Concept Analysis for Darknet Market

Formal contexts $\mathcal{K} = (G, M, I)$ are defined over transaction categories G and keywords M with incidence relation I. The attribute closure $A' = \{m \in M \mid \forall g \in A, (g, m) \in I\}$ (Eq. 2) and object closure $B' = \{g \in G \mid \forall m \in B, (g, m) \in I\}$ (Eq. 3) induce formal concepts $\mathcal{C} = (A, B)$, forming a concept lattice ordered by $(A_1, B_1) \leq (A_2, B_2) \Leftrightarrow A_1 \subseteq A_2$ (Eq. 4). Each concept is encoded as a frequency vector $\mathbf{v}_{A,B} = [\text{freq}(m_1), \ldots, \text{freq}(m_k)], m_i \in B$ (Eq. 5) capturing structural patterns for darknet slang recognition. Attribute optimization through closures identifies cross-category keyword associations, enhancing semantic understanding.

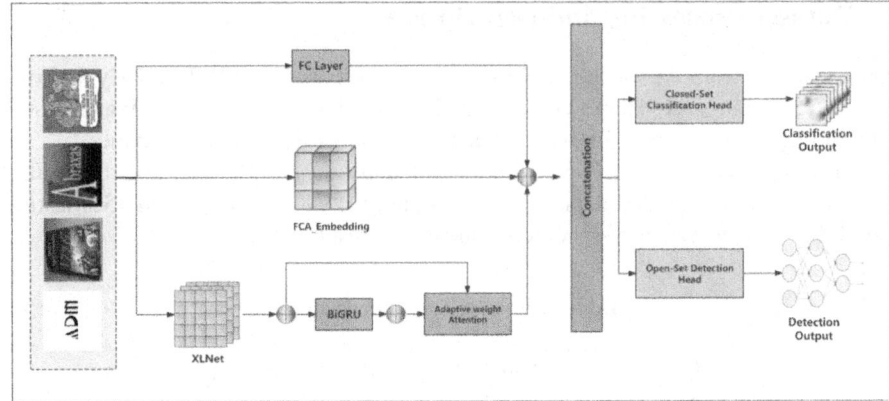

Fig. 1. Framework architecture.

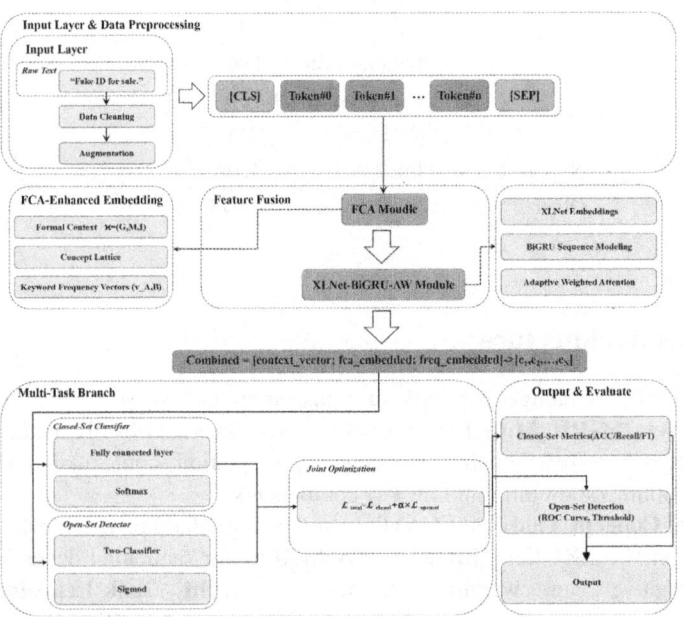

Fig. 2. Detailed workflow.

4.2 Handling Unknown Categories

For emerging illicit activities , we implement uniform labeling to enable joint closed-set/open-set detection within a unified framework.

4.3 XLNet-BiGRU-AW Module

Our **XLNet-BiGRU-AW Module** integrates XLNet, BiGRU, and AW-Attention to detect illicit transactions. For input sequence $X = \{x_1, \ldots, x_T\}$, it first generates XLNet embeddings:

$$\mathbf{H}^{(\text{xlnet})} = [\mathbf{h}_1^{(\text{xlnet})}, \ldots, \mathbf{h}_T^{(\text{xlnet})}] \tag{6}$$

BiGRU processes these to capture bidirectional dependencies:

$$\mathbf{H}^{(\text{gru})} = [\mathbf{h}_1^{(\text{gru})}, \ldots, \mathbf{h}_T^{(\text{gru})}] \tag{7}$$

AW-Attention then computes attention scores and weights:

$$\text{attn\_scores} = \text{matmul}(\mathbf{X}, \text{attention\_weights})\text{squeeze}(-1) \tag{8}$$

$$\text{aw\_weights} = \text{softmax}(\text{attn\_scores}) \tag{9}$$

$$\theta = \sigma(\text{aw\_param}) \tag{10}$$

$$\text{attn\_\tilde{w}eights}_t = \text{attn\_weights}_t \cdot \theta \tag{11}$$

The final context vector aggregates key features:

$$\text{context} = \sum_{t=1}^{L} \text{attn\_\tilde{w}eights}_t \mathbf{x}_t \tag{12}$$

suppressing noise in darknet texts.

4.4 Multi-Task Learning Strategy

The framework jointly performs **closed-set classification** (Weighted Cross-Entropy loss) and **open-set detection** (Binary Cross-Entropy loss). The multi-task loss is:

$$\mathcal{L}_{\text{total}} = \mathcal{L}_{\text{closed}} + \alpha_{\text{openset}} \mathcal{L}_{\text{openset}} \tag{13}$$

with α_{openset} balancing tasks. We optimize with:

- **AdamW** with explicit weight decay
- **ReduceLROnPlateau** scheduler using validation F1-score
- **Mixed Precision Training** for efficient GPU usage

Closed-set classification and open-set detection complement each other: the former provides stable feature constraints, while the latter ensures sensitivity to emerging threats. Shared representations (BiGRU outputs, AW-Attention context vectors, FCA embeddings) enhance robustness to unseen darknet trends.

5 Experiments

We evaluate **FCA_XLNet_BiGRU_MultiTask** on closed-set classification and open-set detection against baselines (BERT, RoBERTa, DarkBERT) and LLMs (PHI3, Falcon, Aya, Gemma, DeepSeek, LLaMA). Experiments cover open-set recognition, low-resource adaptation, and ablation studies.

5.1 Experimental Setup

Tests ran on an **NVIDIA Tesla V100 GPU** with **Python 3.9/PyTorch 2.0**. FCA used `concepts` library. Evaluation metrics:

- **Accuracy (ACC)**: Proportion of correctly classified instances over total predictions.
- **Recall**: Ability to identify all relevant instances (minimizing false negatives).
- **Precision**: Proportion of true positives among predicted positives (reducing false alarms).
- **F1-Score**: Harmonic mean of precision and recall, balancing both metrics for imbalanced data.

5.2 Overall Performance

Closed-Set Classification Table 2 shows results: **Key:** Our model outperforms baselines by 3–4% ACC/F1, showing strong low-resource adaptability.

Table 2. Closed-Set Classification

Data	Model	ACC	Recall	F1
Raw	BERT	87.16%	87.30%	87.16%
	RoBERTa	86.35%	86.07%	86.35%
	DarkBERT	86.39%	86.58%	86.39%
	Ours	**90.42%**	**90.45%**	**90.51%**
Enhanced	BERT	89.73%	89.60%	89.73%
	RoBERTa	88.78%	88.48%	88.78%
	DarkBERT	88.74%	88.68%	88.74%
	Ours	**91.68%**	**91.53%**	**91.67%**

Open-Set Detection Table 3 results: **Key:** Superior recall/F1 confirms multi-task effectiveness for unknown categories.

Table 3. Open-Set Detection

Model	ACC	Recall	F1
BERT	86.48%	86.12%	86.56%
RoBERTa	87.85%	87.74%	87.85%
DarkBERT	88.61%	88.54%	88.61%
Ours	**91.68%**	**88.12%**	**89.23%**

Table 4. LLM Comparison

Task	Model (Size)	ACC	F1
7*Closed-Set	PHI3 (3.8B)	54.08%	52.03%
	Falcon (7B)	60.67%	56.20%
	Aya (8B)	65.21%	57.65%
	Gemma (9B)	63.42%	62.07%
	DeepSeek (32B)	75.99%	72.78%
	LLaMA (70B)	76.31%	71.48%
	Ours	**91.68%**	**91.67%**
7*Open-Set	PHI3 (3.8B)	53.93%	55.88%
	Falcon (7B)	81.71%	81.98%
	Aya (8B)	77.44%	77.57%
	Gemma (9B)	88.12%	87.99%
	DeepSeek (32B)	85.57%	86.27%
	LLaMA (70B)	63.73%	66.37%
	Ours	**91.68%**	**89.23%**

LLM Comparison Table 4 shows LLMs underperform in darknet semantics:

Open-Set Analysis

- **Detection Rate:** Our model leads in recall (Table 4)
- **Threshold Balance:** Adaptive thresholds reduce false negatives without increasing false positives

Low-Resource Performance. Augmentation boosts all models (1–3% ACC gain), bu

6 Ablation Study and Error Analysis

We conducted an ablation study to assess component impact. Table 5 shows performance variations in classification and detection tasks.

Key findings:

- BiGRU boosts XLNet, confirming sequential modeling importance
- Attention enhances F1 via semantic focusing
- FCA integration yields highest scores for terminology recognition

Misclassifications stem from ambiguous slang. Advanced parsing could refine performance.

Table 5. Ablation Study Results

Task	Model	Prec.	Rec.	F1
4*Closed-Set	XLNet	88.16%	88.16%	88.04%
	+BiGRU	89.60%	89.56%	89.60%
	+Att	89.87%	89.58%	89.87%
	+FCA	**91.68%**	**91.54%**	**91.67%**
4*Open-Set	XLNet	87.54%	87.41%	87.54%
	+BiGRU	87.15%	87.08%	87.15%
	+Att	88.17%	88.05%	88.17%
	+FCA	**92.44%**	**92.80%**	**83.36%**

7 Conclusion and Future Work

We proposed **FCA_XLNet_BiGRU_MultiTask**, integrating FCA, XLNet, BiGRU, and adaptive attention. It excels in darknet classification and detection, outperforming baselines in noisy, low-resource settings. Ablation confirmed FCA and attention's importance.

7.1 Key Contributions

1. **Unified Multi-Task Learning Framework:** By jointly addressing classification and detection tasks, the framework enhances adaptability to unknown categories and enables efficient knowledge transfer.
2. **Domain Knowledge Enhancement:** Leveraging FCA to reinforce embedding representations significantly improves the recognition of darknet-specific terminology.
3. **Adaptive Attention Mechanism:** Dynamically focusing on key terms effectively reduces noise interference and enhances the model's generalization capabilities.

7.2 Future Work

We plan to explore three key directions: (1) **Cross-Language and Cross-Platform Expansion**, extending the framework's adaptability to multilingual environments and non-text modalities (e.g., images, watermarks) to broaden its coverage; (2) **Dynamic Adaptive Learning**, implementing continuous model updating mechanisms to address the rapid evolution of darknet slang and illicit techniques, ensuring long-term effectiveness; and (3) **Efficient Deployment and Real-Time Monitoring**, applying model compression and distributed deployment techniques to enable large-scale real-time surveillance capabilities.monitoring for practical applications.

Acknowledgments. This work was supported by the National Natural Science Foundation of China (Grant Nos. 72274096, 72301136 and 72174087), and the Foreign Cultural and Educational Expert Program of the Ministry of Science and Technology of China (Grant No. G2022182009L).

References

1. Per Hakon, M., Fahmy, Y.F.B., Guttorm, S.: The ransomware-as-a-service economy within the darknet. Comput. Secur. **92**, 101762 (2020)
2. Alnabulsi, H., Islam, R.: Identification of illegal forum activities inside the dark net. In: International Conference on Machine Learning. (2018)
3. Seyler, D., Liu, W., Wang, X., Zhai, C.: Towards dark jargon interpretation in underground forums. In: ECIR (2), pp. 393–400 (2021)
4. Al-Nabki, M.W., Fermé, E., Amigó, E., de Pablo, I.: Classifying illegal activities on tor network based on web textual contents. In: Conference of the European Chapter of the Association for Computational Linguistics. (2017)
5. He, S., He, Y., Li, M.: Classification of illegal activities on the dark web. In: Proceedings of the 2nd International Conference on Information Science and Systems, pp. 73–78 (2019)
6. Wang, C., Li, Z., Wang, W., Cai, Q., Yin, M., Feng, X.: Large-scale Evaluation of Malicious Tor Hidden Service Directory Discovery. In: IEEE Conference on Computer Communications. (2022)
7. Ammar, H., Miled, N., Mtibaa, M.: Survey on formal concept analysis based supervised classification techniques. In: International Conference on Machine Learning, pp. 21–29 (2020)
8. Jin, Y., et al.: DarkBERT: a Language Model for the Dark Side of the Internet. Comput. Res. Repository, 7515–7533 (2023)
9. Srivatsav, V., Rezaei, N., Diepenbroek, G.V., Siolas, G.: VendorLink: an NLP approach for identifying and linking vendor migrants and potential aliases on darknet markets. In: Annual Meeting of the Association for Computational Linguistics, pp. 8619–8639 (2023)
10. Liang, K., Chen, X., Wang, H.: An unsupervised detection framework for chinese jargons in the darknet. In: Web Search and Data Mining. (2022)
11. Faizan, M., Khan, R.A.: Exploring and analyzing the dark web: a new alchemy. First Monday (2019)

Knowledge-Driven Superpixel Shortest Path Optimization for Image Stitching

Renping Xie, Chenxi Pang, and Ming Tao(✉)

School of Computer Science and Technology, Dongguan University of Technology, Dongguan 523808, China
{xierenping,pangchenxi9,taom}@dgut.edu.cn

Abstract. UAV and remote sensing image stitching has significant value in agricultural monitoring, environmental surveillance, and urban inspection. However, traditional stitching methods often suffer from visual artifacts caused by imperfect seam-line selection, as well as inefficiency and limited precision in complex scenarios. This paper proposes a knowledge-driven seamline optimization framework that integrates superpixel segmentation, edge saliency analysis, and shortest-path algorithms. First, SLIC superpixel segmentation partitions images into homogeneous regions, reducing computational redundancy through semantic-aware knowledge modeling and improving computational efficiency through adaptive superpixel seed distribution, priority queue acceleration, and parallelization. Second, edge saliency analysis extracts high-frequency structural features as prior knowledge to avoid seamlines crossing prominent edges. Finally, a multi-feature fusion mechanism combining color consistency, edge significance, and spatial continuity guides the Dijkstra shortest-path algorithm to optimize seamline placement for natural transitions, enabling knowledge-based integration of heterogeneous visual cues. Furthermore, the proposed method incorporates a parallelized shortest-path search and dynamically adjusted superpixel constraints to further refine seamline placement. Experimental results on multiple high-resolution remote sensing and UAV datasets demonstrate that the method not only enhances the perceptual quality of stitched images but also effectively reduces visible artifacts.

Keywords: Superpixel segmentation · Edge saliency analysis · Multi-feature fusion · Seamline path planning

1 Introduction

Remote sensing and unmanned aerial vehicle (UAV) image have become indispensable tools for large-scale geospatial applications, including precision agriculture, disaster assessment, and urban development [1]. A fundamental challenge is stitching multiple overlapping images into seamless mosaics to provide comprehensive spatial coverage. Although existing methods rely on feature matching and geometric alignment, they often do not address critical issues in complex scenarios [2]: inadequate seamline placement causing visible artifacts, high computational costs for high-resolution images, and sensitivity to texture variations and illumination changes [3].

Recent advances in superpixel segmentation and graph-based optimization offer promising avenues to improve seam-line quality [4]. Superpixels reduce processing complexity by grouping pixels into perceptually uniform regions with embedded spatial knowledge, while shortest-path algorithms efficiently navigate these regions to identify optimal seams through structured knowledge reasoning [5].

However, existing methods still face considerable challenges in complex environments due to insufficient integration of multidimensional features (e.g., edge saliency and color coherence), resulting in suboptimal seamlines. For instance, when dealing with large-scale water bodies, forests, or dense urban structures, traditional approaches struggle to avoid seamlines crossing critical objects, leading to noticeable artifacts such as visible discontinuities along roads, buildings, or other prominent structures, ultimately degrading the visual consistency of stitched images. To address these issues, this paper proposes a knowledge-driven superpixel-based seamline optimization framework that enhances the naturalness of stitched images by leveraging edge saliency and multi-feature fusion to guide seamline placement.

Our contributions to the knowledge-driven superpixel framework can be summarized as follows:

- Robust edge saliency extraction uses an enhanced RNFA (Robust Non-maximum Feature Alignment) algorithm, leveraging edge knowledge to suppress noise while preserving structural continuity.
- Adaptive SLIC superpixel segmentation with gradient-guided seed initialization and boundary refinement, ensuring precise alignment with image semantics.
- Multi-feature fused shortest-path optimization, combining color deviation, edge significance, and spatial constraints as knowledge constraints to steer seamlines along natural boundaries.

2 Related Work

2.1 Edge Feature-Based Seam Line Optimization

Edge features are critical for locating natural seam lines in image stitching. Traditional methods often rely on edge detection algorithms such as Canny; however, these approaches tend to generate redundant edges in high-resolution images, leading to high computational complexity and fragmented structural information. Recent advancements focus on improved edge extraction techniques. For instance, the Robust Non-maximum Feature Alignment (RNFA) algorithm enhances edge continuity and saliency through non-maximum suppression and chain tracking. By integrating edge saliency analysis, Pak et al. [6] construct edge cost maps to quantify the visual importance of edge regions, guiding seam line selection. However, it should be noted that existing methods are not without limitations. Firstly, edge chain fragmentation in complex scenes has been shown to reduce the reliability of cost maps. Secondly, the sensitivity of traditional edge detection to illumination variations may introduce bias in saliency computation, thereby compromising the global optimality of seam lines.

2.2 Superpixel Segmentation-Driven Image Representation

Superpixel segmentation partitions images into perceptually homogeneous regions, substantially reducing computational complexity in subsequent processing [7]. The Simple Linear Iterative Clustering (SLIC) algorithm, a widely adopted method, generates superpixels via iterative clustering based on color and spatial proximity [8]. However, its fixed seed distribution and coarse boundaries limit its precision in stitching applications. Improved methods address these issues through adaptive seed adjustment and boundary refinement techniques (e.g., local color mean fusion), enhancing segmentation quality [9]. Despite the evident advances in this field, there are still several challenges that require attention. Firstly, the efficiency of computation for high-resolution images is suboptimal [10]. Secondly, uniform superpixels are not adaptable enough to complex textures. Third, there is insufficient exploration of the potential synergy between superpixel features (e.g., color variance, edge alignment) and seam line optimization.

2.3 Multi-feature Fusion for Seam Line Optimization

Seam line optimization requires balancing texture continuity, edge alignment, and visual saliency. Early geometric cropping methods are computationally efficient but fail to handle non-rigid deformations. Global optimization approaches like GraphCut improve seam quality via energy minimization but suffer scalability issues. Shortest-path-based methods (e.g. Dijkstra's algorithm) enable efficient local optimization by constructing superpixel adjacency graphs with edge cost and color difference weights [11]. Zhao et al. [12] proposed a multi-modality image fusion method based on correlation-driven dual-branch feature decomposition, which enhances feature cross-channel dependencies and extracts modality-specific features. Compared with this, our multi-feature fusion mechanism combines color deviation, edge significance, and spatial constraints, more effectively guiding seamlines along natural boundaries. However, the existing methods encounter several challenges, including insufficient utilization of superpixel semantic information, resulting in deviations from natural boundaries, dependence on empirical parameter tuning for multi-feature weight allocation, and redundant computations in high-resolution images, impeding real-time performance. These limitations underscore the need for a novel framework that integrates edge saliency guidance with adaptive superpixel weighting [13].

3 Method

This section presents a robust image stitching framework that addresses the computational inefficiency and suboptimal seam line selection of traditional methods through three key steps: edge feature extraction, superpixel segmentation, and seam line optimization. This framework integrates multiple algorithmic innovations to achieve efficiency and accuracy in high-resolution image stitching applications.

3.1 RNFA-Based Edge Feature Extraction

Traditional edge detectors like the Canny algorithm often produce redundant edges in high-resolution images, increasing computational costs. To mitigate this, we employ the Robust Natural Feature Analysis (RNFA) algorithm, which integrates gradient magnitude and orientation information for reliable feature detection, as shown in Fig. 1.

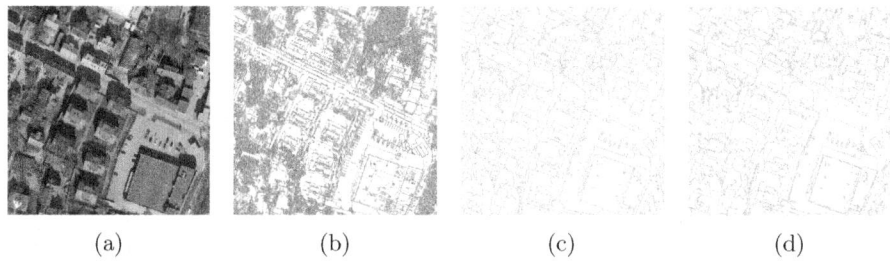

(a) (b) (c) (d)

Fig. 1. Original Image and Boundary Detection Comparison: Canny vs. RNFA with Gaussian Kernel Variations, (a) original image, (b) Canny edges, (c) RNFA edges with bad parameters($\sigma=1.5$), (d) RNFA edges with good parameters($\sigma=1.0$)

The RNFA algorithm applies Gaussian blurring (5×5 kernel, $\sigma = 1.0$) to suppress noise while preserving edge sharpness for accurate gradient computation (G_x, G_y via Sobel operators). Smaller σ (1.0) prevents over-smoothing critical edges (e.g., building contours), whereas $\sigma = 1.5$ (Fig. 1(c)) degrades gradient precision, causing fragmented edges. Non-maximum suppression (16 orientation bins) and eight-neighborhood connectivity analysis enhance structural continuity, validated by the NFA framework (with a threshold of 60.0). Furthermore, the gradient orientation $O(s)$ for the extraction of HOG characteristics is computed as:

$$O(s) = arctan(\frac{G_y(s)}{G_x(s)}), \qquad (1)$$

where $G_x(s)$ and $G_y(s)$ denote horizontal and vertical gradient magnitudes. HOG-based texture complexity $\Gamma(s)$ is then calculated using a sliding window(11×11) and normalized histogram bins ($B = 12$):

$$\Gamma(s) = \frac{\sum_{i=1}^{B} H_i(s) - \sum_{i=1}^{B} min(H_i(s), \bar{H}(s))}{Y + \sum_{i=1}^{B} H_i(s)}, \quad (2)$$

where $\bar{H}(s)$ is the average histogram value and Y is a regularization constant set to 10^{-6} to prevent division-by-zero errors and stabilize feature responses in low-texture regions. As shown in Fig. 1(d), RNFA ($\sigma = 1.0$) outperforms Canny (Fig. 1(b)) and $\sigma = 1.5$ (Fig. 1(c)) by preserving high-frequency gradients (G_x, G_y) for coherent edges while suppressing noise, avoiding Canny's redundant edges and $\sigma = 1.5$'s fragmentation from blurred gradients.

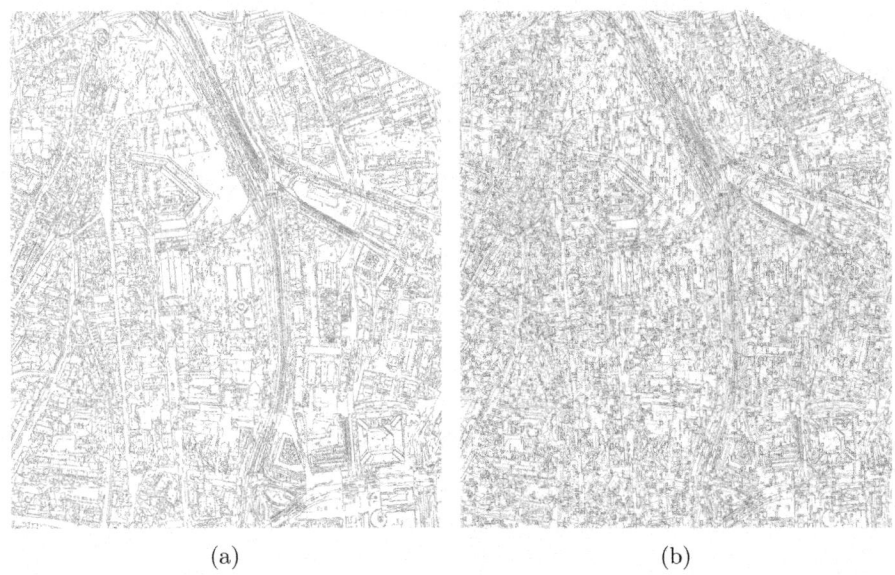

(a)   (b)

Fig. 2. (a) Refined Superpixel Boundaries Using Adaptive Segmentation, (b) Edge Cost Map Derived from Edge Saliency Analysis(blue lines): Overlay on top of the Superpixel Boundaries(a) map in the same image. (Color figure online)

To further refine extracted features, an edge saliency analysis module is introduced. It incorporates spatial distribution analysis via a sliding window (size: 50 pixels) and intensity variation measurements considering color and gradient differences. The resulting edge cost map (Fig. 2(b)) normalizes the values to [0,1], ensuring consistent weighting in the downstream processing. This cost map improves seam line selection by prioritizing dominant structural edges while minimizing the influence of weak or noisy edges.

The integration of RNFA with edge saliency analysis provides a robust edge extraction process, ensuring that detected edges align with meaningful structural elements. By incorporating multiscale feature tracking, adaptive thresholding, and spatial consistency constraints, the proposed approach significantly improves the reliability of seam placement in high-resolution image stitching.

3.2 Enhanced SLIC-Based Superpixel Segmentation

To address the computational inefficiency and boundary inaccuracy of traditional SLIC, we introduce several key enhancements to improve both segmentation quality and processing speed.

Adaptive Seed Distribution: Instead of using a fixed grid, initial superpixel seeds are distributed adaptively based on local gradient features. The process begins with a 5 × 5 initial grid set via the self written function. The seed positions are then adjusted using a gradient-weighted approach with a search radius of 10 pixels, ensuring better alignment with the image structures. A density control mechanism prevents over-segmentation in homogeneous regions, improving segmentation consistency.

Boundary Refinement: To enhance boundary accuracy, we introduce an optimization strategy using the drawBoundary function. This includes a local 3 × 3 window analysis, where the mean color values are computed for each superpixel. Pixels near region boundaries are reassigned based on color similarity and spatial connectivity, ensuring that superpixel edges closely follow natural image structures. Small regions (less than 25 pixels) are merged with the most similar neighboring superpixels in a post-processing stage, further refining segmentation results. Of which, superpixel similarity is quantified via Normalized Cross-Correlation (NCC) within local 5 × 5 windows:

$$NCC(x) = \frac{\sum (f(i,j) - \bar{f})(g(i,j) - \bar{g})}{\sqrt{\sum (f(i,j) - \bar{f})^2 \sum (g(i,j) - \bar{g})^2}}, \tag{3}$$

where (i, j) denote the pixel coordinates within the local 5 × 5 window, $f(i, j)$ and $g(i, j)$ represent the grayscale intensities of the superpixel regions f and g, respectively, and $\bar{f}$ and $\bar{g}$ mean grayscale values within the window. A threshold $P_0 = 0.4$ is applied to classify foreground pixels, ensuring that merged regions exhibit high structural coherence.

As illustrated in Fig. 2(a), these enhancements allow the refined boundaries to align more accurately with key image edges while maintaining computational efficiency. The iterative optimization dynamically adjusts the compactness factor based on local image structures, ensuring convergence when label changes fall below 1% or after 10 iterations. These improvements significantly enhance superpixel segmentation performance, making it more robust for high-resolution image processing tasks.

3.3 Multi-feature Fusion for Seam Line Optimization

We propose a multi-feature fusion framework that integrates color consistency, edge saliency, and spatial continuity for efficient and precise seam line selection.

Multi-feature Fusion Mechanism: The proposed framework integrates three complementary constraints for the fusion of features. First, the color-difference constraint calculates CIELAB color space discrepancies between adjacent superpixels using the superPixelCost function, preventing seam lines from crossing high-contrast regions. Second, edge saliency guidance maps gradient-based costs to superpixel weights, directing seam paths away from structurally salient areas. Finally, the spatial continuity constraint prioritizes vertical adjacency connections in the graph model through directional penalties, ensuring smooth transitions while discouraging excessive horizontal offsets.

Efficient Path Search Optimization: The optimization strategy combines enhancements to computational efficiency with post-processing refinement. Among them, the energy function $E(f)$ for seam line optimization integrates data and smoothness terms:

$$E(f) = E_{data}(f) + E_{smooth}(f), \qquad (4)$$

where $E_{data}(f) = \sum_x p_j(x)$ penalizes label assignments outside valid regions, and $E_{smooth}(f)$ enforces consistency between adjacent superpixels:

$$E_{smooth}(f) = \sum_{(s,s')} \eta(L(s), L(s'))exp(-\frac{(\mu(s) - \mu(s'))^2}{2\delta^2}), \qquad (5)$$

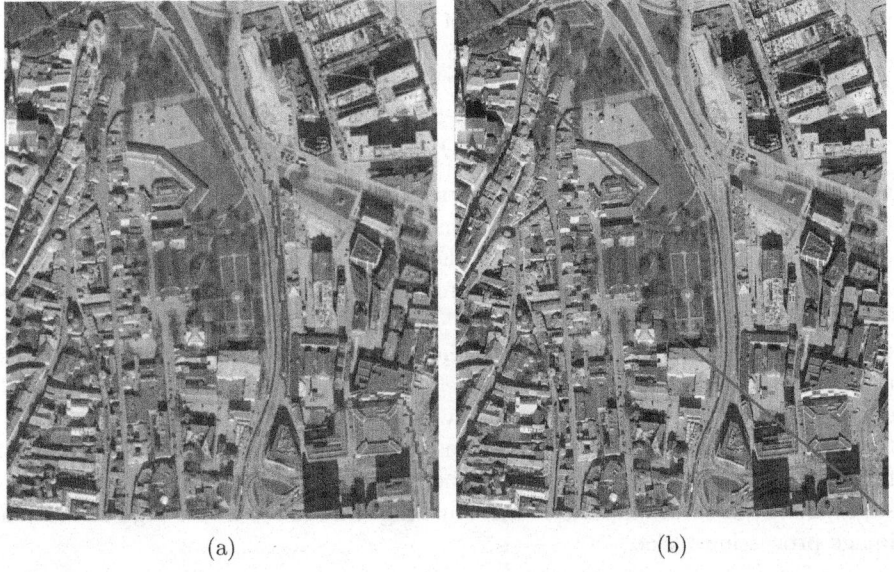

(a)   (b)

Fig. 3. Proposed Method VS Commercial Software PTGui, (a) Proposed Method: Seam Line Alignment Along Natural Boundaries, (b) Commercial Software PTGui: Seam Line Trajectories in Complex Scenes.

where $\mu(s)$ is the mean grayscale of superpixel s, and δ controls the penalty strength. $\eta(L(s), L(s'))$ is a label compatibility function that returns 1 if the superpixels s and s' are assigned different labels (i.e., they lie on opposite sides of the seam), and 0 otherwise. This formulation ensures that seam lines align with homogeneous regions.

Additionally, using a priority queue with a min-heap reduces path search complexity from $O(n^2)$ to $O(nlog(n))$. Parallel processing accelerates feature computation by 40%. Boundary refinement uses local 3 × 3 window analysis and merges small superpixel regions.

As shown in Fig. 3, this approach demonstrates improved alignment with natural boundaries (e.g., roads and buildings) compared to commercial tools like PTGui, effectively avoiding artifacts in textured regions through combined global constraints and local adjustments.

4 Experimental

4.1 Datasets and Implementation Details

Datasets: For experimental evaluation, we employed two datasets. The first dataset comprises Brandenburg (Germany) RGBN orthophotos at a 20 cm resolution from Google Earth Engine, which offers a vast collection of orthophotos from various regions worldwide. From this dataset, we selected several images from specific regions (named Brandenburg1 for region 589542 and Brandenburg2 for region 589569) and applied our stitching algorithm. The second dataset, the Katowise dataset, was provided by the Heilongjiang Mapping Institute and consists of a sequence of consecutive images consecutively captured by the same device. This dataset is particularly well-suited for assessing the performance and robustness of our image stitching approach.

Preprocessing: Input images are down-sampled using pyrDown to 1/4 resolution, retaining key features while reducing noise and computation.

Environment: Experiments were conducted on Windows 11 with an Intel i5-13400 CPU, implemented in C++ using OpenCV.

4.2 Stitching Performance

In this subsection, we present a detailed qualitative evaluation of the stitching performance of the proposed method. As shown in Fig. 4(a), the method demonstrates highly effective handling of complex scenes by achieving seamless transitions across image boundaries. The integration of superpixel segmentation and shortest-path optimization enables the precise placement of seam lines, which consistently follow natural image boundaries (e.g., roads, water bodies, and building edges) and reduce visual artifacts.

As shown in Fig. 4(b), a notable advantage of the proposed approach is its robust edge saliency analysis, which is pivotal for ensuring that the seam lines

Fig. 4. High-Resolution Texture Stitching: Proposed Method's Seam Line Path (a) Panoramic diagram of seam line, (b) Detail Visualization: Seam Line Optimization.

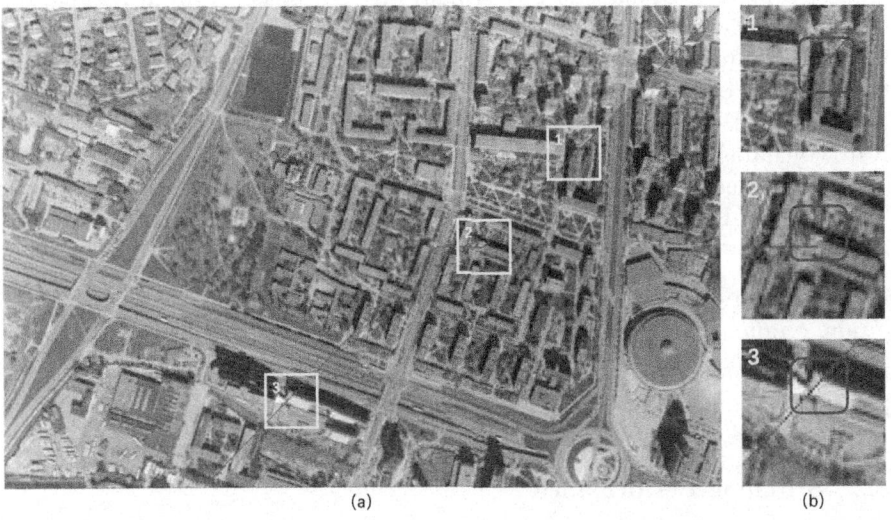

Fig. 5. High-Resolution Texture Stitching: Commercial Software's Seam Line Path, (a) Panoramic diagram of seam line, (b) Detail Visualization: Seam Line Artifacts Near Building and Road Boundaries.

are placed in regions with minimal perceptual significance. In contrast to conventional methods that rely on global intensity blending—often resulting in ghosting effects and color discrepancies—the proposed method employs a multi-feature fusion mechanism. This mechanism carefully fuses structural and textural infor-

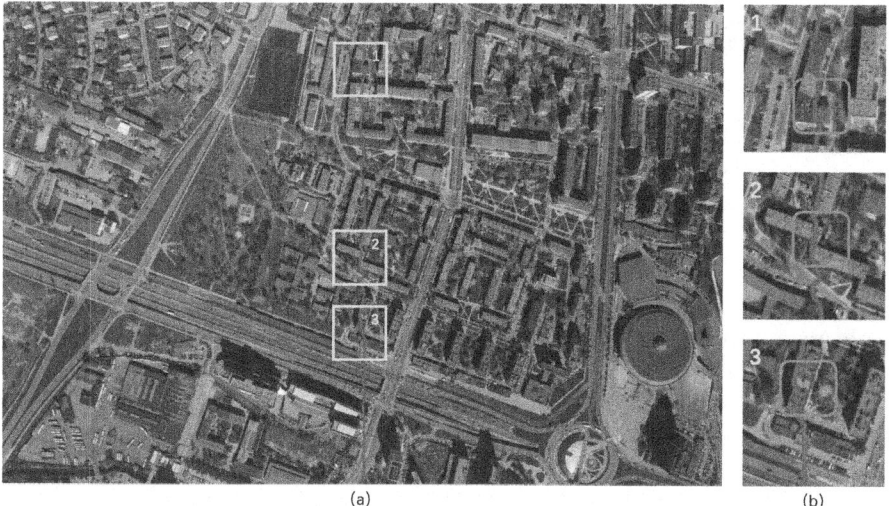

Fig. 6. High-Resolution Texture Stitching: Traditional Shortest-Path Algorithm's Seam Line Path, (a) Panoramic diagram of seam line, (b) Detail Visualization: Boundary Misalignment in Traditional Shortest-Path Algorithm.

mation from the overlapping regions, thereby preserving high-resolution details and minimizing abrupt transitions between stitched segments.

Moreover, visual comparisons (refer to Fig. 4(a), Fig. 5(a) and Fig. 6(a)) reveal that traditional methods and some commercial software tend to generate seam lines that frequently traverse critical objects such as buildings and vehicles. Such crossings lead to visible misalignments and structural distortions in the final mosaic (refer to Fig. 5(b) and Fig. 6(b)). In contrast, our method significantly mitigates these issues by incorporating adaptive superpixel segmentation, which intelligently segments the image into perceptually homogeneous regions. The use of spatial continuity constraints further ensures that the seam lines are routed away from high-saliency regions, thereby maintaining the integrity of prominent structures. Although the inclusion of semantic segmentation increases the computational burden, the overall efficiency is enhanced through priority queue acceleration and parallel computation techniques, ensuring that the method remains computationally feasible for high-resolution aerial image.

4.3 Quantitative Evaluation

For a rigorous quantitative assessment, two primary metrics were employed: the Structural Similarity Index (SSIM) and the count of seam line crossings through critical objects. These metrics provide a dual perspective on the quality of the image stitching process—evaluating both the preservation of structural details and the minimization of visual artifacts.

Table 1. SSIM index comparison between traditional method and proposed method on three datasets.

Method	Brandenburg1	Brandenburg2	Katowise	Average
Traditional Method	0.9083	0.8219	0.1388	0.6230
Proposed Method	0.9411	0.9762	0.4805	0.7993

As shown in **Table 1**, the SSIM index, which quantifies the structural similarity between the stitched output and the original overlapping images, achieved an average value of 0.7993 with the proposed method. This value represents a significant improvement over the traditional method, which recorded an average SSIM of 0.6230. The enhancement in SSIM is attributed to the multi-feature fusion mechanism, which adeptly guides the seam lines to align with natural boundaries. As a consequence, the structural integrity of the image is better preserved, and the occurrence of abrupt transitions is substantially reduced.

Table 2. Counts of seam lines crossing critical objects between commercial software and the proposed method on three datasets (unit: number). The smaller the value, the better the performance.

Method	Brandenburg1	Brandenburg2	Katowise	Average
Commercial Software	12	23	43	26
Proposed Method	5	8	16	9.7

In addition to SSIM, the evaluation also focused on the number of seam line crossings through critical objects such as buildings and vehicles. Results presented in Table II indicate that the proposed method reduces these undesirable crossings by 65.38% when compared with commercial software solutions (**Table 2**). This substantial reduction is primarily due to the effective combination of edge saliency analysis and adaptive superpixel segmentation. These techniques collectively ensure that the seam lines are preferentially routed along less significant regions, thereby minimizing the intersection with important structural elements.

Furthermore, despite the additional processing required for semantic segmentation, the overall computational efficiency remains competitive. The optimization strategies implemented, including the use of a priority queue for the shortest-path computation and parallel processing, enable the method to outperform conventional Dijkstra-based approaches in both runtime and scalability. This efficiency, coupled with the superior visual quality of the stitched images, underscores the practicality of the proposed method for large-scale remote sensing and unmanned aerial vehicle (UAV) image applications.

In summary, the experimental results confirm that the proposed method not only produces aesthetically superior mosaics with seamless transitions and well-preserved structural details but also offers a quantifiable advantage over traditional stitching techniques and commercial software. The enhancements in both SSIM and seam line placement demonstrate the method's efficacy in addressing the common challenges encountered in high-resolution image stitching tasks, thereby validating its potential for practical deployment in demanding imaging scenarios.

5 Conclusion

In this paper, we proposed an image stitching framework for remote sensing and UAV image that integrates adaptive superpixel segmentation with shortest-path optimization, significantly reducing the computational complexity of high-resolution image processing while ensuring smooth transitions in seam regions. Experimental results demonstrate notable improvements, with a 17.6% increase in SSIM and a 65.38% reduction in visible artifacts in critical regions. This work provides a knowledge-enhanced and efficient solution for high-precision image stitching in complex scenes, with potential applications in large-scale geospatial analysis and intelligent knowledge systems for Earth observation. However, at a macro level, the proposed method still exhibits slight discontinuities under extreme lighting or significant color differences, and its real-time performance on ultra-large-scale images remains a challenge—limitations that hinder its broader application.

References

1. Tao, M., Li, X., Yuan, H., Wei, W.: UAV-Aided Trustworthy Data Collection in Federated-WSN-Enabled IoT Applications. Inf. Sci. **532**, 155–169 (2020)
2. Xu, Y., Luo, Y., Yang, K., Shang, C.: Research on image mosaic of low altitude UAV based on Harris corner detection. In: IEEE International Conference on Electronic Measurement and Instruments, pp. 639–645 (2019)
3. Tao, M., Li, X., Feng, J., Lan, D., Du, J., Wu, C.: Multi-agent cooperation for computing power scheduling in UAVs empowered aerial computing systems. IEEE J. Sel. Areas Commun. **42**(12), 3521–3535 (2024)
4. Yuan, Y., Fang, F., Zhang, G.: Superpixel-Based seamless image stitching for UAV images. IEEE Trans. Geosci. Remote Sens. **58**, 1–12 (2020)
5. Miao, X., Qu, T., Chen, X., He, C.: Superpixel-Based Foreground-Preserving Image Stitching. Mach. Vis. Appl. **34**, 17 (2023)
6. Pak, M., Bayazit, U.: Regional bit allocation with visual attention and distortion sensitivity. Multimedia Tools Appl. **79**(15), 10551–10571 (2020)
7. Yusupov, O., Eshonqulov, E., Yusupov, R., Sattarov, K.: Analysis of superpixel segmentation approaches in remote sensing images. In: AIP Conference Proceedings, pp. 040026 (2024)
8. Dong, Z., Wang, M., Li, D.: A high resolution remote sensing image segmentation method by combining superpixels with minimum spanning tree. Acta Geodaetica et Cartographica Sinica **46**(6), 734–742 (2017)

9. Yu, H., Jiang, H., Liu, Z., Zhou, S., Yin, X.: EDTRS: A superpixel generation method for SAR images segmentation based on edge detection and texture region selection. Remote Sensing **14**(21), 5589 (2022)
10. Lati, A., Belhocine, M., Achour, N.: Fuzzy correlation based algorithm for UAV image mosaic construction. Multimedia Tools Appl. **83**(1), 3285–3311 (2024)
11. He, L., Li, X., He, X., Li, J., Song, S., Plaza, A.: VSP-Based warping for stitching many UAV images. IEEE Trans. Geosci. Remote Sens. **61**, 1–13 (2023)
12. Zhao, Z., et al.: CDDFuse: correlation-driven dual-branch feature decomposition for multi-modality image fusion. In: Proceedings of the IEEE/CVF Conference on Computer Vision and Pattern Recognition (CVPR), pp. 5906–5916 (2023)
13. Zhu, S., Zhang, Y., Zhang, J., Hu, H., Zhang, Y.: ISGTA: an effective approach for multi-image stitching based on gradual transformation matrix. SIViP **17**, 3811–3820 (2023)

Edge-Knowledge-Driven Smoke Removal Based on Infrared and Visible Image Fusion

Hengye Xu, Renping Xie, and Ming Tao(✉)

Dongguan University of Technology, Dongguan, Guangdong, China
{hengyexu,xierenping,taom}@dgut.edu.cn

Abstract. In smoky environments, the fusion of infrared and visible images leverages the smoke-penetrating property of infrared imaging to remove smoke from visible images. However, due to the lower exposure of infrared images, the suppression of visible images in the smoke region of the fused image can result in unnatural transitions between smoke and non-smoke regions, leading to pronounced boundary artifacts. To address this issue, we propose a Multi-slice Poisson Edge Softening Algorithm (MPEA) that uses edge knowledge to ensure a smooth and natural transition between smoke and non-smoke regions in the fused image. Furthermore, we introduce the quadrangle attention transformer module (QATransformer) as a decoder to preserve the detailed textures in non-smoke regions during feature reconstruction. Finally, we integrate these components into the proposed smoke removal fusion network, enabling edge-knowledge-driven adaptive fusion of infrared and visible information. Comparative and ablation experiments demonstrate the effectiveness of the proposed method.

Keywords: Image Fusion · Smoke Removal · Edge Knowledge · Edge Transition · Transformer

1 Introduction

Infrared and visible image fusion (IVF) aims to integrate the complementary information of multi-source modalities to enhance scene representation capabilities. Infrared images, by capturing thermal radiation characteristics, can highlight salient targets under low visibility conditions, while visible images can provide rich texture details and spatial context information under sufficient exposure. The fusion of them has high application value in fields such as night-time surveillance, autonomous driving, and military reconnaissance [1]. Traditional IVF methods, such as multi-scale decomposition and sparse representation, mostly rely on manually designed fusion rules and struggle to balance multi-modal features in complex scenes like smoke obstruction adaptively.

In recent years, deep learning-based fusion methods, such as convolutional neural networks CNN and generative adversarial networks GAN, have improved the quality of fused images through data-driven feature learning. In smoke scenes, smoke particles scatter visible bands, causing serious loss of texture information in visible images, while infrared sensors, due to their long-wavelength characteristics, are not disturbed by smoke texture. Therefore, the fusion of infrared and visible images leverages the smoke-penetrating property of infrared imaging to remove smoke from visible images. However, existing dynamic weight allocation strategies, such as suppressing the weight of visible in smoke regions and enhancing infrared response, tend to produce weight abrupt changes at the boundaries between smoke and non-smoke regions, resulting in unnaturally transitional fusion boundaries and affecting the performance of downstream tasks.

To solve the above problems, this paper proposes an edge-knowledge-driven smoke removal image fusion method. Firstly, by designing a Poisson gradient-guided fusion weight smoothing algorithm, the proportion of infrared-visible information at smoky boundaries is progressively adjusted through edge knowledge to achieve a natural transition. Secondly, leveraging the advantage of Transformer in modeling long-range dependencies [2,3], a QATransformer decoder with a quadrangle attention mechanism is adopted to replace the traditional CNN structure, overcoming the receptive field limitations of CNN. An end-to-end edge-knowledge-driven smoke removal fusion network can be constructed to more thoroughly remove the smoke of the fused images while preserving the texture and spatial details in the non-smoke region.

Our contributions can be summarized as follows:

- We have developed an edge-knowledge-driven infrared and visible image fusion network to solve the prominent edge issue in the smoky region of the fused image after softening.
- We design a Multi-slice Poisson edge softening algorithm (MPEA) to smooth the boundaries between smoke and non-smoke regions in the fused image, thus overcoming the obvious edge transition issues caused by the incompatibility of infrared and visible modalities.
- We introduce a QATransformer decoder to enhance the infrared target information in the smoke region and visible texture information in non-smoke region.

2 Related Work

2.1 Edge Smoothing Method in Image Fusion

In recent years, the issue of edge blurring in smoke softened regions in image fusion has emerged as a new research direction. To tackle this problem, scholars have proposed various smoothing methods to maintain or enhance edge structures during the fusion process. For instance, Wang et al. [4] proposed a gradient operator fusion scheme based on relaxation iteration. Leveraging the complementary gradient detection characteristics significantly improves edge quality and ensures real-time performance. At the algorithm level, Al-nasrawi et al. [5] introduce edge-preserving constraints, balancing the needs of smoothing and edge sharpening, which is particularly suitable for high-noise scenarios. Although traditional methods are capable of preserving edges, they have limited computational efficiency and multi-scale adaptability. Moreover, in the image fusion of smoke scenes, there is currently no appropriate solution to the problem of smoke region edge protrusion caused by cross-modal incompatibility.

2.2 Infrared and Visible Image Fusion Method Based on Deep Learning

Deep learning-based infrared and visible image fusion (IVF) [6] methods have demonstrated remarkable progress. Convolutional neural network (CNN)-driven methods typically employ end-to-end architectures with hierarchical convolutional layers to extract complementary features, including visible texture details and infrared salient targets, followed by multi-scale feature fusion mechanisms. For instance, Zhang et al. [7] introduced a CNN-based generic fusion framework that leverages dual-stacked convolutional blocks to hierarchically capture salient features from multi-modal inputs. Autoencoder (AE)-based methodologies adopt encoder-decoder paradigms, where the encoder compresses dual-modal representations into latent embeddings, and the decoder reconstructs fused images with enhanced informational fidelity. Tang et al. [8] incorporated an illumination-aware sub-network to probabilistically estimate spatial illumination distributions for adaptive feature aggregation.

Generative adversarial network (GAN)-oriented solutions utilize adversarial training between generators and discriminators to align fusion results with natural image distributions. Notably, Wang et al. [9] developed a unified frequency adversarial learning framework, integrating discrete wavelet transform with frequency-compensated generators to decompose spatial features into multi-band frequency components. Transformer-based IVF architectures exploit self-attention mechanisms to model global contextual dependencies, while hybrid CNN-Transformer designs synergistically combine local receptive fields of CNNs with long-range dependency modeling of transformers. For example, Zhao et al. [10] proposed a dual-branch network incorporating transformer modules for global feature interaction and CNN blocks for local detail preservation, achieving enhanced semantic consistency in cross-modal fusion tasks.

3 Method

In this section, we proposed a cross-modal edge-smoothing smoke removal fusion network. Specifically, we first designed a multi-slice Poisson edge softening algorithm (MPEA), which is shown in Fig. 1.

3.1 Smoke Softening and Double Branch Extractor

Smoke Softening Stage. To address the significant smoke masking in fused images, we introduce a series of smoke-softening algorithms and dual double-branch feature extractors. As visible information in smoke regions consists of

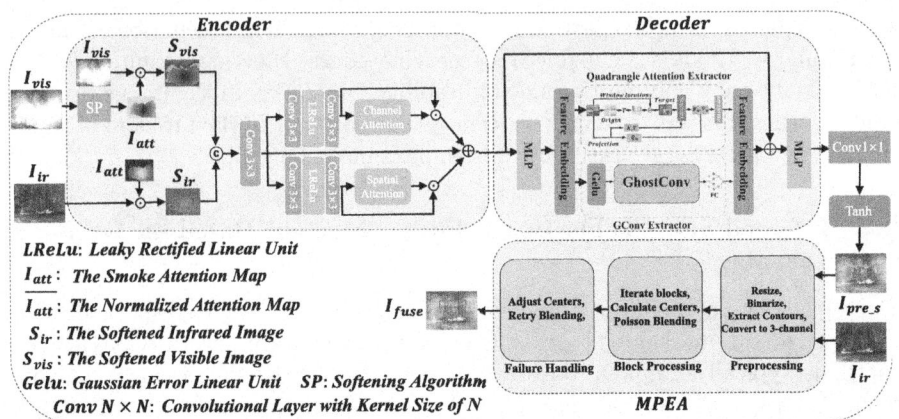

Fig. 1. The framework of the proposed smoke removal fusion network.

smoke textures, which causes significant target blur. The smoke softening algorithm can dynamically reduce smoke by lowering the weight of visible information and increasing infrared information proportions during fusion, achieving a dynamic smoke removal fusion effect. As illustrated in Fig. 1, Xie et al. [11] construct an attention map I_{att} via the smoke softening algorithm to characterize smoke concentration distribution, which is assigned differentially to infrared and visible modalities. This process is formulated as:

$$S_{ir} = I_{att} \odot S_{ir}, \quad S_{vis} = (1 - I_{att}) \odot S_{vis}, \tag{1}$$

where $\odot$ denotes element-wise multiplication, enabling adaptive suppression of infrared interference while preserving visible structural details in smoke-occluded regions.

Double Branch Extractor. In the feature extraction stage, to achieve the dual objectives of preserving high-fidelity texture details in non-smoke regions of fused images while enhancing the infrared salient target information within smoke regions and smoothing edge transitions between these regions, we introduce a double branch encoder incorporating spatial and channel attention mechanisms. Given the input image set $S_{in} = \{S_{vis}, S_{ir}\} \in \mathbb{R}^{H \times W \times 2}$, we first process it through a shallow feature extraction backbone for preliminary feature extraction and bifurcation, expressed as:

$$S_{mid} = BFE(S_{in}), \tag{2}$$

where $BFE(.)$ denotes a composite structure consisting of one 3×3 convolutional layer followed by two parallel branches, each comprising a 3×3 convolutional layer, LReLU activation, and another 3×3 convolutional layer in sequence. The initially extracted visible and infrared features are subsequently fed into channel attention (CAM) and spatial attention (SAM) modules respectively for dimensional-wise feature enhancement. These attention-enhanced features are then element-wise multiplied with S_{mid}, followed by residual connections with the original input S_{in}, ultimately yielding the refined output features:

$$S_{out} = C_{3\times3}(S_{in}) + CAM(S_{mid}) \odot S_{mid} + SAM(S_{mid}) \odot S_{mid}, \tag{3}$$

where, $CAM(.)$ and $SAM(.)$ represent the channel attention module and spatial attention module respectively, while S_{mid} denotes the intermediate features generated by the BFE structure. The $\odot$ operator indicates element-wise multiplication, and $C_{3\times3}$ refers to a standard 3×3 convolutional layer.

3.2 QATransformer Decoder

During the decoder phase, the smoke region softening process for visible image I_{vis} and infrared image I_{ir} partially compromises the preservation of detailed textures in non-smoke regions and the proportional weighting of infrared information within these regions. Therefore, we introduce the quadrangle attention mechanism module [2] in the decoder to enhance the fusion model's capability to capture features in non-smoke region images and balance the contributions of infrared and visible information inside and outside the regions. Unlike spatial and channel attention, quadrangle attention employs quadrangular tensor decomposition to jointly model cross-dimensional dependencies, which significantly enhances feature synergy capture efficiency. First, the encoded fusion feature is fed into a multilayer perceptron for nonlinear mapping. Subsequently, the feature embedding $E = \text{Embed}(S_{out}) \in \mathbb{R}^{H \times W \times D}$ is passed to the proposed quadrangle attention extractor and GConv extractor branches.

For the Quadrangle attention extractor branch, feature transformation proceeds as follows: E is projected along the H, W, D, and diagonal directions to generate four groups of attention features:

$$Q_h = EW_h^Q, \quad K_h = EW_h^K, \tag{4}$$

$$U = EW_U, \tag{5}$$

where W_h^Q and W_h^K are learnable parameters, and h, w, d denote the height, width, and diagonal directions. Similarly, Q_w, K_w and Q_d, K_d are derived.

Next, a quadrangle attention calculation is performed. Long-range dependencies are modeled along the main diagonal, with attention calculated as:

$$A_d = \text{Softmax}\left(\frac{Q_d K_d + U}{\sqrt{D}}\right), \quad O_d = A_d V_d + O_w, \tag{6}$$

A_h, O_h and A_w, O_h can be obtained similarly. Finally, a gating mechanism integrates the quad-directional outputs:

$$O_{att} = \text{LayerNorm}\left(\sigma(G) \odot O_d + (1 - \sigma(G)) \odot E\right), \tag{7}$$

where G is O_{att} processed by a 3×3 convolution layer, $\sigma(\cdot)$ denotes the sigmoid activation, and $\odot$ represents element-wise multiplication.

For the GConv Extractor branch, which focuses on local image features, the input E is first activated by a GELU layer. The features are then decomposed via GhostConv into F_m and F_c, followed by channel-wise concatenation and a fully connected layer for mapping:

$$O_{conv} = \text{Concat}(F_m, F_c)W_{fc} + b_{fc}, \tag{8}$$

where W_{fc} and b_{fc} are the weight matrix and bias term.

Finally, the outputs O_{conv} and O_{att} are combined with the fused feature E via residual connections. By a series of non-linear operations, we can obtain the preliminary edge-enhanced fused image I_{pre_s}.

3.3 Multi-slice Poisson Edge Softening Algorithm

Due to the incompatibility of cross-modal information between infrared and visible images, the initial fusion results in I_{pre_s} with distinct edge boundaries in the smoke regions after the softened smoke texture and enhancement of infrared salient features in the feature extraction stage.

To address this issue, we designed a smoke region edge smoothing algorithm (MPEA). First, we aimed to smooth the edges of the smoke regions in I_{pre_s}. Therefore, based on the smoke segmentation algorithm in **Section** 3.1, we obtained the smoke region segmentation mask M, and further extracted the regional contours to get the smoke region contour mask M_d.

As smoke texture information does not belongings to the scope of the infrared modality and we only smoothed a few pixel-level regions at the edges, we selected the corresponding contour region infrared image and assigned it to the contour edges of I_{pre_s}, ensuring a smooth transition between the smoke and non-smoke region. In addition, we dilated the contour mask M_d by 3 pixels, which could further ensure the complete fit of the smoothing region and reduce the loss of edge detail textures. Among them, Poisson fusion is an image fusion technique that employs the Poisson equation to adjust the source image's gradient to match the target, achieving natural image integration. Based on it, we transform the fusion smoothing problem into a gradient optimization problem, balancing the detail retention and color consistency in the smoke and non-smoke regions. We employ Poisson fusion to integrate the infrared features of the edge regions into the corresponding regions of I_{pre_s} for smoothing.

By setting the step size $\triangle l$, M_d was divided into multiple patches, and patches not involving the contour regions were discarded. The reason for choosing the multi-slice strategy to Poisson fusion was that the irregularity of the M_d contour region causes the center point (c_x, c_y) of the fusion region to deviate from the range of M_d. As for the patches with fusion failure, we could adjust the region center (c_x, c_y) to ensure the success rate. The Poisson fusion process can be represented as:

$$\triangle_{I_f} = div(\triangledown f), \ I_f|\partial\Omega = g, \tag{9}$$

where f represents the gradient field of the infrared image, g represents the color around the boundary of I_{pre_s}, and Ω represents the effective fusion region corresponding to each patch. In this way, we could obtain the fusion image I_f with smoothed regional edges.

4 Experiment

4.1 Datasets and Implementation Details

- **Dataset:** Our experiments employ three popular image fusion datasets: MSRS, M^{3}FD, and TNO. During the training stage, 1,083 smoke texture images with diverse geometric shapes were Poisson-blended into visible images from the MSRS dataset, which aims to generate sufficient smoke scenario IVF data. For testing stage, 20 image pairs from M^{3}FD and TNO datasets were selected to evaluate the effectiveness of our method.
- **Implementation Details:** The experiments were conducted on a platform with an Intel®Xeon®Platinum 8352V CPU @2.10GHz and two NVIDIA GeForce RTX 3090 GPUs. Training samples were randomly cropped into 128 × 128 patches with a stride of 10 and normalized to [0,1]. We adopted the adam optimizer with a fixed learning rate of 0.001. The training epoch was set to 150, and the batch size was 128.

4.2 The State-of-the-Art Fusion Methods

- CNN-based fusion methods: **SEAF** [12] and **PIAF** [8].
- AE-based fusion methods: **DF** [13] and **RFN** [14].
- GAN-based fusion methods: **FGAN** [15] and **LRRN** [16].
- Transformer-based fusion methods: **YDTR** [17], **CMT** [18], **CDDF** [10], **DAT** [19], **SWF** [20].

4.3 Evaluation Metrics

In this experiment, we employed the following 6 metrics to evaluate the fused images of smoke softening in terms of detail preservation and edge smoothing. Among them, visual information fidelity (VIF), information entropy (EN), spatial frequency (SF), Average Gradient (AG), standard deviation (SD), and edge preservation-based fusion quality index (Q_{abf}). Higher values of these metrics indicate better quality of the fused image.

4.4 Performance Comparison

As illustrated in Fig. 2, the results demonstrate significant improvements outside the smoke region detail retention and the smoothness of the smoke region boundaries on the M^{3}FD dataset. In contrast, other fusion methods leave too much residual smoke texture in the smoke region. SWF (columns 4 and 8) exhibits noticeable blockiness along the smoke region edges, distorting the transition between the smoke region and the non-smoke region. Due to smoke with

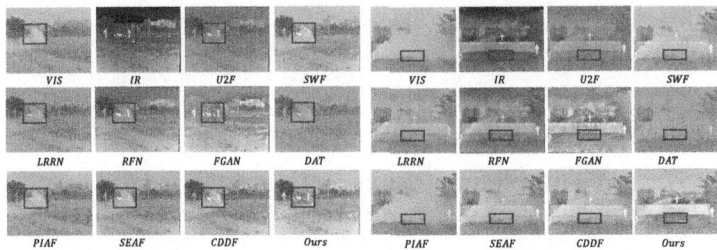

Fig. 2. Visual performance comparison with state-of-the-art methods on M^{3}FD dataset.

irregular density, PIAF (columns 1 and 5) struggles to preserve the finer details within the smoke region, resulting in an overly smoothed, unnatural edge transition. Furthermore, most state-of-the-art methods, such as the RFN (columns 2 and 6) and FGAN (columns 3 and 7), demonstrate satisfactory smoke-softening effects in smoke regions. However, their insufficient consideration of proportional balance in cross-modal information allocation between smoke region and non-smoke region, which leads to a significant loss of detailed texture information in non-smoke regions. In contrast, our proposed method achieves superior smoke region softening while maintaining great detail texture in the non-smoke region. This can be attributed to the QATransformer decoder's capability in focusing on detail texture reconstruction in non-smoke regions during feature restoration processes.

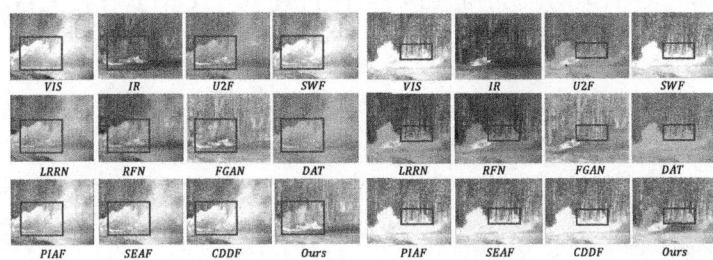

Fig. 3. Visual performance comparison with state-of-the-art methods on TNO dataset.

For the TNO dataset, which presents more complex and diverse smoke in military scenarios, the superiority of the proposed method is even more apparent. The smoke region exhibits a highly smooth edge, ensuring that it blends seamlessly with the non-smoke region while maintaining critical infrared features such as sniper in Fig. 3. LRRN (columns 1 and 5) introduces noticeable edge artifacts in the smoke region, leading to a sharp and jagged appearance. SEAF(columns 2 and 6) fails to retain the finer details of the smoke's inner infrared feature, leading to an overly prominent edge between the smoke and non-smoke regions.

Table 1. Performance Comparison of metrics with state-of-the-art methods on M³FD and TNO Datasets.

Model	M³FD Dataset						TNO Dataset					
	VIF	EN	SF	AG	SD	Qabf	VIF	EN	SF	AG	SD	Qabf
YDTR [17]	0.72	6.47	10.50	3.71	24.68	0.54	0.60	6.29	5.94	2.15	25.18	0.37
DF [13]	0.62	6.31	6.98	2.71	20.72	0.31	0.55	6.13	4.89	1.93	21.52	0.31
RFN [14]	0.62	6.98	7.62	3.11	33.23	0.40	0.65	6.87	5.26	2.36	35.54	0.38
CMT [18]	0.76	6.96	11.50	4.45	32.08	0.60	0.76	6.91	8.37	3.38	36.33	0.51
CDDF [10]	0.87	6.81	14.41	5.28	33.02	0.63	0.83	7.03	10.05	3.82	45.58	0.53
DAT [19]	0.60	6.10	12.94	4.39	20.52	0.50	0.66	6.20	7.68	2.73	22.40	0.43
U2F [21]	0.58	6.42	7.87	3.12	23.78	0.36	0.56	6.37	4.94	2.13	25.44	0.35
SEAF [12]	0.79	6.77	14.92	5.63	32.29	0.62	0.78	7.06	9.83	3.95	40.79	0.49
PIAF [8]	0.84	6.63	14.31	5.31	29.12	0.61	0.81	6.85	9.50	3.77	40.79	0.57
SWF [20]	0.87	6.63	13.17	8.01	30.06	0.63	0.77	6.75	9.52	3.46	38.92	0.54
FGAN [15]	0.86	6.88	7.49	10.31	30.89	0.30	0.75	6.60	8.92	3.62	27.87	0.34
LRRN [16]	0.61	6.48	10.87	4.03	25.47	0.50	0.64	6.88	7.45	2.95	39.53	0.40
Ours	0.92	6.99	14.83	5.64	34.57	0.64	0.81	7.47	10.43	3.97	45.97	0.58

The quantitative comparison results of the proposed method on the M³FD and TNO datasets are shown in **Table 1**, we keep all quantitative metrics to two decimal places for easier statistical analysis. Our method outperforms other comparative methods in several key metrics. For instance, on the M³FD dataset, our method achieves the highest VIF (0.921) and SF (14.834), effectively preserving details in non-smoke regions while avoiding over-smoothing and artifacts at the smoke region boundaries. On the TNO dataset, our method still demonstrates superior performance, especially in SF (10.43) and EN (7.472). During the fusion process, the weight of visible smoke information was suppressed, resulting in partial gradient loss at transitional boundaries between smoke and non-smoke regions. This accounts for our method's inferiority to SEAF in both AG and SF metrics. However, the proposed method excels in edge smoothness and detail preservation in the smoke region, avoiding the blurring and artifacts seen in methods such as DF and SEAF.

4.5 Ablation Study

In this section, we set a series of ablation experiments to verify the effectiveness of the proposed Poisson edge softening algorithm and QATransformer decoder.

Qualitative and Quantitative Analysis. Among them, W/o Poisson edge softening represents eliminating the Poisson edge softening algorithm, which primarily impacts the smooth transition of edges between the smoke and non-smoke

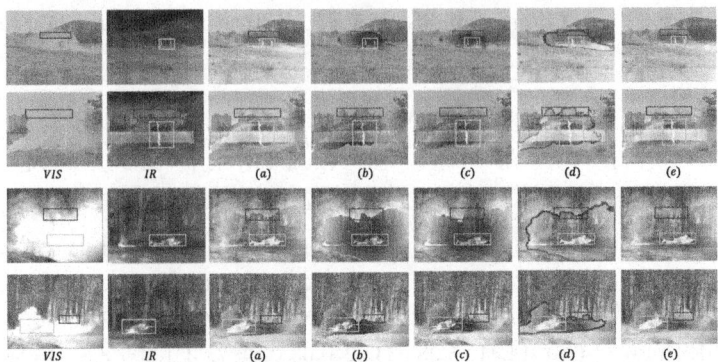

Fig. 4. Visual performance comparison with every ablation methods on M³FD and TNO dataset. From left to right represent different methods: (a), (b), (c) and (d) show the result of W/o Poisson edge softening, W/o QATransformer with Poisson edge softening, W/o QATransformer and our method, respectively.

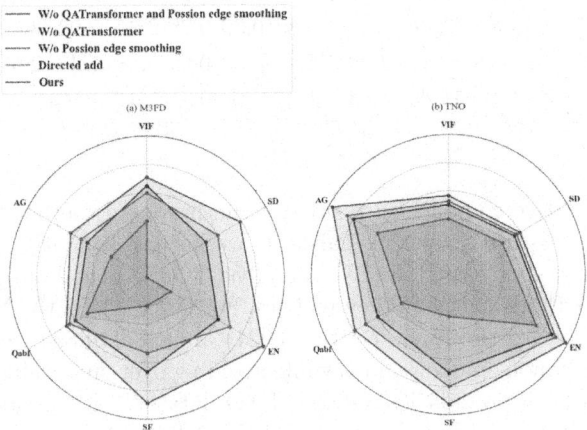

Fig. 5. Metric performance comparison with every ablation methods on M³FD and TNO dataset.

regions. W/o QATransformer represents replacing the QATransformer decoder with the traditional transformer decoder. W/o QATransformer and Poisson edge softening indicates the ablation of the Poisson edge softening algorithm based on W/o QATransformer. Directed adding denotes adopting direct superposition to smooth the edges inside and outside the smoke region.

As shown in Fig. 4, Our method (e) showed better edge transitions after softening the smoke region, and also well-preserved the infrared features within the smoke region and the visible texture features outside the smoke region. Furthermore, the quantitative metrics curve of the ablation experiment is shown in Fig. 5. We can observe that our method (e) outperforms the other ablation groups across key metrics like VIF, EN, and SF. Due to the lack of edge transitions between smoke regions, (a) presents an unnatural sense of boundaries, which is seen in the decreased SF and Q_{abf} value in Fig. 5.

W/o QATransformer (c) presents a significant infrared feature loss in the smoke regions and the yellow boxes in the images highlight this effect. Additionally, when both the QATransformer and Poisson edge softening algorithm are removed (b), the fusion quality deteriorates further, with visible artifacts in both the smoke and non-smoke regions. Directed Adding (d) fails to maintain a natural edge between smoke and non-smoke regions.

Compared with (a), our comprehensive method (d) achieves natural edge transitions between smoke and non-smoke regions, and also achieves better quantitative metrics. This is attributed to the proposed Poisson edge softening algorithm. Moreover, after the QATransformer decoder's feature reconstruction in the smoke and non-smoke regions, our fusion result not only attains a good smoke-softening effect in the smoke region but also significantly preserves the texture details in the non-smoke region. This can be reflected by comparing with (c).

5 Conclusion

In this paper, we designed a Multi-slice Poisson Edge softening Algorithm (MPEA) to smooth the transition of cross-modal information between the smoke and non-smoke regions in fused images. Additionally, we introduced a QATransformer module as a decoder to preserve the detailed texture information outside the smoke regions during the feature reconstruction process. Eventually, we integrated these into the proposed cross-modal edge smoothing smoke removal fusion network, which enables it to adaptively fuse information from different modalities based on the weights of infrared and visible smoke regions. Extensive comparative and ablation experiments have verified the effectiveness of the proposed method.

References

1. Tao, M., et al.: Bidding-Enabled resource pricing for computation offloading in 6G Vehicle-to-Edge networks. IEEE Trans. Intell. Transp. Syst. (2025)
2. Zhang, Q., Zhang, J., Xu, Y., Tao, D.: Vision transformer with quadrangle attention. IEEE Trans. Pattern Anal. Mach. Intell. **46**(5), 3608–3624 (2024)
3. Tao, M., et al.: Multi-Agent cooperation for computing power scheduling in UAVs empowered aerial computing systems. IEEE J. Sel. Areas Commun. (2024)
4. Lopez-Morina, G., Monteiro, J., Bustillo, H., Baets, B.: Self-Adapting weighted operators for multiscale gradient fusion. Inf. Fusion **44**, 136–146 (2018)
5. Al-Insarawi, M., Deng, G., Thai, B.: Edge-Aware smoothing through adaptive interpolation. SIViP **12**, 347–354 (2018)
6. Liao, L., Tao, M., Dong, A., Xie, R., and Zhang, Y.: Graph-Convolutional-Network-Enabled task offloading for industrial image recognition in digital twin edge networks. IEEE Internet Things J. (2025)

7. Zhang, Y., et al.: IFCNN: a general image fusion framework based on convolutional neural network. Inf. Fusion **54**, 99–118 (2020)
8. Tang, L., Yuan, J., Zhang, H., Jiang, X., Ma, J.: PIAFusion: a progressive infrared and visible image fusion network based on illumination aware. Inf. Fusion **53**, 79–92 (2022)
9. Wang, Z., Zhang, Z., Qi, W., Yang, F., and Xu, J.: FreqGAN: infrared and visible image fusion via unified frequency adversarial learning. IEEE Trans. Circuits Syst. Video Technol. (2024)
10. Zhao, Z., et al.: CDDFuse: correlation-driven dual-branch feature decomposition for multi-modality image fusion. In: Proceedings of the IEEE/CVF Conference on Computer Vision and Pattern Recognition, pp. 5906–5916 (2023)
11. Xie, R., Xu, H., Tao, M., He, C., and Chen, M.: Data-Driven smoke segmentation and removal for visible image. In: 2024 IEEE International Symposium on Parallel and Distributed Processing with Applications (ISPA), pp. 621–636, IEEE (2024)
12. Tang, L., Yuan, J., Ma, J.: Image fusion in the loop of high-level vision tasks: a semantic-aware real-time infrared and visible image fusion network. Information Fusion **82**, 28–42 (2022)
13. Li, H., Wu, X.-J.: Densefuse: a fusion approach to infrared and visible images. IEEE Trans. Image Process. **28**(15), 2414–2523 (2018)
14. Li, H., Wu, X.-J., Kittler, J.: RFN-Nest: an end-to-end residual fusion network for infrared and visible images. Inf. Fusion **73**, 72–86 (2021)
15. Ma, J., Yu, W., Liang, P., Li, C., Jiang, J.: FusionGAN: a generative adversarial network for infrared and visible image fusion. Inf. Fusion **48**, 11–26 (2019)
16. Li, H., Xu, T., Wu, X.-J., Lu, J., Kittler, J.: LRRNet: a novel representation learning guided fusion network for infrared and visible images. IEEE Trans. Pattern Anal. Mach. Intell. **45**(9), 11040–11052 (2023)
17. Tang, W., He, F., Liu, Y.: YDTR: infrared and visible image fusion via y-shape dynamic transformer. IEEE Trans. Multimedia **25**, 5413–5428 (2022)
18. Park, S., Vieu, A.G., Lee, C.: Cross-Modal transformers for infrared and visible image fusion. IEEE Trans. Circuits Syst. Video Technol. **34**(2), 770–785 (2023)
19. Tang, W., He, F., Liu, Y., Duan, Y., Si, T.: DATFuse: infrared and visible image fusion via dual attention transformer. IEEE Trans. Circuits Syst. Video Technol. **33**(7), 3159–3172 (2023)
20. Ma, J., et al.: SwinFusion: cross-domain long-range learning for general image fusion via Swin transformer. IEEE/CAA J. Automatica Sinica **9**(7), 1200–1217 (2022)
21. Xu, H., Ma, J., Jiang, J., Guo, X., Ling, H.: U2Fusion: a unified unsupervised image fusion network. IEEE Trans. Pattern Anal. Mach. Intell. **44**(1), 502–518 (2020)

HDRIU-B: Hierarchical Data Rights Confirmation and Incremental Update Mechanism Based on NFT and SBT in Blockchain

Sudan Hu[1], Zening Zhao[1,2(✉)], and Hongwei Zhang[3(✉)]

[1] Tianjin University of Technology, Tianjin, China
2022269@stud.tjut.edu.cn, znzhao@email.tjut.edu.cn
[2] National Computer Virus Emergency Response Center, Tianjin 300457, China
[3] Tianjin 360 Hongteng Technology Co. Ltd, Tianjin, China
zhanghongwei1@360.cn

Abstract. As a new production factor, the value of data hinges on efficient data circulation and robust rights confirmation mechanisms. However, existing data rights confirmation schemes often struggle with insufficient security and low resource utilization during data updates. To address these challenges, this paper proposes a hierarchical data rights confirmation and incremental data update mechanism based on Non-Fungible Tokens (NFTs) and Soulbound Tokens (SBTs) on the blockchain, named HDRIU-B. In HDRIU-B, data owners upload their data to the Inter Planetary File System (IPFS), and the Content Identifier (CID) generated for each piece of data in IPFS is bound to an NFT, enabling efficient management of data usage rights. To further clarify data ownership, users can bind existing NFTs to SBT. The core innovation of HDRIU-B lies in its incremental data update mechanism: when new NFTs are bound to the same SBT, it signifies an incremental update to the dataset which is bound to the SBT. Additionally, once an NFT is bound to an SBT, it cannot be bound to another SBT, ensuring data integrity and immutability. We conducted experiments to evaluate the gas consumption and time costs of the proposed scheme on the blockchain. The results show that HDRIU-B improves the efficiency of data update and resource utilization while ensuring data security and integrity. Compared with the traditional methods, the mechanism proposed in this paper reduces the time consumption from 6701ms to 2023ms when processing this task, achieving an efficiency improvement of approximately 69.8%.

Keywords: NFT · SBT · data rights confirmation · dynamic update · data security · blockchain

1 Introduction

In the absence of a perfect data rights confirmation system, the circulation and sharing of data resources are significantly hindered, limiting their potential to fully realize value as a new production factor. In 2022, Lu Zhipeng et al. [1] from China Electronics proposed the innovative concept of "data components" for the problem of data ownership classification. By separating the personality rights of information from the property rights of data, and further dividing the property rights into ownership and operation rights, the problem of unclear data ownership was effectively solved. However, although the data ownership has been resolved to a certain extent, it still faces new technical challenges when the confirmed data needs to be added. At present, NFT is widely used in data rights confirmation scenarios [2], but there are still obvious limitations in the existing research on the dynamic update of confirmed data. For example, the NFT right confirmation method based on digital watermarking proposed by Saeed Ranjbar Alvar et al. [3] only supports static images, and the traceable data exchange scheme proposed by Song R et al. [4] by binding data to NFT does not fully consider the dynamic update requirements of confirmed data. Therefore, there is a pressing need to develop mechanisms that support incremental updates and dynamic management of data on the base of data rights confirmation.

1.1 Related Works

Among the existing data rights confirmation schemes, NFT and SBT, as two important digital credential technologies [5,6], have shown extensive application potential in the field of data rights confirmation. However, most of the existing studies [7] focus on the uniqueness and non-tampering of NFT to realize data rights confirmation, or use the non-transferability of SBT to bind data ownership [8], and the discussion on how to combine NFT and SBT to build a more perfect data rights confirmation system is still limited. Therefore, how to integrate the advantages of NFT and SBT to improve the integrity of data rights confirmation and dynamic management capabilities is still a problem to be solved. To further analyze this problem, this paper reviews the existing data rights confirmation schemes based on NFT and SBT respectively, and summarizes their limitations in data incremental update.

Data Rights Confirmation Based NFT. In the NFT based right confirmation work, Dalla Preda M and Masaia F [9] pointed out that although the uniqueness of NFT provides technical foundation for data rights confirmation, due to the easy replicability of data, there is a risk of fraud in right confirmation. In order to improve the authenticity of NFT, some studies [10] have explored the integration of digital watermarking techniques to enhance the ability of data provenance. However, such approaches may cause data loss in the process of data updating, reducing the integrity and reliability of the data. In addition, Liu et al. [11] proposed an efficient tracking mechanism based on blockchain to manage the change of data asset rights. DART [12] data circulation scheme enhances the fluidity of data rights confirmation through cross-chain NFT technology, and provides a feasible scheme for data circulation in multi-chain environment. However, these studies mainly focus on the application of NFT in data rights confirmation and circulation, and there is still a lack of effective solutions for the incremental update of data whose right have been confirmed.

Data Right Confirm Based SBT. Unlike NFT, SBT possess inherent non-transferability, which grants them unique advantages in managing data ownership. However, research on SBT [13]mostly focus on the application in digital identity authentication and personal reputation evaluation. N Tanwar et al. [14] proposed a data rights confirmation and privacy protection scheme combining NFT and SBT to enhance the security and credibility of data in the blockchain environment. Nevertheless, the data circulation process remains vulnerable to tampering risks [15], and the applicability of this scheme in dynamic data management and circulation scenarios still has certain limitations. Therefore, how to take advantage of the non-transferability of SBT to support the dynamic update of data under the premise of ensuring data security is still a problem worthy of further research.

In general, although NFT and SBT have made important progress in the field of data rights confirmation, there are still some limitations in existing research on the incremental update of data whose right has been confirmed and the tamper-proof protection during data circulation. Specifically, there is still a lack of systematic research on how to effectively combine the unique characteristics of NFT and SBT to simultaneously achieve data rights confirmation, dynamic update and secure data circulation.

1.2 Motivation

Data rights confirmation is a key link in data circulation. while current NFT-based schemes provide some ideas, they remain susceptible to malicious tampering during data circulation processes. As a non-transferable token, has been utilized in identity verification scenarios but has yet to be fully explored for applications in data rights confirmation and dynamic management. Consequently, how to combine the characteristics of NFT and SBT to build a unified framework for data rights confirmation, dynamic update, and secure circulation remains an open research problem. This paper proposes a data rights confirmation mechanism combining NFT and SBT, which records the right to use data through NFT and the ownership of data through SBT, and proposes an incremental update mechanism to realize efficient data update and ownership management. This approach not only reduces the time and gas costs associated with data update on the blockchain but also enhances the security and integrity of data.

1.3 Contributions

The contributions of this paper are as follows:

(1) We propose a dynamic data update mechanism,HDRIU-B, which combines NFT and SBT. In this framework, NFT serves are utilized to manage data

usage rights, while SBT serves as non-transferable certificate to establish data ownership. This approach effectively distinguishes the right to use data from the ownership, enabling hierarchical management of data rights.
(2) HDRIU-B supports incremental data update, users can cast the new data into a new NFT, and update the data set by binding with SBT, avoiding the high cost of overall data upload, significantly improving the efficiency of data update while reducing resource consumption.
(3) Through theoretical analysis and experimental verification, the proposed HDRIU-B scheme has high security in the process of data incremental update, and can effectively prevent the repeated confirmation of data rights. Experimental results show that HDRIU-B exhibits low Gas consumption and time overhead in the data update process.

2 Proposed HDRIU-B

2.1 System Overview

In this scenario, NFT is used to manage the right to use the data, and SBT is used to manage the ownership of the data.

SC: Data Storage Center, consisting of IPFS and Hash library. The hash library stores the hash values of received packets for data verification. Once verified, the data is uploaded to IPFS, which can create a content-addressable Hash for the data, known as a content identifier (CID). CID ensures that legitimate users can obtain specified data from IPFS and that the data remains untampered with.

User: A participant in HDRIU-B, either a data seller or a data demander.

The program mainly includes the following five steps: data upload, NFT issuance, application for SBT, update SBT for data incremental update.

As shown in Fig. 1, once the User completes data collection, the data undergoes a cleaning process, and metadata is extracted. Following data processing, the User uploads the data D_A to SC. Firstly, SC verifies the uniqueness of D_A. Upon successful verification, the SC uploads the data to IPFS, which generates a unique CID for each data to ensure the immutability and uniqueness of the data. After CID generation, SC invokes the smart contract to mint a NFT for the packet D_A. Once minted, the NFT is stored in the User's digital wallet. To further clarify data ownership, the User can choose to bind the NFT to a SBT by calling a smart contract. This binding mechanism facilitates hierarchical management of data ownership, effectively distinguishing between data usage rights and ownership. When Users want to update a data set, they can upload the new data, generate a new CID, and cast a new NFT. Subsequently, the User can choose to bind this new NFT with the SBT corresponding to the target dataset to complete the incremental update of the data. Notably, if the User selects the leased NFT and the NFT has been bound to the original owner's SBT, the binding operation will fail, ensuring the data integrity and security. The following smart contracts are used in HDRIU-B. These contracts realize the life cycle management functions of data right confirmation, update, transaction and corresponding NFT/SBT on the chain, including the registration, authority binding, transfer and recovery of data assets:

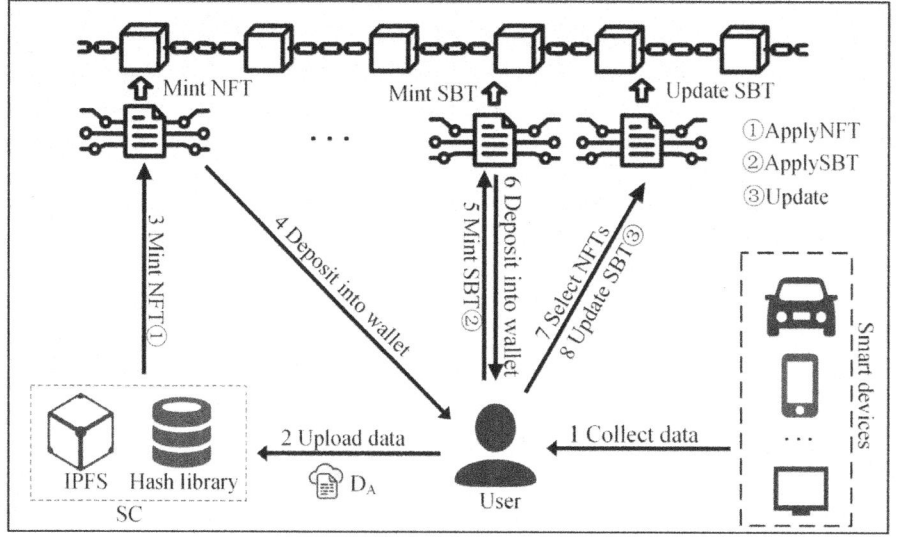

Fig. 1. General scheme programming.

1. **ApplyNFT**(D_*, $Wallet_*$, $JSON_*$): This smart contract allocates an NFT for each data confirmation and sends it to ∗'s digital wallet. The output is an array storing the ids of all NFTs.
2. **ApplySBT**($NFTs_{select}$, info:): The smart contract judges the binding status of NFTs and synthesizes the selected set of eligible NFTs and SBT-related information to generate a unique *tokenId* as output for identifying a specific SBT.
3. **Update**(SBT_{select}, $NFTs_{select}$): This smart contract uploads and associates the new NFT set with the selected SBT, completes the data update, and outputs the ID of the SBT.
4. **Transfer**($NFTs_{selected}$, $Wallet_*$, price) This smart contract will perform the NFT locking and transfer process to transfer the selected NFT to ∗'s digital wallet and deduct the corresponding amount of tokens from it.
5. **Revoke**(NFT, Compensation): This smart contract performs the revocation operation of NFT, which is invoked by the data owner to reclaim the authorized NFT and deduct the amount owed by the data user.
6. **Return**(NFT, $Wallet_*$): The smart contract will automatically execute the NFT return process at the end of the authorization period, returning the NFT to ∗'s digital wallet.

2.2 Data Upload

Data Processing. Relying on a variety of smart hardware, such as smartphones and various sensors, User can obtain data resources spanning multiple categories. In the proposed dynamic data rights confirmation scheme based on

NFT and SBT, the data processing process is first completed by User to collect the original data, the data processing workflow begins with User collecting raw data. Subsequently, the data undergo a cleaning process to remove invalid or erroneous records and is formatted into a standardized structure. Following this, the key features are extracted from the cleaned data, and corresponding metadata is generated. The metadata is typically stored in a JSON file, which comprehensively documents the fundamental attributes and characteristics of the data, such as the data type, the time of collection, and data volume. Under the premise of ensuring that user privacy is properly protected, the metadata must accurately capture the core characteristics of the original data, thereby providing a foundation for subsequent operations such as associating metadata with NFT.

Data Validation with IPFS Upload. During the data upload process, the SC performs verification on the uploaded data. The primary objective of data verification is to prevent the inclusion of duplicate or tampered data within the system, thereby ensuring the security and integrity of data rights confirmation and circulation.

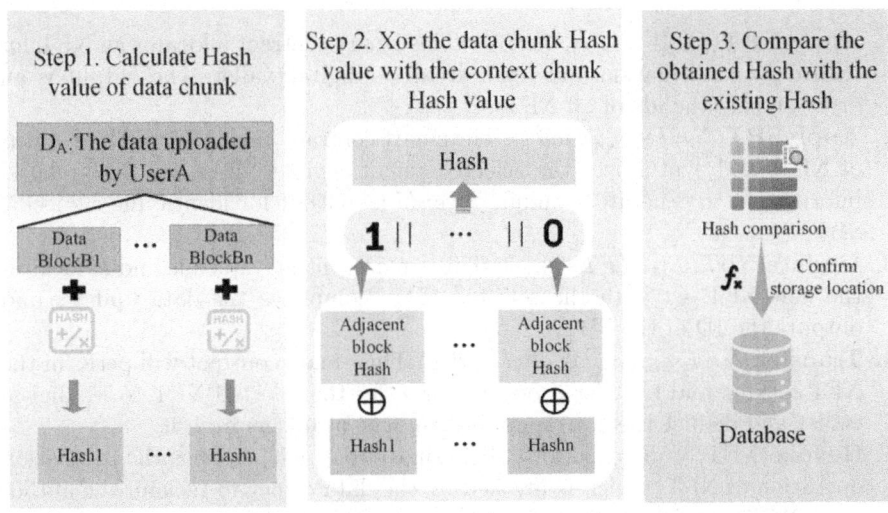

Fig. 2. Data validation.

Data Validation. As illustrated in Fig. 2, it is assumed that UserA has completed processing and is prepared to upload the packet D_A. User first transfers the data D_A to the SC. To ensure data integrity and authenticity, SC performs verification on the received data D_A. SC maintains a hash library that stores the hash values of all previously received data packets. Suppose that D_A is a packet of length

L. Upon receiving D_A, SC divides it into n blocks and adopts a sliding window of size w with a sliding step of s. The starting position of the i−th block is $(i-1) \times s$, and the ending position is $(i-1) \times s + w - 1$. Thus, the data of the i−th block can be represented as follows:

$$B_i = D_A[start_i : end + 1] = [(i-1) \times s + w - 1] \tag{1}$$

Next, a hash function is applied to compute the hash value for each block B_i:

$$H(B_i) = SHA256(SHA256(B_i)) \tag{2}$$

Then, the position of the block in the packet and its context information are considered. To capture the context information, the context trigger function T_i is introduced, which is expressed as the XOR operation of the hash value of the current block B_i and the hash values of its neighboring blocks:

$$T(B_i) = \bigoplus_{j=i-1}^{3} h(B_i), \tag{3}$$

where $\bigoplus$ denotes the XOR operation. For boundary cases(i.e., $i = 1$ or $i = n$), only existing adjacent blocks are considered.

Finally, the context-triggered hash value is further hashed using a locality sensitive hashing(LSH) function to map it into a smaller hash space:

$$LSH(D_A) = H(T_1(B_1)||T_2(B_2)||...||T_n(B_n)) \tag{4}$$

Subsequently, SC compares the calculated hash value $LSH(D_A)$ with the existing hash values in the hash library. If the verification is successful, that is, $LSH(D_A)$ does not conflict with any hash value in the library, SC stores $LSH(D_A)$ in the hash library and records the storage location of data D_A in the database:

$$Loc(D_A) = Record(LSH(D_A), Position(D_A)) \tag{5}$$

Here, $Loc(D_A)$ represents the location record of data D_A, $Record$ is the recording function, and $Position(D_A)$ denotes the specific location of data D_A within the SC. If the difference between $LSH(D_A)$ and some hash value $LSH(D_{exist})$ in the hash library is found to be less than a predefined threshold δ,i.e.,

$$\Delta(LSH(D_A), LSH(D_{exist})) < \delta \tag{6}$$

where δ denotes the hash value difference calculation function, SC will identify data D_A as illegal data and refuse to issue NFT for it.

Data Is Uploaded to IPFS With CID Generation. After the data validation is completed successfully, SC uploads the data packet D_A to IPFS. IPFS will generate a unique CID for each uploaded data, which serves as the fingerprint to uniquely identify the data content. Following CID generation, SC binds the CID to the metadata of the packet D_A, typically stored in a JSON file. The metadata includes essential attributes of the data, such as data type, collection time, data volume and other information, which can be used to trace the origin of the data and ensure its uniqueness.

2.3 NFT Distribution and Circulation

Once the data is uploaded to IPFS, the SC invokes the smart contract and generates a unique ID to identify the NFT using the ERC-721 protocol:

$$NFT = Apply(D_A, Wallet_A, JSON(D_A), CID) \qquad (7)$$

Here, $Wallet_A$ represents UserA's digital wallet, $JSON(D_A)$ represents the JSON file containing the data D_A, and CID is the Content identifier generated by IPFS. By binding CID to NFT, a unique and immutable relationship between the NFT and the data is established.

Once the NFT is successfully created, UserA can query and verify the newly minted NFT and its corresponding dataset D_A in the blockchain network to ensure the authenticity of the NFT and the integrity of the data. At this stage, UserA can call the smart contract to sell or lease the NFT. The smart contract according to the corresponding unique NFT: $NFT(Wallet_A, ID, LSH(D_A))$ automatically verifies the information related to the NFT, and after confirming that UserA has control over the NFT, the request to sell or lease the above NFT is broadcast to the entire blockchain network.

When UserB receives the NFT sale request, they can initiate a purchase request. The smart contract will automatically verify the legitimacy of the UserB's address and confirm whether the account balance exceeds the price of the NFT. If the verification is successful, the smart contract transfers the NFT from UserA's address to UserB's address, granting UserB control over the NFT. Simultaneously, an equivalent amount of tokens is deducted from UserB's account and transferred to UserA's account.

2.4 Apply for SBT

As a representation of data ownership, the application process for SBT is the key step in data rights confirmation. By applying for an SBT, UserA can establish clear ownership of the data, thereby preventing unauthorized tampering or misuse. Assume that UserA owns a total of γ NFTs, denoted as $NFTs_{total} = \{NFT_1, NFT_2, \ldots, NFT_\gamma\}$, which includes all NFTs obtained through applications or purchases. UserA selects δ NFTs from its account, denoted as $NFTs_{select} = \{NFT_1, NFT_2, \ldots, NFT_\delta\}$, and calls smart contract to upload the identifiers of these δ NFTs. After verifying the ownership of these

NFTs, the smart contract generates a unique $tokenId$ to identify the specific SBT and issues the SBT as follows:

$$tokenId = ApplySBT(NFT_{select}, info) \qquad (8)$$

Upon successful issuance, data ownership is locked, meaning the bound NFT can no longer be bound to any new SBT, but can still be transferred as a lease.

2.5 Update SBT for Incremental Data Update

When the dataset requires updating, the user can upload the new data to the SC, following the aforementioned steps, obtain a new set of NFTs denoted as $NFTs_{new} = \{NFT_1, NFT_2, \ldots, NFT_n\}$, where n is the number of newly obtained NFTs. The user can then select the target SBT for updating and append the chosen NFTs to complete the data update process:

$$UpdateSBT = Update(SBT_{select}, NFTs_{select}) \qquad (9)$$

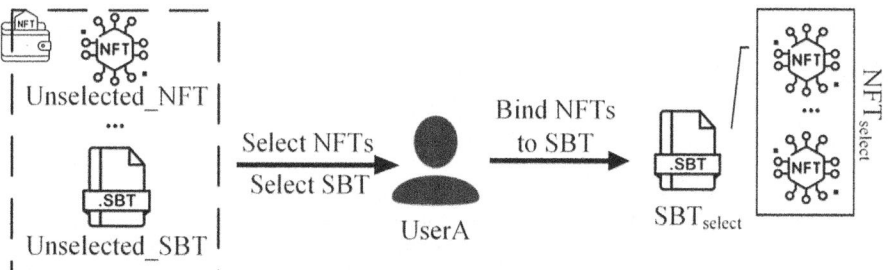

Fig. 3. SBT update.

As illustrated in Fig. 3, the selected NFT are denoted as NFT_{select} and SBT_{select}, respectively. When NFT_{select} is bound to SBT_{select}, it represents an incremental update to the dataset, incorporating the data associated with NFT_{select} into the dataset represented by SBT_{select}. Additionally, NFT_{select} can still be leased to others (e.g., UserB), but UserB is restricted from binding it to their own SBT. This mechanism not only ensures dataset integrity and clarifies ownership but also enhances the flexibility of NFT_{select}.

The algorithm for updating SBT is as follows, where UpdateSBT denotes the updated status of SBT and SBT_{select} denotes the SBT selected for updating. Through the aforementioned mechanism, HDRIU-B enables incremental updates to dataset while ensuring efficient data updates. Simultaneously, the binding mechanism between SBT and NFT prevents duplicate rights confirmation and resolves potential ownership conflicts.

Algorithm 1. Update SBT

Input: Selected SBT SBT_{select}, New NFTs $NFTs_{select}$, User Account Acc
1: **Contract** UPDATE(SBT_{select}, $NFTs_{select}$, Acc)
2:   **for** each NFT in $NFTs_{select}$ **do**
3:     Verify that Acc owns the NFT
4:     Associate each NFT with SBT_{select}
5:   **end for**
6:   Emit an event indicating the SBT has been updated
7:   Mark $NFTs_{select}$ as bound to SBT_{select}
8: **end Contract**

---

3 Security and Performance Analysis

3.1 Security Theory Analysis

In this section, we construct a relational mapping table based on the HDRIU-B design. Let $U = \{u_1, u_2, \ldots, u_k\}$ represent the set of users in the system, $C = \{c_1, c_2, \ldots, c_k\}$ denote the set of Content Identifiers (CIDs) generated after data is uploaded to IPFS, and $D = \{d_1, d_2, \ldots, d_k\}$ represent the set of data packets. The set of Non-Fungible Tokens (NFTs) in the system is denoted as $N = \{n_1, n_2, \ldots, n_k\}$, while the set of SBTs is represented as $S = \{s_1, s_2, \ldots, s_k\}$. Furthermore, the set of binding relationships between NFT and SBT is defined as $Sn = \{n_1, n_2, \ldots, n_m\}$, where $S_n \subseteq N$, denoting the set of NFTs that have been bound to SBT. The relational mapping table is presented in Table 1:

Table 1. Formal expression of mapping relationship

Relationship name	Formalization
Output CID	$\mathcal{O} : \mathrm{CID}(d) \to c$
Mint NFT	$\mathcal{C} : \mathrm{MintNFT}(c, u) \to n$
Mint SBT	$\mathcal{C} : \mathrm{MintSBT}(u, n) \to s$
Bind NFT to SBT	$\mathcal{C} : \mathrm{BindNS}(n, s) \to \mathrm{True/False}$
Data Access Control	$\mathcal{O} : \mathrm{AccessControl}(u, n) \to \{\mathrm{True, False}\}$

Theorem. HDRIU-B can resist attacks of adversary $\mathscr{A}$ attempting to perform repeated rights confirmation, ensuring the uniqueness of data and the uniqueness of data ownership.

Proof. To prove that HDRIU-B can resist the attacks that adversary $\mathscr{A}$ attempting to perform repeated rights confirmation on the data, we divide the proof into the following steps:

Step 1. Data Uniqueness Verification Mechanism. HDRIU-B adopts $\mathscr{A}$ data uniqueness verification mechanism before data upload. When adversary $\mathscr{A}$ attempts to upload a duplicate data packet D'_A, the system utilizes a sliding window and context-sensitive hashing technique to compute a unique hash value $LSH(D_A)$, and compares it with the existing hash values in the system. Any attempt to upload the same or highly similar data will be rejected. Formally:

$$\forall D_A, D'_A \in D : \Delta(LSH(D_A), LSH(D'_A)) < \delta \Rightarrow Reject(D_A) \qquad (10)$$

Step 2. CID Generation and NFT Binding. Once data D_A passes the uniqueness verification, it is uploaded to IPFS, generating a unique CID. Specifically:

$$\forall d_i \in D, \forall c_i \in C : CID(d_i) = c_i \land (\forall d'_i \neq d_i, CID(d'_i) \neq c_i) \qquad (11)$$

Subsequently, the SC calls the smart contract to bind the CID with the newly minted NFT for a unique association:

$$Bind(D_A, CID(D_A)) \Rightarrow MintNFT(CID(D_A), u) = n \qquad (12)$$

Step 3. NFT and SBT Binding Restrictions. In HDRIU-B, if an adversary $\mathscr{A}$ attempts to bind the same NFT to multiple SBTs for repeated right confirmation, the binding will fail. Once an NFT is bound to an SBT, it cannot be bound to another SBT. The smart contract will reject $\mathscr{A}$'s binding request, ensuring that each data packet D_A has only one unique owner, thereby guaranteeing the uniqueness of data ownership.

Suppose that adversary $\mathscr{A}$ attempts to perform repeated rights confirmation by uploading a duplicate packet D'_A that is identical or highly similar to an existing packet D'_A. The following scenarios will be prevented:

Case 1. $\mathscr{A}$ directly uploads D'_A. During the data uniqueness verification in Step 1, the system computes $LSH(D'_A)$ and the detects that its difference from $LSH(D'_A)$ is below the threshold δ. Consequently, the system rejects D'_A and prevents $\mathscr{A}$ from minting a new NFT for D'_A.

Case 2. $\mathscr{A}$ attempts to bind the same NFT to multiple SBTs. If $\mathscr{A}$ obtains an NFT already bound to an SBT, $\mathscr{A}$ may try to bind it to another SBT. Due to the binding restriction mechanism, the smart contract verifies the legitimate owner of the SBT to which the NFT is bound. If $\mathscr{A}$ is not the legitimate owner, the smart contract rejects the binding request, thereby preventing $\mathscr{A}$ from performing repeated rights confirmation on D_A.

Through the above steps, HDRIU-B ensures that adversary $\mathscr{A}$ cannot successfully execute repeated rights confirmation attacks, thereby guaranteeing the uniqueness of the data and the uniqueness of data ownership.

3.2 Performance Analysis

The experimental environment is configured as follows: the hardware setup includes an AMD Ryzen 7 5800HS Creator Edition processor with a base clock speed of 3.20 GHz, 16 GB of RAM, and Windows 10 as the operating system. For the software environment, Ganache is employed to simulate a blockchain network, providing a local development and testing environment, while IPFS

(Kubo version) serves as a distributed file storage system for data storage and retrieval. Smart contracts are written in Solidity v0.8.0 and deployed on the local Ethereum test network provided by Ganache. The network configuration consists of a locally running IPFS node using Kubo v0.33.1, with the blockchain network hosted on Ganache's local test environment, operating on the default port 7545.

Security of The Scheme. We conducted an experimental comparison for the uniqueness of ownership, and the results are presented in Table 2:

Table 2. Comparison of two types of contract deployment

Scene	Data update restrictions	Deployment contract Gas consumption (unit: Gas$\times 10^5$)
1	False	2.5
2	True	4.2

As shown in Table 2, in the absence of permission control, the structure of smart contracts is simpler, resulting in a lower gas consumption during deployment($2.5 \times 10^5 Gas$). However, with the introduction of the SBT mechanism and the addition of permission controls, the complexity of smart contracts increases, leading to higher Gas consumption during deployment($4.2 \times 10^5 Gas$). Given the critical importance of data security, this increase in Gas consumption is justified, as the enhanced security outweighs the additional cost. Therefore, in data update scenarios, data security takes precedence over deployment costs, and the increased Gas consumption is deemed acceptable.

The Advancement of The Scheme. This article compares two cases of data update in the validation scheme used in OpenSea, **samp1** and **samp2**. samp1 scheme needs to upload the updated data as a whole and bind it with a new NFT when the data is updated. In the pure NFT scenario, samp2 achieves dataset update by modifying the CID bound to NFT. We evaluated the time and Gas consumption of both schemes, with results averaged over multiple repeated experiments.

The horizontal axis "Number of data items" in Figs. 4 and 5 represents the total number of data items that users have cumulatively authorized. In this experiment, 10 pieces of data with a single piece size of 47 bytes were uploaded in each batch. The time consumption and Gas overhead of the three different schemes(HDRIU-B, samp1, and samp2) in the process of data rights confirmation were evaluated successively to analyze their performance change trends. The Experimental results demonstrate that the time and Gas consumption of samp1 scheme increase almost linearly with the growth in data volume. In constrast,

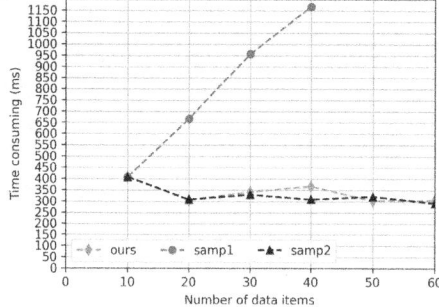 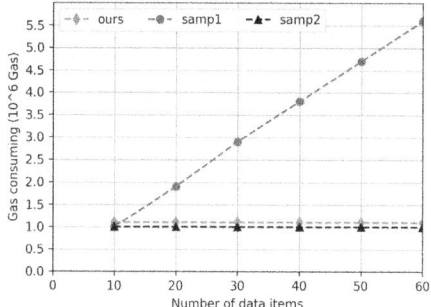

Fig. 4. Comparison of time required for data update.

Fig. 5. Comparison of Gas required for data update.

the time consumption of HDRIU-B scheme and samp2 schemes is nearly identical and significantly lower than that of samp1. Specifically, when the number of data items is 30, the time consumption of samp1 is $957ms$, while the proposed HDRIU-B scheme and samp2 require $341ms$ and $307ms$, respectively. This difference mainly stems from the incremental update mechanism of HDRIU-B, which avoids the high time cost of overall data upload.

In terms of Gas consumption, samp2 exhibits the lowest Gas consumption, followed by HDRIU-B. Although samp2 performs best in terms of Gas efficiency, it suffers from limitations such as the risk of data pollution and insufficient permission controls. While samp1 can avoid data pollution, its time cost and Gas consumption are significantly higher, especially during a small amount of data needs to be updated to the dataset, leading to resource inefficiency. In contrast, HDRIU-B, through its incremental update mechanism, significantly reduces both time and Gas consumption while ensuring data security and integrity, providing an efficient and secure solution for data update.

Scalability of The Scheme. In the process of uploading data to IPFS and binding it with NFT, the Gas consumption is mainly related to the number of uploaded data entries, as each piece of data on IPFS generates a Hash value (CID) of the fixed length. Specifically, the length of the hash value generated after uploading data to IPFS is constant, and the computational consumption of its generation is independent of the data content size, but only depends on the number of data entries. Based on this observation, this experiment aims to explore the scalability of data binding with NFT, especially analyzing the impact of increasing the number of data entries on blockchain Gas costs and time consumption.

As illustrated in Figs. 6 and 7, during the experiment, both Gas costs and time consumption exhibit a steady increase with the growth in data volume, indicating that the proposed method demonstrates strong scalability in the process of binding data to NFT. As the number of data entries increases, the system can

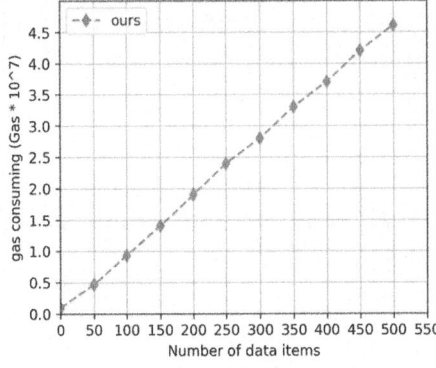 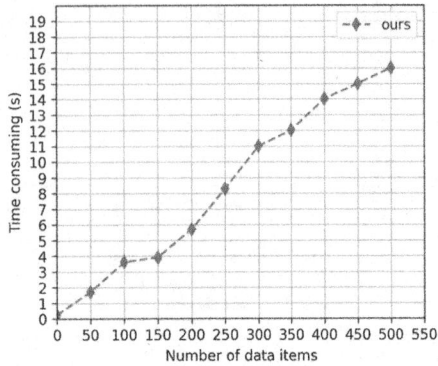

Fig. 6. Comparison of time required for data update.

Fig. 7. Comparison of Gas required for data update.

effectively manage larger data loads without encountering performance bottlenecks. Therefore, the proposed scheme exhibits robust scalability and is well-suited to accommodate future demands for large-scale data processing.

4 Conclusion

In this paper, we proposed a hierarchical data rights confirmation and incremental data update scheme based on NFT and SBT, named HDRIU-B. This scheme address the challenges of insufficient security and low resource utilization during incremental data update. By combining the hierarchical management mechanism of NFT and SBT, HDRIU-B achieves a clear distinction between data ownership and usage rights. As the core medium of access control, SBT ensures the security during data update and prevents unauthorized data pollution. Additionally, the proposed incremental update mechanism reduces the time cost and Gas consumption associated with data update, enhancing the overall efficiency and resource utilization of the system.

Acknowledgments. The work was supported by the National Key Research and Development Program of China [grant number 2021YFB3300900]; the Key Research and Development Program of Tianjin [grant number 23YFZCSN00240]; and the Innovation and Entrepreneurship Training Program for college students [grant number 202410060024].

References

1. Xiaoming, T., et al.: "Data component: an innovative framework for information value metrics in the digital economy." China Commun.**21**(5), 17–35 (2024). https://doi.org/10.23919/JCC.fa.2023-0781.202405

2. Zhang, C., Cheng, J., Zhang, H., Wang, J., Shi, K.: "Data rights verification in the industrial internet: a securing progressive scheme with locked-NFTS and adaptive federated learning." In: *2023 IEEE 29th International Conference on Parallel and Distributed Systems (ICPADS)*. IEEE, pp. 1785–1792 (2023). https://doi.org/10.1109/ICPADS60453.2023.00247
3. Ranjbar Alvar, S., Akbari, M., Yue, D., Zhang, Y.: "NFT-based data marketplace with digital watermarking." In: *Proceedings of the 29th ACM SIGKDD Conference on Knowledge Discovery and Data Mining*, pp. 4756–4767 (2023). https://doi.org/10.1145/3580305.3599876
4. Song, R., Gao, S., Song, Y., Xiao, B. : A traceable and privacy-preserving data exchange scheme based on non-fungible token and zero-knowledge. In: *2022 IEEE 42nd International Conference on Distributed Computing Systems (ICDCS)*. IEEE, pp. 224–234 (2022). https://doi.org/10.1109/ICDCS54860.2022.00030
5. Ali, O., Momin, M., Shrestha, A., Das, R., Alhajj, F., Dwivedi, Y.K.: A review of the key challenges of non-fungible tokens. Technol. Forecast. Soc. Chang. **187**, 122248 (2023). https://doi.org/10.1016/j.techfore.2022.122248
6. Ohlhaver, P., Weyl, E. G., Buterin, V.: "Decentralized society: finding web3's soul." *Available at SSRN 4105763* (2022). https://doi.org/10.2139/ssrn.4105763
7. ÄŐuriška, M., Neradilová, H., Fedorko, G., Molnár, V., Mikušová, N.: Use of non-fungible tokens for proof of ownership and originality of simulation model in logistics. Simul. Model. Pract. Theory **134**, 102949 (2024). https://doi.org/10.1016/j.simpat.2024.102949
8. Joo, Y., Seo, J.: "User authentication techniques using a dynamic soulbound token." J. Web Eng. **23**(5), 717–733 (2024). https://doi.org/10.13052/jwe1540-9589.2356
9. Dalla Preda, M., Masaia, F.: "Exploring NFT validation through digital watermarking," In: *Proceedings of the 18th International Conference on Availability, Reliability and Security*, pp. 1–6 (2023). https://doi.org/10.1145/3600160.3605063
10. Mouris, D., Tsoutsos, N. G.: "NFTs for 3D models: sustaining ownership in industry 4.0." *IEEE Consumer Electron. Mag.* **13**(2) (2022). https://doi.org/10.1109/MCE.2022.3164221
11. Liu, Y., Zhang, J., Ding, X., Guo, B., Hu, D., Jiang, Y.: "Efficient data asset right provenance for data asset trading based on blockchain," In: *International Conference on Knowledge Science, Engineering and Management*. Springer, pp. 151–162 (2024). https://doi.org/10.1007/978-981-97-5501-1_12
12. Zhao, H., Zhang, X., Shi, J., Li, R., Dart: A low-cost and secure cross-chain scheme for popular digital assets." In: IEEE Wireless Communications and Networking Conference (WCNC). IEEE, vol. 2024, pp. 1–7 (2024). https://doi.org/10.1109/WCNC57260.2024.10571060
13. Cabot-Nadal, M.À., Playford, B., Payeras-Capellà, M.M., Gerske, S., Mut-Puigserver, M., Pericàs-Gornals, R.: "Private identity-related attribute verification protocol using soulbound tokens and zero-knowledge proofs.âĂİ In: 7th Cyber Security in Networking Conference (CSNet). IEEE, vol. 2023, pp. 153–156 (2023). https://doi.org/10.1109/CSNet59123.2023.10339754
14. Tanwar, N., Thakur, J.: Patient-centric soulbound NFT framework for electronic health record (EHR). J. Eng. Appl. Sci. **70**(1), 33 (2023). https://doi.org/10.1186/s44147-023-00205-9
15. Cho, H., Zhang, L., Jiang, X.: "Secure cryptographic technology framework for data element circulation transactions." In: *2024 IEEE 11th International Conference on Cyber Security and Cloud Computing (CSCloud)*. IEEE, pp. 187–193 (2024). https://doi.org/10.1109/CSCloud62866.2024.00040

A Blockchain Transaction Tracking Method Based on Dynamic Graph Link Prediction

Chi Jiang[1], Jinglin Wang[1], Manhua Shi[1], Ke Zhang[1(✉)], and Yin Zhang[1,2]

[1] School of Information and Communication Engineering, University of Electronic Science and Technology of China, Chengdu 611731, China
zhangke@uestc.edu.cn
[2] Yunnan Key Laboratory of Service Computing, Yunnan University of Finance and Economics, Kunming 650221, China

Abstract. This paper proposes a transaction tracking method based on dynamic graph link prediction to tackle the challenges posed by blockchain's anonymity, which facilitates money laundering, fraud, and other illicit activities. By constructing a dynamic transaction graph and combining Temporal Graph Neural Networks with Transformer models, the method effectively predicts transaction links and uncovers potential transactional relationships. Experimental results show that the proposed method outperforms existing approaches in terms of Accuracy, F1-score, and AUC, providing significant support for blockchain transaction regulation and financial crime prevention.

Keywords: Blockchain Transaction Tracking · Link Prediction · Graph Neural Networks

1 Introduction

Blockchain transaction tracking is vital for regulation, combating illicit activities like money laundering enabled by inherent anonymity (e.g., Bitcoin, Ethereum) [1]. It traces funds, identifies suspicious behavior, and provides law enforcement evidence, ensuring market stability and compliant blockchain development.

Existing techniques face limitations: Heuristic methods rely on static rules; taint analysis struggles with complexity; importance ranking (e.g., PageRank) is computationally heavy; link prediction uses static snapshots, missing dynamic changes and long-term trust.

To address this, we propose a dynamic graph link prediction method. It constructs temporal transaction snapshots, extracts features, and uses a Temporal Graph Neural Network for structural features and a Transformer for dynamic relationships. Combining these enables effective future link prediction.

The main contributions of this paper are summarized as follows:

1) We use a temporal GNN structure encoder and a Transformer relationship encoder to jointly model dynamic features.

2) We integrate dynamic structure and relationship features to enhance transaction graph link prediction.
3) Experiments on Ethereum data show our method's effectiveness in blockchain transaction tracking.

2 Related Works

Common blockchain transaction tracking methods include heuristic approaches, taint analysis, importance ranking, and link prediction.

Heuristic methods use expert rules, such as Huang et al.'s co-spending clustering for ransomware [2] and Phetsouvanh et al.'s improved BFS for suspicious flows [3].

Taint analysis tracks 'tainted' funds, with strategies like Poison and Haircut [4], LIFO and TIHO [5], and Wu et al.'s TPP-based Ethereum tracking [6].

Importance ranking uses graph algorithms to assess account influence, e.g., Wu et al.'s Push-Pop personalized PageRank [1] and TRacer [7].

Link prediction models temporal data to forecast links, including random walks with Word2Vec [8], time-weighted multigraphs [9], GCN-based BT^2 [10], and DNLP-TCT's temporal self-attention with BiLSTM [11].

3 Methodology

3.1 Preliminaries

The dynamic transaction graph $G = \{G_1, \ldots, G_t\}$ captures the blockchain network's evolution, with $G_t = (V_t, E_t)$ representing nodes (accounts) and edges (transactions) at time t.

Link prediction forecasts the chance of a transaction between nodes v_i and v_j at future time $t + k$, using a function $f(v_i, v_j)$ compared against threshold λ as in Eq. 1:

$$\hat{y}_{ij}^{t+k} = \begin{cases} 1 & \text{if } f(v_i, v_j) > \lambda \\ 0 & \text{otherwise} \end{cases} \quad (1)$$

Here, $f(v_i, v_j)$ represents the probability of a transaction link forming between nodes v_i and v_j at time $t + k$, and $\hat{y}_{ij}^{t+k}$ is the link prediction outcome.

3.2 Model Architecture

The model architecture of the dynamic graph link prediction method based on structural and relationship encoding proposed is shown in Fig. 1.

In dynamic graph construction, blockchain data is converted into snapshots, with node and relationship features extracted to form a relationship matrix.

In structure encoding, a temporal GNN processes node features enhanced by causal convolution, then uses LSTM to capture long-term dependencies and generate structural features.

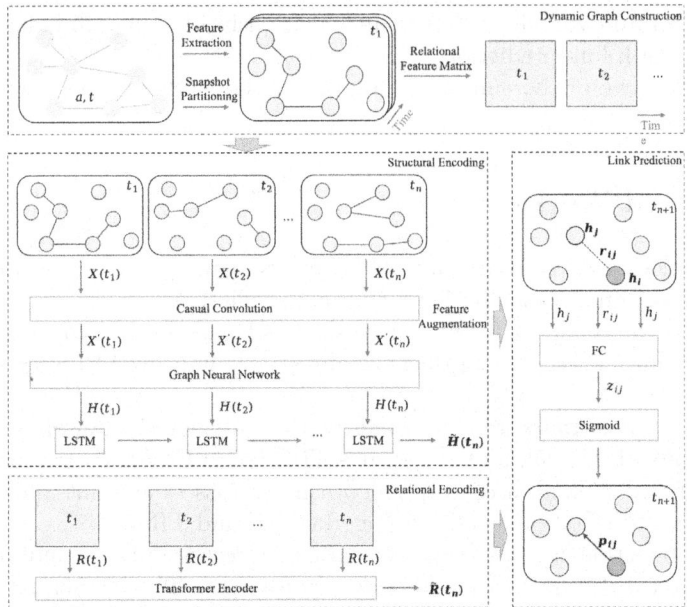

Fig. 1. This is the blockchain transaction tracking model architecture, which consists of four main parts: dynamic graph construction, structure encoding, relationship encoding, and link prediction.

In relationship encoding, the relationship matrix is fed into a Transformer encoder to model evolving interactions, producing relationship features.

In link prediction, structural and relationship features are fused via a fully connected layer, and future links are predicted using a Sigmoid function.

Dynamic Graph Construction. In this phase, a dynamic transaction graph $G = \{G(t_1), G(t_2), \ldots, G(t_n)\}$ is constructed from blockchain data as time-based snapshots. Each snapshot $G(t_i)$ includes nodes (accounts) and edges (transactions), generated via a sliding window to reflect network changes over time.

For each $G(t_i)$, node features $X(t_i)$ are extracted, covering activity (volume, duration, frequency) and wealth (input/output, balance). Four directional relationship features—transaction count, total and average amount, and time span—form a sparse matrix $R(t_i)$, where $r_{mn}(t_i)$ denotes the interaction from node v_m to v_n.

The snapshot representation is shown in Eq. 2, capturing the dynamic evolution of the blockchain network for link prediction tasks.

$$G(t_i) = (V(t_i), E(t_i), X(t_i), R(t_i)) \qquad (2)$$

Structure Encoder. The structure encoder uses a temporal GNN to extract dynamic features. Node features $X(t_i)$ are enhanced by causal convolution over past K steps to address low-activity periods, as shown in Eq. 3:

$$X'(t_i) = \sum_{k=0}^{K-1} W_k \cdot X(t_{i-k}) \qquad (3)$$

The enhanced $X'(t_i)$ is then input to a GNN that aggregates neighborhood information, as shown in Eq. 4:

$$H^{(l)}(t_i) = \sigma\left(W^{(l)}(t_i) \cdot \mathrm{Agg}(H^{(l-1)}(t_i), A(t_i))\right) \qquad (4)$$

With $H^{(0)}(t_i) = X'(t_i)$, the output $H(t_i)$ is fed into an LSTM to model temporal dependencies, as shown in Eq. 5:

$$\tilde{H}(t_i) = \mathrm{LSTM}(H(t_i), \tilde{H}(t_{i-1})) \qquad (5)$$

In this equation, $\tilde{H}(t_i)$ is the updated structural feature at time t_i, capturing the network's dynamics and serving as input for the next step. The final output $\tilde{H}(t_n)$ is used as the dynamic structural representation for link prediction.

Relationship Encoder. The Transformer encoder extracts dynamic features, adding positional encoding $PE(t_i)$ for temporal order, as in Eq. 6:

$$PE(t_i, 2j) = \sin\left(\frac{t_i}{10000^{2j/d}}\right), \quad PE(t_i, 2j+1) = \cos\left(\frac{t_i}{10000^{2j/d}}\right) \qquad (6)$$

Here, d is the relationship feature dimension and j its index. This encoding is added to $R(t_i)$ to form the enhanced matrix $R'(t_i)$ in Eq. 7:

$$R'(t_i) = R(t_i) + PE(t_i) \qquad (7)$$

The relationship matrix with positional encoding is processed via self-attention, which computes weighted relations among query Q, key K, and value V for the sequence $R' = [R'(t_1), R'(t_2), \ldots, R'(t_n)]$, as shown in Eq. 8:

$$Q = R'W_Q, \quad K = R'W_K, \quad V = R'W_V \qquad (8)$$

The attention score matrix is the scaled dot product of query Q and key K, normalized by Softmax, then multiplied by value V to get the attention output in Eq. 9:

$$\hat{R} = \mathrm{Softmax}\left(\frac{QK^T}{\sqrt{d_k}}\right)V \qquad (9)$$

In the multi-head attention mechanism, the query, key, and value vectors are mapped into multiple subspaces, with the outputs concatenated and transformed into the final representation space, as shown in Eq. 10:

$$\tilde{R} = \mathrm{Concat}(\hat{R}^{(1)}, \hat{R}^{(2)}, \ldots, \hat{R}^{(h)})W_O \qquad (10)$$

The attention output at time t_n, $\tilde{R}(t_n)$, serves as the dynamic relationship feature for link prediction tasks.

Link Prediction. Link prediction forecasts future links by combining dynamic structural features h_i, h_j and relationship features r_{ij} of node pair (v_i, v_j) via a fully connected layer, producing the integrated feature z_{ij} as in Eq. 11:

$$z_{ij} = W_1 \cdot [h_i \parallel h_j \parallel r_{ij}] + b \tag{11}$$

where W_1 is a learnable weight, b is the bias, and $\parallel$ denotes concatenation. The link probability is computed using the Sigmoid function in Eq. 12:

$$p_{ij} = \text{Sigmoid}(z_{ij}) \tag{12}$$

During training, positive samples are real links and negatives are random non-links. The model minimizes cross-entropy loss in Eq. 13:

$$\mathcal{L} = -\sum_{(i,j)\in\mathcal{T}} [y_{ij}\log(p_{ij}) + (1-y_{ij})\log(1-p_{ij})] \tag{13}$$

where $y_{ij} \in \{0, 1\}$ indicates whether a link exists.

4 Experiments and Results

4.1 Datasets and Evaluation Metrics

The experiments use the Ethereum transaction dataset from [12], containing source and target node IDs, transaction amounts, and timestamps. It includes three subsets—EthereumG1, EthereumG2, and EthereumG3—representing different-scale Ethereum subgraphs. Details are in Table 1:

Table 1. Statistical Information of the Ethereum Transaction Dataset

Dataset	Nodes	Edges	Average Degree	Average Clustering Coefficient	Time Span (Months)
EthereumG1	9855	14144	2.870	0.029	41.20
EthereumG2	23847	31312	2.626	0.018	41.60
EthereumG3	103916	118440	2.280	0.016	41.70

In the experiments, three metrics are adopted to evaluate the performance of the method, namely AUC (Area Under the Curve), Accuracy, and F1-score.

4.2 Experimental Setup

In this section, the following methods are selected as reference baselines for subsequent method evaluation:

(1) Heuristic Methods (Similarity Metrics): CN [13], LHN [14], RA [15].(2) Static Feature Learning Methods: MLP [16].(3) Static Graph Learning Methods: T-EDGE [17], GCN [18], GAT [19], GraphSAGE [20].(4) Dynamic Feature Learning Methods: LSTM [21], Transformer Encoder [22].(5) Dynamic Graph Learning Methods: EvolveGCN [23], DNLP-TCT [11].

Dynamic methods use snapshots and static methods use the full graph.

Unlike random splits in traditional link prediction, dynamic graphs use chronological splitting: 70% embedding set for encoder training, 30% training-test set with equal negatives.

Experiments use PyTorch with 8 snapshots, 10% overlap. Convolution kernels of sizes 2, 3, 4 are used for EthereumG1G3. GraphSAGE has 2 layers, 16-unit ReLU hidden layers, plus an LSTM. The Transformer has 2 layers, 4 heads. Adam optimizer with 0.01 learning rate; training epochs are 120, 180, 200 for EthereumG1G3.

4.3 Experimental Results and Analysis

Performance Comparison. This section compares link prediction performance on EthereumG1G3 (Table 2). Feature and graph learning methods outperform heuristic ones (e.g., CN, RA) that rely on local topology. In contrast, methods like MLP, LSTM, and GCN extract richer features, improving accuracy. Graph learning, especially dynamic models (e.g., EvolveGCN, DNLP-TCT), outperform general feature learners by better modeling complex node relations. Static models like GraphSAGE miss temporal patterns, while dynamic ones (e.g., LSTM, EvolveGCN) capture evolving behaviors. The proposed method outperforms EvolveGCN and DNLP-TCT by jointly modeling structure, dynamics, and long-term relationships via the relationship encoder, enhancing prediction performance.

Table 2. Performance Comparison of Link Prediction Methods

Methods	EthereumG1			EthereumG2			EthereumG3		
	AUC	Acc	F1	AUC	Acc	F1	AUC	Acc	F1
CN	0.286	0.296	0.143	0.333	0.335	0.174	0.410	0.416	0.258
LHN	0.274	0.302	0.040	0.308	0.313	0.024	0.396	0.372	0.080
RA	0.290	0.501	0.003	0.347	0.501	0.005	0.428	0.503	0.013
T-EDGE	0.716	0.716	0.755	0.605	0.605	0.393	0.811	0.811	0.771
MLP	0.934	0.851	0.855	0.897	0.824	0.793	0.926	0.862	0.846
GCN	0.938	0.872	0.874	0.888	0.793	0.795	0.881	0.821	0.814
GAT	0.937	0.862	0.865	0.904	0.808	0.820	0.883	0.791	0.770
GraphSAGE	0.966	0.908	0.910	0.981	0.931	0.933	0.976	0.920	0.921
LSTM	0.962	0.911	0.910	0.966	0.886	0.885	0.977	0.925	0.923
Transformer Encoder	0.965	0.906	0.909	0.967	0.904	0.907	0.972	0.917	0.915
EvolveGCN	0.969	0.925	0.923	0.980	0.923	0.926	<u>0.985</u>	<u>0.936</u>	<u>0.939</u>
DNLP-TCT	<u>0.976</u>	<u>0.926</u>	<u>0.928</u>	<u>0.986</u>	<u>0.935</u>	<u>0.938</u>	0.979	0.932	0.934
Proposed Method	**0.992**	**0.972**	**0.972**	**0.994**	**0.970**	**0.970**	**0.996**	**0.979**	**0.979**

Ablation Study. This section conducts ablation studies on variants of the proposed method: (1) SE w/o TL structure encoder without temporal learning (no snapshot partitioning); (2) SE w/o FE structure encoder without feature enhancement; (3) SE structure encoder; (4) RE (LSTM) relationship encoder with LSTM; (5) RE (TE) relationship encoder with Transformer; (6) Full Model all modules included.

Table 3. Comparison of Performance with Different Variants of the Proposed Method

Method Variants	AUC	Acc	F1
SE w/o TL	0.9759	0.9201	0.9209
SE w/o FE	0.9858	0.9401	0.9398
SE	0.9883	0.9498	0.9503
RE (LSTM)	0.8281	0.7928	0.8283
RE (TE)	0.8476	0.8473	0.8204
Full model	**0.9956**	**0.9776**	**0.9775**

Table 3 shows link prediction results of model variants. The full model performs best, confirming all modules' synergy.

Removing temporal learning or feature enhancement reduces performance, showing their key roles in capturing dynamics and enhancing weak features.

Transformer Encoder in relationship encoding outperforms LSTM by better managing sparse data with self-attention; LSTM struggles with zeros.

5 Conclusion

This paper proposes a dynamic graph link prediction method for blockchain tracking, combining a temporal GNN structure encoder and a Transformer-based relationship encoder. By capturing dynamic features, it effectively predicts future transactions. Experiments show it outperforms existing methods, aiding blockchain regulation and enhancing transaction security and transparency.

Acknowledgments. This work was supported in part by Sichuan Science and Technology Program under Grant No.2024YFHZ0321, and the Foundation of Yunnan Key Laboratory of Services Computing under Grant No.YNSC24101.

References

1. Wu, Z., Liu, J., Wu, J., Zheng, Z.: Transaction tracking on blockchain trading systems using personalized PageRank. arXiv preprint arXiv:2201.05757 (2022)
2. Huang, D.Y., et al.: Tracking ransomware end-to-end. In: 2018 IEEE Symposium on Security and Privacy (SP), pp. 618–631. IEEE (2018)
3. Phetsouvanh, S., Oggier, F., Datta, A.: EGRET: extortion graph exploration techniques in the bitcoin network. In: 2018 IEEE International Conference on Data Mining Workshops (ICDMW), pp. 244–251. IEEE (2018)

4. Möser, M., Böhme, R., Breuker, D.: Towards risk scoring of bitcoin transactions. In: Financial Cryptography and Data Security: FC 2014 Workshops, BITCOIN and WAHC 2014, Christ Church, Barbados, March 7, 2014, Revised Selected Papers 18, pp. 16–32. Springer (2014)
5. Tironsakkul, T., Maarek, M., Eross, A., Just, M.: Probing the mystery of cryptocurrency theft, an investigation into methods for cryptocurrency tainting analysis. In: Cryptocurrency Research Conference 2019 (2019)
6. Wu, J., et al.: Toward understanding asset flows in crypto money laundering through the lenses of Ethereum heists. IEEE Trans. Inf. Forensics Secur. **19**, 1994–2009 (2023)
7. Wu, Z., Liu, J., Wu, J., Zheng, Z., Chen, T.: TRacer: scalable graph-based transaction tracing for account-based blockchain trading systems. IEEE Trans. Inf. Forensics Secur. **18**, 2609–2621 (2023)
8. Wei, W., Zhang, Q., Liu, L.: Bitcoin transaction forecasting with deep network representation learning. IEEE Trans. Emerg. Top. Comput. **9**(3), 1359–1371 (2020)
9. Lin, D., Chen, J., Wu, J., Zheng, Z.: Evolution of Ethereum transaction relationships: toward understanding global driving factors from microscopic patterns. IEEE Trans. Comput. Soc. Syst. **9**(2), 559–570 (2021)
10. Li, Z., He, E.: Graph neural network-based bitcoin transaction tracking model. IEEE Access **11**, 62109–62120 (2023)
11. Ding, J., Huang, J.: DNLP-TCT: a dynamic network link prediction framework for tracking cryptocurrency transactions. In: 2024 14th Asian Control Conference (ASCC), pp. 159–164. IEEE (2024)
12. Lin, D., Wu, J., Yuan, Q., Zheng, Z.: Modeling and understanding Ethereum transaction records via a complex network approach. IEEE Trans. Circuits Syst. II Expr. Briefs **67**(11), 2737–2741 (2020)
13. Newman, M.E.: Clustering and preferential attachment in growing networks. Phys. Rev. E **64**(2), 025,102 (2001)
14. Leicht, E.A., Holme, P., Newman, M.E.: Vertex similarity in networks. Phys. Rev. E—Statist. Nonlinear Soft Matter Phys. **73**(2), 026,120 (2006)
15. Zhou, T., Lü, L., Zhang, Y.C.: Predicting missing links via local information. The Europ. Phys. J. B **71**, 623–630 (2009)
16. Rumelhart, D.E., Hinton, G.E., Williams, R.J.: Learning representations by backpropagating errors. nature **323**(6088), 533–536 (1986)
17. Lin, D., Wu, J., Yuan, Q., Zheng, Z.: T-Edge: temporal weighted multidigraph embedding for Ethereum transaction network analysis. Front. Phys. **8**, 204 (2020)
18. Kipf, T.N., Welling, M.: Semi-supervised classification with graph convolutional networks. In: International Conference on Learning Representations (2017)
19. Veličković, P., Cucurull, G., Casanova, A., Romero, A., Liò, P., Bengio, Y.: Graph attention networks. In: International Conference on Learning Representations (2018)
20. Hamilton, W., Ying, Z., Leskovec, J.: Inductive representation learning on large graphs. Adv. Neural Info. Process. Syst. **30** (2017)
21. Hochreiter, S., Schmidhuber, J.: Long short-term memory. Neural Comput. **9**(8), 1735–1780 (1997)
22. Vaswani, A., et al.: Attention is all you need. Adv. Neural Info. Process. Syst. **30** (2017)
23. Pareja, A., et al.: EvolveGCN: evolving graph convolutional networks for dynamic graphs. In: Proceedings of the AAAI Conference on Artificial Intelligence, vol. 34, pp. 5363–5370 (2020)

Online-Learning Based Task Scheduling in Industrial Internet-of-Things: Tackling Resource Skew with Dynamic Optimization

Jian Zhang, Xueqiang Li, Qunjian Chen, and Ming Tao(✉)

School of Computer Science and Technology, Dongguan University of Technology, Dongguan 523808, China
{zjian,lixq,chenqunjian,taom}@dgut.edu.cn

Abstract. With the rapid development of mobile edge computing, more and more tasks require substantial communication and computing resources, which makes resource management in Industrial Internet of Things (IIoT) face the challenge of resource skew. Resource skew can affect the efficiency of task execution, as overloading of edge servers can significantly degrade the system performance. To address this issue, an Online-Learning based Task Scheduling framework is proposed to optimize task scheduling. The framework can accurately sense the task and edge server states in the network and select the optimal allocation scheme, thereby reducing the total energy consumption of task execution. By modeling the optimization problem as a Markov Decision Process (MDP), an Online-Learning based Task Scheduling algorithm, combining with the Upper Confidence Bound (UCB) strategy to enable efficient decision-making in task scheduling, is designed to provide a effective solution. Experimental results show that the proposed method is superior to the compared methods in terms of delay and energy consumption.

Keywords: Online-Learning · Task Scheduling · Resource Management · Upper Confidence Bound · Industrial Internet of Things

1 Introduction

In recent years, the emergence of mobile edge computing has driven the rapid advancement in IIoT. In this context, critical tasks such as device status monitoring, anomaly detection, and fault diagnosis require more and more communication and computing resources [1,2]. These tasks often have stringent real-time requirements, which creates challenges for resource management in the IIoT. However, heterogeneous edge servers and dynamic task loads often result in resource skew. Server overload caused by resource skew significantly increases energy consumption, which reduces the efficiency of task execution [3,4].

Optimizing resource management is crucial to mitigate resource skew [5]. Existing research primarily depended on static assumptions to design task allocation strategies. However, these strategies ignore the dynamic changes in real-time resources and workloads, causing the strategy to be less effective in dynamic scenarios [6]. These limitations highlight the demand for task scheduling methods that respond to real-time changes in dynamic scenarios [7,8].

To address this challenge, we propose an Online-Learning based Task Scheduling framework. By sensing the states of tasks and edge servers in the network, this framework can select a scheme for task segmentation and allocation based on dynamic changes in real-time resources and workloads. This scheduling scheme prevents servers overload, which reduces the energy consumption of task execution and ensures that tasks in IIoT can be executed efficiently. Specifically, by evaluating the state of the edge server in combined with the UCB strategy, the task is segmented into two task modules and accurate task allocation is achieved. Compared with non-segmentation strategies, Greedy algorithms and Random algorithms, our framework reduces the execution time and energy consumption of tasks, proving the effectiveness of its optimized task scheduling strategy.

The remainder of this paper is organized as follows. Section 2 reviews existing resource allocation algorithms. Section 3 introduces the defined model. Section 4 establishes the optimization problem of minimizing energy consumption. Section 5 details the proposed algorithm. Section 6 presents the experimental results and performance evaluation. Section 7 concludes the paper.

2 Related Works

In the IIoT, the challenge of resource management caused by resource-skew has attracted significant attention from both academia and industry. To address this challenge, research about optimized resource allocation has received increasing attention [9]. Hlaing et al. proposed a static independent task scheduling method on virtualized servers in cloud computing environments, which minimizes the execution cost while maximizing the total execution time [10]. However, these approaches ignore the dynamic characteristics of tasks and servers, which would limit the effectiveness in IIoT with dynamically changing environments. Coito et al. propose a dynamic scheduling and re-scheduling solution integrating information technology and operations techniques to support personalized production operations and improve real-time system adaptability [11]. In addition, there are studies focusing on optimizing resource allocation through resource pricing mechanisms or multi-agent cooperation [12,13].

To improve the efficiency of task execution in mobile computing, Kang et al. segmented deep neural networks into front-end and back-end on a layer-by-layer basis, thereby optimizing the computation and data transfer for mobile computing [14]. Inspired by this approach, we extend this thought process to task segmentation, designed to adapt to dynamic changes in the characteristics of tasks and servers in IIoT. By segmenting tasks into smaller, manageable task modules, it is more efficient to adapt to changing environments [15].

3 System Model

In the IIoT, many tasks have multi-stage or multi-modal structures. For example, image processing tasks can be divided into submodules such as preprocessing and feature extraction, thereby enabling parallel scheduling across devices. As shown in Fig. 1, consider the task scheduling problem in a multi-slot IIoT. There are n tasks in the system, denoted as $q = \{q_1, q_2, \ldots, q_n\}$, which will be allocated to m edge servers, denoted as $S = \{S_1, S_2, \ldots, S_m\}$. To fully utilize the capabilities of the edge server, each task q_i is segmented into two task modules, q_{i1} and q_{i2}, through different segmentation schemes, thereby transforming the task into two parallel-scheduled task modules while preserving the dependency constraints. To facilitate the observation of the real-time scheduling process, all scheduling decisions are stored in the segmentation decision table $\mathcal{T}_{\text{seg}}$ and the allocation decision table $\mathcal{T}_{\text{all}}$.

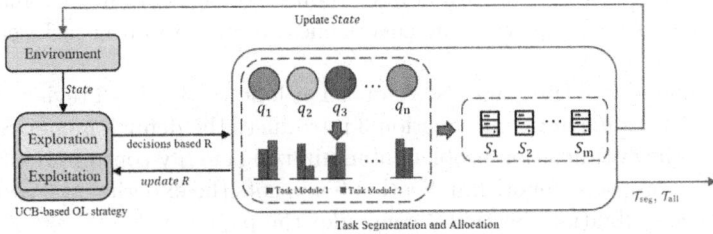

Fig. 1. Dynamic Task scheduling.

Edge servers in IIoT are heterogeneous and have imbalanced loads, which leads to differences in energy consumption and requires energy-optimized scheduling strategies. To accurately quantify the latency and energy consumption caused by task scheduling, it is necessary to consider the effects of task features and edge server states on task scheduling. To optimize task scheduling decisions, we define task, edge server, energy consumption and task execution models.

3.1 Task Model

We characterize each task by $q_i = (d_i, c_i, l_i, n_i)$, where d_i denotes the data size of task q_i and c_i denotes the computing requirements of task q_i. Each task q_i can be segmented into two task modules, $q_{i,1} = (d_{i,1}, c_{i,1})$ and $q_{i,2} = (d_{i,2}, c_{i,2})$, where $d_i = d_{i,1} + d_{i2}$ and $c_i = c_{i,1} + c_{i,2}$. The delay constraint l_i for task q_i is required to be satisfied by the last completed task module after segmentation, and the number of available segmentation schemes n_i is considered as an intrinsic property of the task.

The amount of data completed for transmission and the amount of computation completed during the scheduling of the task module $q_{i,k}, k \in \{1, 2\}$

are defined as $q_{i,k}^{\text{tran}}$ and $q_{i,k}^{\text{comp}}$. It is further specified that $q_{i,k}^{\text{tran}}(t)$ and $q_{i,k}^{\text{comp}}(t)$ denote the amount of data transmission completed and the computing completed by the task module $q_{i,k}$ in the time interval $(t-1,t]$. It noted that the task q_i transmits completely, it is required that the total data transmitted over all time intervals is equal to the data size of the task. This can be defined as $\sum_t [q_{i,1}^{\text{tran}}(t) + q_{i,2}^{\text{tran}}(t)] = d_i$. Similarly, it noted that the task is completely computed by requiring that the amount of computation accumulated over all time slots must be equal to the computational requirements of the task. This can be defined as $\sum_t [q_{i,1}^{\text{comp}}(t) + q_{i,2}^{\text{comp}}(t)] = c_i$.

To ensure that each task module can be executed correctly on the edge server, the binary decision for task scheduling is represented as

$$\delta_{i,k}^j = \begin{cases} 1, & \text{if task module } q_{i,k} \text{ is assigned to edge server } S_j, \forall k \in \{1,2\}, \\ 0, & \text{otherwise.} \end{cases} \quad (1)$$

3.2 Edge Server Model

Considering the limited computing power and communication resources of edge servers in IIoT, the state of edge server S_j within the time interval $(t-1,t]$ is defined as

$$S_j(t) = \left(B_j^{\max}, R_j^{\max}, P_j^{\text{comp}}, P_j^{\text{tran}}, P_j^{\text{standby}}, B_j^{\text{assign}}(t), R_j^{\text{assign}}(t)\right), \quad (2)$$

where $B_j^{\max}$ represents the communication resources of S_j, $R_j^{\max}$ represents the computing power of S_j, P_j^{comp} is used to calculate the computing energy consumption of S_j, P_j^{tran} is used to calculate the communication energy consumption of S_j, and P_j^{standby} is used to calculate the operating energy consumption of S_j. $B_j^{\text{assign}}(t)$ is the communication resource consumed by S_j during the time interval $(t-1,t]$. It can be defined as

$$B_j^{\text{assign}}(t) = \sum_{i=1}^{n} \left[q_{i,1}^{\text{tran}}(t)\delta_{i,1}^j + q_{i,2}^{\text{tran}}(t)\delta_{i,2}^j\right], \quad \forall j = 1,2,\ldots,m. \quad (3)$$

$R_j^{\text{assign}}(t)$ is the computing resources consumed by S_j in the time interval $(t-1,t]$. It can be defined as

$$R_j^{\text{assign}}(t) = \sum_{i=1}^{n} \left[q_{i,1}^{\text{comp}}(t)\delta_{i,1}^j + q_{i,2}^{\text{comp}}(t)\delta_{i,2}^j\right], \quad \forall j = 1,2,\ldots,m. \quad (4)$$

3.3 Energy Consumption Model

The energy consumption generated during task scheduling includes communication energy consumption, computing energy consumption, and energy consumption to maintain server operation. The communication energy consumption of task q_i during transmission can be defined as

$$E_{q_i}^{\text{tran}} = E_{q_{i,1}}^{\text{tran}} + E_{q_{i,2}}^{\text{tran}}, \quad (5)$$

where $E_{q_{i,1}}^{\text{tran}} = \frac{d_{i,1}}{q_{i,1}^{\text{tran}}(t)} \cdot P_j^{\text{tran}}$ represents the communication energy consumption generated by the transmission of task module $q_{i,1}$ to edge server S_j, while $E_{q_{i,2}}^{\text{tran}} = \frac{d_{i,2}}{q_{i,2}^{\text{tran}}(t)} \cdot P_j^{\text{tran}}$ represents the communication energy consumption generated by the transmission of task module $q_{i,2}$ to edge server S_j.

The computing energy consumption of task q_i during execution can be defined as

$$E_{q_i}^{\text{comp}} = E_{q_{i,1}}^{\text{comp}} + E_{q_{i,2}}^{\text{comp}}, \tag{6}$$

where $E_{q_{i,1}}^{\text{comp}} = \frac{c_{i,1}}{q_{i,1}^{\text{comp}}(t)} \cdot P_j^{\text{comp}}$ represents the computing energy consumption of executing the task module $q_{i,1}$ on the edge server S_j, while $E_{q_{i,2}}^{\text{comp}} = \frac{c_{i,2}}{q_{i,2}^{\text{comp}}(t)} \cdot P_j^{\text{comp}}$ is the computing energy consumption of executing the task module $q_{i,2}$ on the edge server S_j.

The energy consumption generated by maintaining the edge server S_j operating during task scheduling can be defined as

$$E_{\text{standby}} = T_{\text{end}}^{\text{max}} \cdot P_j^{\text{standby}}, \tag{7}$$

where $T_{\text{end}}^{\text{max}} = \max(T_{\text{end}}^{\text{comp}}(q_{i,1}), T_{\text{end}}^{\text{comp}}(q_{i,2}))$, denotes the time interval when the last task completed scheduling.

3.4 Task Execution Model

To facilitate the research the task scheduling process, the continuous scheduling process is divided into equal-length time-slot units. The time when task q_i starts scheduling is denoted as $T_{\text{arrive}}(q_i)$. During the transmission of the task, the transmission start time of task modules $q_{i,1}$ and $q_{i,2}$ are denoted as $T_{\text{start}}^{\text{tran}}(q_{i,1})$ and $T_{\text{start}}^{\text{tran}}(q_{i,2})$, respectively. The transmission completion time of the task module $q_{i,1}$ is given by $T_{\text{end}}^{\text{tran}}(q_{i,1}) = T_{\text{start}}^{\text{tran}}(q_{i,1}) + \frac{d_{i,1}}{q_{i,1}^{\text{tran}}(t)}$, where $\frac{d_{i,1}}{q_{i,1}^{\text{tran}}(t)}$ denotes the time required for data transmission. Similarly, the transmission completion time of the task module $q_{i,2}$ is given by $T_{\text{end}}^{\text{tran}}(q_{i,2}) = T_{\text{start}}^{\text{tran}}(q_{i,2}) + \frac{d_{i,2}}{q_{i,2}^{\text{tran}}(t)}$, where $\frac{d_{i,2}}{q_{i,2}^{\text{tran}}(t)}$ denotes the time required for data transmission.

The computational start times of the task modules $q_{i,1}$ and $q_{i,2}$ are denoted as $T_{\text{start}}^{\text{comp}}(q_{i,1})$ and $T_{\text{start}}^{\text{comp}}(q_{i,2})$, respectively. The computation completion time of task module $q_{i,1}$ is given by $T_{\text{end}}^{\text{comp}}(q_{i,1}) = T_{\text{start}}^{\text{comp}}(q_{i,1}) + \frac{c_{i,1}}{q_{i,1}^{\text{comp}}(t)}$, where $\frac{c_{i,1}}{q_{i,1}^{\text{comp}}(t)}$ denotes the time required for computation. Similarly, the computation completion time of the task module $q_{i,2}$ is given by $T_{\text{end}}^{\text{comp}}(q_{i,2}) = T_{\text{start}}^{\text{comp}}(q_{i,2}) + \frac{c_{i,2}}{q_{i,2}^{\text{comp}}(t)}$, where $\frac{c_{i,2}}{q_{i,2}^{\text{comp}}(t)}$ denotes the time required for computation.

4 Problem Formulation

To achieve efficient task scheduling in IIoT scenarios, the objective is to minimize the total energy consumption during task execution, which includes the energy consumption of data transmission, computation execution, and the maintenance energy consumption of edge servers. The objective function is expressed as

$$\mathcal{P}: \min \sum_{i=1}^{n} \left(E_{q_i}^{\text{tran}} + E_{q_i}^{\text{comp}}\right) + E_{\text{standby}}$$
$$\text{s.t.} C_1 : T_{\text{end}}^{\text{comp}}(q_{i,2}) - T_{\text{arrive}}(q_i) \leq l_i,$$
$$C_2 : R_j^{\text{assign}}(t) \leq R_j^{\max},$$
$$C_3 : B_j^{\text{assign}}(t) \leq B_j^{\max}, \qquad (8)$$
$$C_4 : \sum_{j=1}^{m} \left(\delta_{i,1}^j + \delta_{i,2}^j\right) \leq 2, \quad \forall i = 1, 2, \ldots, n,$$
$$C_5 : T_{\text{end}}^{\text{comp}}(q_{i,1}) \leq T_{\text{start}}^{\text{comp}}(q_{i,2}).$$

C_1 is to ensure that the scheduling time of task q_i can satisfy the delay requirement l_i. C_2 and C_3 are to ensure that the edge server S_j is not overloaded at any time interval t. C_4 is to ensure that each task q_i is correctly allocated to the edge server. C_5 is to ensure that the dependencies between task modules are maintained.

5 Solution

5.1 Markov Decision Process

To optimize system performance through task scheduling, we transfer the task scheduling problem to a discrete MDP process and define the following corresponding components.

State: The state of the edge server and the features of the task q_i are observed when making decisions about task segmentation and allocation. Thereby, the environment information for executing task q_i at time interval $(t-1,t]$ is obtained. The state of the edge server at time interval $(t-1,t]$ is defined as $S(t) = \{S_1(t), S_2(t), \ldots, S_j(t)\}$. Therefore, the environment information for executing task q_i at time interval t can be defined as

$$\text{State}_i(t) = \{q_i, S(t)\}. \qquad (9)$$

Action: To achieve optimization objectives, it is necessary to determine an appropriate segmentation and allocation strategy for each task q_i. Therefore, the actions of the tasks can be defined as segmentation decisions a_{seg} and allocation decisions a_{all}, where $a_{\text{seg}} \in \{0, 1, 2, \ldots, n_i\}$, $a_{\text{split}} = 0$ means no segmentation. The decision to allocate the task module is $a_{\text{all}}(q_{i,1}) \in \{1, 2, \ldots, j\}, a_{\text{all}}(q_{i,2}) \in \{1, 2, \ldots, j\}$. The action space can be defined as

$$A(q_i) = \{a_{\text{seg}}, \{a_{\text{all}}(q_{i,1}), a_{\text{all}}(q_{i,2})\}\}. \qquad (10)$$

Reward: To achieve an effective task segmentation and allocation strategy, we design a reward function to evaluate the segmentation effect and execution delay of the task segmentation and allocation scheme, and encourage the exploration of more schemes. The reward function can be defined as

$$R(t) = r_i^{\text{seg}}(t) - r_i^{\text{time}}(t) + r_i^{\text{exp}}(t). \tag{11}$$

where $r_i^{\text{seg}}(t)$ indicates the segmentation reward, which is designed to evaluate the effectiveness of task segmentation, and can be defined as

$$r_i^{\text{seg}}(t) = \begin{cases} \alpha, & \text{if } R_j^{\max} - R_j^{\text{assign}}(t) \geq c_{i,k}, \\ & B_j^{\max} - B_j^{\text{assign}}(t) \geq d_{i,k}, \ \forall i,j,k \in \{1,2\}, \\ 0, & \text{otherwise.} \end{cases} \tag{12}$$

$r_i^{\text{time}}(t)$ indicates the time penalty, which is designed to evaluate the execution time of the task scheduling scheme, and can be defined as

$$r_i^{\text{time}}(t) = \beta \cdot \left(\max_{k \in \{1,2\}} T_{\text{end}}^{\text{comp}}(q_{i,k}) - T_{\text{arrive}}(q_i) \right), \ \forall i. \tag{13}$$

$r_i^{\text{exp}}(t)$ indicates the exploration reward, which is designed to encourage the framework to explore more different scheduling schemes, and can be defined as

$$r_i^{\text{exp}}(t) = \gamma \sqrt{\frac{2 \ln N}{N_A}}, \tag{14}$$

where N is the total number of decisions, N_A is the number of times decision A was selected, and γ is the exploration weight.

5.2 Online-Learning Based Task Scheduling

In the IIoT, dynamically changing environment information brings challenges to resource management. Task scheduling strategies that rely on static assumptions have limited effectiveness. To address this issue, we propose an Online-Learning based Task Scheduling framework. The framework dynamically adjusts the task scheduling scheme to adapt to the dynamically changing edge server status and task requirements. Unlike deep reinforcement learning methods that rely on pre-training with static historical datasets, the proposed framework combines a UCB policy to improve the efficiency of task execution and reduce the energy consumption of task scheduling in real time through online learning.

In the initial stage of task scheduling, it is impossible to evaluate different scheduling schemes due to the lack of sufficient environmental information beforehand. To ensure fair competition among all scheduling schemes, the algorithm initializes the optimal reward value to $R^* \leftarrow 0$. This design can avoid the influence of prior bias on decision-making, thereby establishing a fair starting point for subsequent dynamic optimization. In addition, since the tasks in the same scene usually have similar structures, the segmentation action a_{seg} and its

Algorithm 1. Online-Learning based Task Scheduling

1: **Input:** Task list Q, server list S, coefficients α, β, γ, max iterations T
2: Initialize resources, $\mathcal{T}_{\text{seg}} \leftarrow \emptyset$, $\mathcal{T}_{\text{all}} \leftarrow \emptyset$
3: **for** $t = 1$ to T **do**
4:   **for** each $q_i \in Q$ **do**
5:     Parse $q_i = (d_i, c_i, l_i, n_i)$; $R^* \leftarrow 1$, $a_{\text{seg}}^* \leftarrow 0$, $a_{\text{all}}^* \leftarrow \{\emptyset, \emptyset\}$
6:     **for** each segmentation point a_{seg} **do**
7:       Generate $q(i,1), q(i,2)$ with $d(i,k), c(i,k)$, $R_j \leftarrow 0$;
8:       **for** $k = 1, 2$ **do**
9:         Find S_{feasible}^k for $d(i,k), c(i,k)$;
10:         **for** each $s_j \in S_{\text{feasible}}^k$ **do**
11:           Compute $R_j \leftarrow r_{\text{seg}} - r_{\text{time}} + r_{\text{exp}}$;
12:           **if** $R_j > R^*$ **then**
13:             $R^* \leftarrow R_j$, update a_{seg}, update a_{all};
14:           **end if**
15:         **end for**
16:       **end for**
17:     **end for**
18:     Insert $(q_i, a_{\text{seg}}), (q(i,1), a_{\text{all}}[1]), (q(i,2), a_{\text{all}}[2])$ into $\mathcal{T}_{\text{seg}}, \mathcal{T}_{\text{all}}$
19:     Execute task$(q_i, a_{\text{seg}}, a_{\text{all}})$
20:   **end for**
21: **end for**
22: **Output:** $\mathcal{T}_{\text{seg}}, \mathcal{T}_{\text{all}}$

---

corresponding segmentation reward $r_i^{\text{seg}}(t)$ can be used as a reference for the new task. Specifically, when a new task arrives, the reward for its segmentation action directly inherits the segmentation reward of the previous task, thereby accelerating convergence.

The algorithm iterates over all segmentation schemes a_{seg}, each of which generates two task modules $q_{i,1}$ and $q_{i,2}$. The data size $d_{i,k}$ and computing requirements $c_{i,k}$ of the task module are determined by the segmentation points inherent to the task. For each task module, the algorithm determines a set of feasible servers S_{feasible} that satisfy the constraints for allocation, and calculates the reward $r_i^{\text{seg}} - r_i^{\text{time}} + r_i^{\text{exp}}$ for each scheduling scheme. Through comparing the current reward R_j with the optimal reward R, the algorithm dynamically updates the scheduling scheme for each task. If the current scheduling scheme can lead to a higher reward, the globally optimal segmentation decision a_{seg} and the allocation decision a_{all} will be updated accordingly. Finally, all selected scheduling decisions are recorded in the segmentation decision table $\mathcal{T}_{\text{seg}}$ and the allocation decision table $\mathcal{T}_{\text{all}}$.

To encourage exploration of additional scheduling schemes, an exploration term is included in the reward, denoted as $r_i^{\text{exp}}(t) = \gamma \sqrt{\frac{2 \ln N}{N_A}}$. This design uses the UCB strategy to estimate the potential reward of an unknown scheduling scheme. Specifically, the exploration term is positively related to $N_A^{-\frac{1}{2}}$. When a scheduling scheme A is explored less, the exploration term significantly increases the estimated reward, encouraging the algorithm to prioritize exploring these scheduling schemes in the early stages. As N_A increases, the exploration term gradually decays, and the scheduling scheme relies more on the utilization term $r_i^{\text{seg}} - r_i^{\text{time}}$. This exploration mechanism prevents the algorithm from converging to a suboptimal solution by prematurely over-exploring local optima. In terms of the above descriptions, the designed Online-Learning based Task Scheduling can be stated in Algorithm 1.

6 Experiment

6.1 Experimental Settings

To thoroughly evaluate the performance of the proposed framework, experiments were conducted on a system featuring a 12th Gen Intel(R) Core(TM) i5-12600KF 3.70 GHz processor and 32 GB of RAM. The development environment was configured with Python 3.9 and PyTorch 2.4, with PyTorch utilized for implementing and training the models.

In this experiment, a task scheduling scenario with 40 tasks and 3 edge servers is considered. The task data sizes are sampled from a uniform distribution $U(120, 260)$ (in MB), and the computing requirements are sampled from a uniform distribution $U(300, 650)$ (in MIPS). Depending on the intrinsic properties of the tasks, 2 to 5 possible segmentation schemes can be used. The communication resources of each server are sampled from a uniform distribution $U(70, 90)$ (in Mbps), while the computing power is sampled from a uniform distribution $U(45, 65)$ (in MIPS).

6.2 Performance Comparison

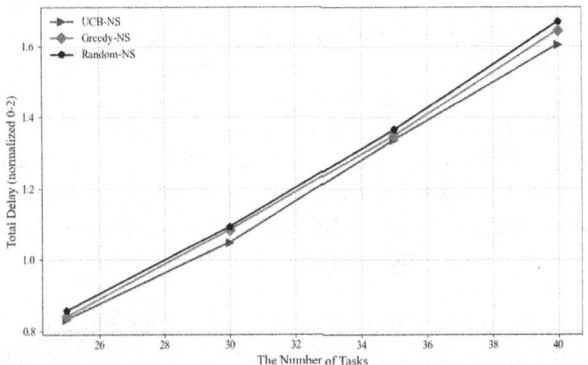

Fig. 2. Delay in task execution for non-segmented strategies.

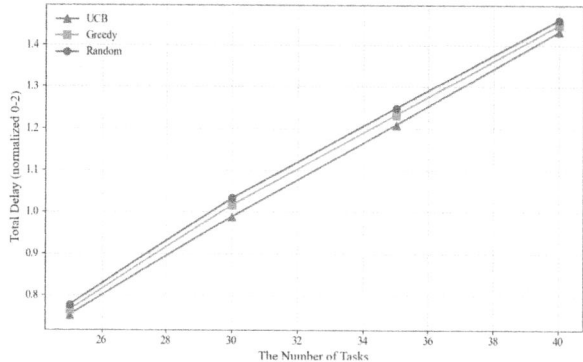

Fig. 3. Delay in task execution for segmented strategies.

Due to the correlation between energy consumption and task delay, delay was also included in the experimental evaluation to reflect energy optimization. To evaluate the effectiveness of the task segmentation strategies in reducing system latency, Figs. 2 and 3 shows the latency of task scheduling with different numbers of tasks. The experimental results show that when the number of tasks increases from 25 to 40, the segmentation-based strategies (UCB, Greedy, and Random) always have lower normalized latency than the non-segmentation strategies (UCB-NS, Greedy-NS, and Random-NS). This advantage becomes more significant when the task size is larger. When the number of tasks reaches 40, the difference between the latencies of the two approaches becomes significant, which shows that parallel scheduling is effective in reducing task execution latency. In addition, the Online Learning algorithm combined with the UCB strategy outperforms the other algorithms at all task sizes, and its latency profile is consistently lower than that of the Greedy algorithms and Random algorithms. It is proved that the Online Learning algorithm can improve the efficiency of task execution. When the number of tasks exceeds 30, the delay growth rate of the Greedy algorithms and Random algorithms with non-segmentation strategy is higher than that of the Online Learning algorithm with non-segmentation strategy, and the maximum gap occurs at 40 tasks. This indicates that the Greedy algorithms and Random algorithms are likely to generate task stacking in complex scheduling scenarios. The steeper latency growth observed in the non-segmented strategy confirms that the task segmentation strategy mitigates task stacking.

To evaluate the effectiveness of the task segmentation strategy in reducing the energy consumption of the system, Figs. 4 and 5 shows the total energy consumption under different numbers of tasks. The experimental results show that the task segmentation strategy has obvious energy saving effect, and this effect becomes more significant with the increase of task size. Specifically, the normalized energy consumption curve of the non-segmented strategies (NS series) is always higher than that of the segmentation-based strategies, and the gap

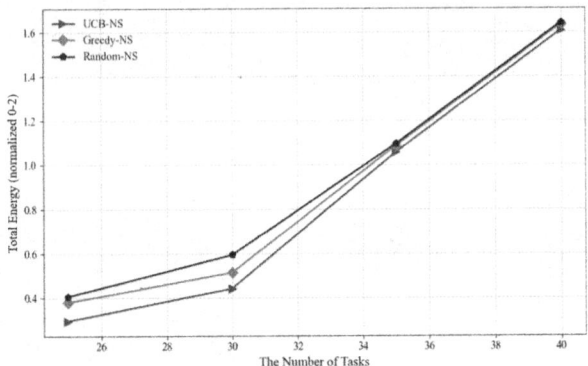

Fig. 4. The energy consumption for task execution of the non-segmentation strategy.

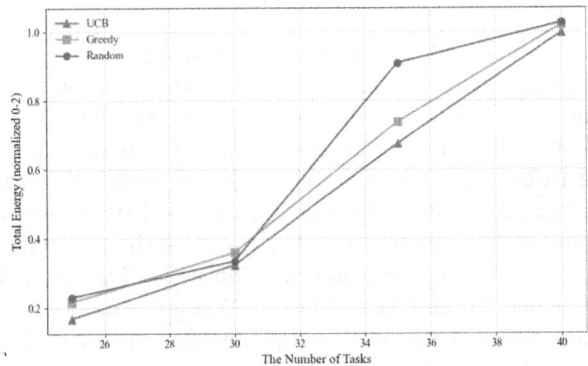

Fig. 5. The energy consumption for task execution of the segmentation strategy.

widens significantly when the number of tasks exceeds 35. This phenomenon can be attributed to the fact that the non-segmented tasks consume a large amount of server resources, forcing the server to operate under high load for a long interval of time. However, segmented tasks enable parallel scheduling, reducing the load on individual servers and lowering energy consumption. At all task sizes, the task scheduling energy consumption of the Greedy algorithm is higher than that of the Online-Learning algorithm combined with the UCB strategy. This indicates that the local optimal strategy leads to unbalanced resource allocation during multi-slot scheduling. The Random algorithm ignores to consider the information of the environment during task scheduling, which leads to higher task scheduling energy consumption. In addition, the lower growth rate of energy consumption of the strategy based on task segmentation proves the advantage of the task segmentation strategy in optimizing resource allocation.

7 Conclusion

To solve the resource skew in IIoT, this paper proposes an Online-Learning based Task Scheduling framework. The framework uses an Online-Learning based Task Scheduling algorithm combined with an UCB strategy to select the optimal task scheduling scheme. Experiments demonstrate that the scheme can improve the task execution efficiency and reduce the task execution energy consumption.

References

1. Huang, H., Ding, S., Zhao, L., Huang, H., Chen, L., Gao, H.: Real-time fault detection for IIoT facilities using GBRBM-based DNN. IEEE Internet Things J. **7**(7), 5713–5722 (2020)
2. Langarica, S., Rüffelmacher, C., Núñez, F.: An industrial internet application for real-time fault diagnosis in industrial motors. IEEE Trans. Autom. Sci. Eng. **17**(1), 284–295 (2020)
3. Zhang, J., et al.: How few Davids improve one goliath: federated learning in resource-skewed edge computing environments. In: Proceedings of the ACM Web Conference 2024, pp. 2976–2985. Association for Computing Machinery, New York (2024)
4. Qian, C., Zhu, J., Shen, Y., et al.: Deep transfer learning in mechanical intelligent fault diagnosis: application and challenge. Neural Process Lett. 54, 2509–2531 (2022)
5. Strumberger, I., Bacanin, N., Tuba, M., Tuba, E.: Resource scheduling in cloud computing based on a hybridized whale optimization algorithm. Appl. Sci. **9**(22), 4893 (2019)
6. Cui, H., Du, Y., Yang, Q., Shao, Y., Liew, S. C.: LLMind: orchestrating AI and IoT with LLM for complex task execution. IEEE Commun. Mag. (2024)
7. Yang, B., Cao, X., Li, X., Zhang, Q., Qian, L.: Mobile-edge-computing-based hierarchical machine learning tasks distribution for IIoT. IEEE Internet Things J. **7**(3), 2169–2180 (2020)
8. Liao, L., Tao, M., Dong, A., Xie, R., Zhang, Y.: Graph-convolutional-network-enabled task offloading for industrial image recognition in digital twin edge networks. IEEE Internet Things J. (2025). https://doi.org/10.1109/JIOT.2025.3543521
9. Wang, Q., Li, W., Mohajer, A.: Load-aware continuous-time optimization for multi-agent systems: toward dynamic resource allocation and real-time adaptability. Comput. Netw. **250**, 110526 (2024)
10. Matos, J.G.D., Marques, C.K.D.M., Liberalino, C.H.P.: Genetic and static algorithm for task scheduling in cloud computing. Int. J. Cloud Comput. **8**(1), 1–19 (2019)
11. Coito, T., et al.: Integration of industrial IoT architectures for dynamic scheduling. Comput. Ind. Eng. **171**, 108387 (2022)
12. Tao, M., Li, X., Ota, K., Dong, M.: Single-cell multiuser computation offloading in dynamic pricing-aided mobile edge computing. IEEE Trans. Comput. Soc. Syst. **11**(2), 3004–3014 (2024)
13. Tao, M., Li, X., Feng, J., Lan, D., Du, J., Wu, C.: Multi-agent cooperation for computing power scheduling in UAVs empowered aerial computing systems. IEEE J. Sel. Areas Commun. **42**(12), 3521–3535 (2024)

14. Kang, Y., et al.: Neurosurgeon: collaborative intelligence between the cloud and mobile edge. In: 22nd International Conference on Architectural Support for Programming Languages and Operating Systems, pp. 615–629. Association for Computing Machinery, Xi'an, China (2017)
15. Gao, M., Shen, R., Shi, L., Qi, W., Li, J., Li, Y.: Task partitioning and offloading in DNN-task enabled mobile edge computing networks. IEEE Trans. Mob. Comput. **22**(4), 2435–2445 (2023)

A Federated Learning Approach for Malware Detection in Data Heterogeneous Environments

Haoyuan Wen, Jingfeng Xue(✉), Wenjie Guo, Liuting Wang, and Wenbiao Du

School of Computer Science and Technology, Beijing Institute of Technology, Beijing, China
{wenhaoyuan,xuejf,wenjieguo,wlt,duwenbiao}@bit.edu.cn

Abstract. Malware detection has become increasingly challenging due to the evolving complexity and diversity of malicious software. Federated learning (FL) provides a promising framework for collaborative model training without sharing sensitive data, making it particularly suitable for malware detection across distributed and heterogeneous data sources. This paper proposes an FL-based malware detection approach that addresses the challenges posed by data heterogeneity. By converting binary malware samples into grayscale images and leveraging convolutional neural networks (CNN), our method achieves effective feature extraction while ensuring cross-platform consistency. To mitigate the impact of non-independent and identically distributed (non-IID) data, we introduce an improved loss function that incorporates a regularization term to align local and global models. Experimental results on the Big2015 dataset demonstrate that the proposed approach outperforms traditional FL methods, such as FedAvg, in scenarios with heterogeneous data distributions. Our findings highlight the effectiveness of combining FL with image-based malware detection techniques in addressing real-world challenges in distributed environments.

Keywords: Malware Detection · Federated Learning · Data Heterogeneity · non-IID · Grayscale Image

1 Introduction

In recent years, the growing complexity of cyberattacks and the rapid evolution of malware techniques have led to increasingly diverse, covert, and sophisticated threats [2]. Modern malware is no longer limited to simple viruses or trojans but has developed into complex variants such as ransomware, spyware, and adware. With the advent of the mobile internet era, malware has extended beyond PC operating systems to mobile devices, IoT devices, and cloud services [5]. Additionally, with the proliferation of app stores, social networks, and online gaming platforms, the channels for malware propagation have become more diverse, including malicious apps, phishing websites, and pop-up ads, significantly increasing the challenges of detection and prevention [3].

As malware samples grow in volume and complexity, the diversity and distribution of data also become increasingly intricate. Traditional centralized malware detection methods require aggregating all data to a single server for processing and training. However, this approach faces significant challenges, including data privacy concerns and limitations in data collection and storage capabilities. Furthermore, malware samples vary significantly across regions and platforms. For instance, app stores, social media platforms, and game development websites often harbor distinct types of malware, creating substantial challenges for traditional data aggregation methods when dealing with distributed and heterogeneous data.

Federated Learning, as an emerging distributed machine learning paradigm, has gained considerable attention in recent years. The core idea of FL is to retain data on local devices or nodes, sharing only model updates (e.g., gradients or weights) for aggregation [7]. This effectively eliminates the need for centralized data storage and transmission, safeguarding data privacy and security. For malware detection, FL enables the utilization of distributed data from various platforms, app stores, and even countries, addressing privacy concerns and leveraging distributed computational resources across multi-terminal and multi-platform environments. This significantly improves computational efficiency and scalability while avoiding reliance on centralized data storage [6].

In current malware detection research, several efforts have attempted to integrate FL with traditional malware detection techniques, using image-based approaches for malware modeling [1]. These methods often convert malware into images and apply CNN for detection. Some studies have combined FL frameworks to enable collaboration across multiple terminal devices, enhancing detection accuracy and system robustness [10]. However, existing research has not adequately addressed the issue of data heterogeneity. In FL, data heterogeneity (i.e., non-IID characteristics) is pervasive in real-world applications, manifesting as variations in data distribution across devices. This leads to challenges in model transferability and adaptation, potentially causing overfitting or underfitting, thereby degrading detection accuracy and generalization performance [12].

This paper proposes an FL-based malware detection method that mitigates data heterogeneity issues. In this approach, binary malware code is converted into grayscale images, ensuring uniform representation of malware samples across different platforms and devices, thereby reducing concept drift during model training. To address inconsistencies in training objectives caused by data heterogeneity, we optimize the loss function to align local and global training objectives. This strategy accelerates training convergence and improves the accuracy and generalization of the global model. By leveraging image recognition techniques and optimizing the model update process, our method enhances the performance of malware detection in FL scenarios while effectively addressing data heterogeneity challenges.

The main contributions of this paper are as follows:

1. This paper proposes a federated learning-based malware detection model that innovatively mitigates the issue of data heterogeneity. By optimizing the loss function in the federated learning process, the model aligns the training objectives of individual clients, significantly improving the training efficiency and performance of the global model. Additionally, the model leverages the advantages of distributed learning, making it well-suited for diverse data scenarios in malware detection.
2. The proposed method converts binary malware code into grayscale image format, ensuring consistent representation of malware samples across different devices and platforms. This image-based strategy not only simplifies data acquisition but also reduces concept drift between devices, minimizing the interference of heterogeneous data during model training.
3. The experiments validate the effectiveness of the proposed method. Results show that under high data heterogeneity scenarios, the proposed approach significantly improves the global model's detection performance and generalization compared to existing methods. Furthermore, the optimized loss function accelerates the training process, demonstrating the practicality and reliability of the method in federated learning settings.

2 Related Work

In recent years, image-based malware detection has attracted widespread attention, especially with the advancement of deep learning technologies, which have proven image processing to be an effective method for malware detection. Nataraj et al. [8] proposed various techniques for converting malware into images and used image recognition techniques for classification and analysis. Pinhero et al. [9] proposed a method that combines image visualization with deep neural networks (DNN), achieving promising classification results using 12 different neural network architectures.

Federated learning (FL) has also become a research hotspot in recent years for malware detection. As a distributed machine learning framework, FL enables multiple participants to collaboratively train a model without sharing data, effectively protecting data privacy. In the context of malware detection, multiple organizations or institutions can use FL to jointly train a global model without exposing their individual malware data. Several studies [1,4,10] have applied FL frameworks to malware detection, achieving promising results.

Despite the progress made in federated learning based malware detection scenarios in recent years, many challenges remain to be addressed in dealing with data heterogeneity. In this paper, we propose an improved strategy that enhances the performance and adaptability of federated learning under data heterogeneity by optimizing the loss function.

3 Methodology

3.1 Problem Formulation

Each client k has its own local data B_k, and its corresponding grayscale image is $I_k = f(B_k)$, represented as f is the conversion function from binary to grayscale image. The goal of each client is to train a model based on local malware samples.

$$I_k = f(B_k) \quad \forall k = 1, 2, \ldots, K \tag{1}$$

where K is the total number of clients.

In this model, the classification goal of malware is to classify grayscale images I_k into one of multiple families of malicious samples instead of just benign and malignant classification. Suppose that the family category of the malicious sample is $F_1, F_2, \ldots, F_M$ (where M is the number of malicious families) and the goal of each client is to bring its image I_k classified as one of these families.

$$y_k = \mathcal{C}_k(I_k) \quad \forall k = 1, 2, \ldots, K \tag{2}$$

where $\mathcal{C}_k$ is the classification model of client k, and $y_k \in \{F_1, F_2, \ldots, F_M\}$ denotes the malware family to which the image belongs.

For each client k, its local loss function $\mathcal{L}_k$ can be used to measure the classification performance of the model using the cross-entropy loss function. The cross-entropy loss function is commonly used in multi-class classification problems. For each sample, the cross-entropy loss function can be expressed as follows.

$$\mathcal{L}_k\left(\mathcal{C}_k; I_k, y_k\right) = -\sum_{c=1}^{M} \mathbb{I}\left(y_{k,i} = F_c\right) \log\left(p_c\right) \tag{3}$$

where p_c is the probability that the model predicts that sample i belongs to family F_c, and $\mathbb{I}(y_{k,i} = F_c)$ is the indicator function, which is 1 if the true label is family F_c, and 0 otherwise.

In federated learning, the goal is to train a global model $\mathcal{C}_{global}$ that can effectively fuse information from different clients. Each client computes the gradient updates $\Delta \mathcal{C}_k$ k for the local model and sends these updates to the central server, which aggregates the updates from all clients to produce the global model. Assuming that the gradient update computed by each client is $\Delta \mathcal{C}_k$, the global optimization objective can be expressed as follows.

$$\mathcal{C}_{global} = \arg\min_{\mathcal{C}} \sum_{k=1}^{K} w_k \mathcal{L}_k\left(\mathcal{C}_k; I_k, y_k\right) \tag{4}$$

where w_k is the weight of client k.

In order to alleviate the problem of data heterogeneity, this paper improves the loss function of federated learning and introduces a regularization item to alleviate the excessive offset of local model update.

$$\mathcal{C}_{global} = \arg\min_{\mathcal{C}} \sum_{k=1}^{K} w_k [\mathcal{L}_k\left(\mathcal{C}_k; I_k, y_k\right) + \lambda \left\|\mathcal{C}_k - \mathcal{C}_{global}\right\|^2] \tag{5}$$

where λ is a hyperparameter used to regulate the learning process between the local model and the global model.

3.2 Methodological Framework

This paper proposes an FL-based malware detection framework, which converts binary malware files into grayscale images and uses CNN for image recognition, forming a novel distributed learning approach. The pipeline of the method is shown in Fig. 1.

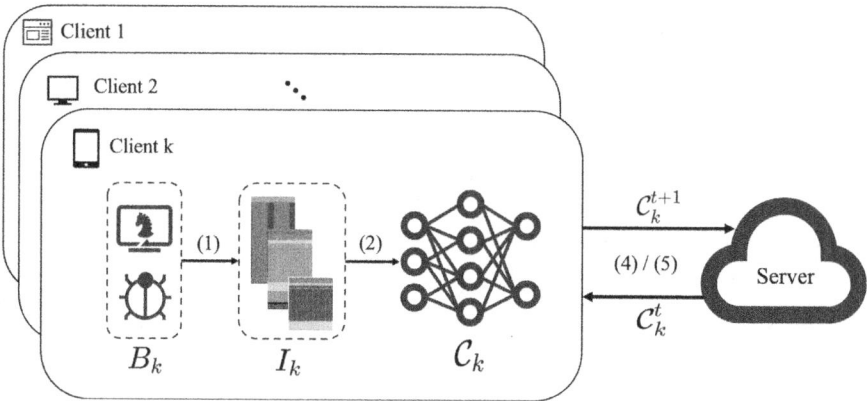

Fig. 1. An overview of the proposed method. Each client trains local data and uploads parameters to the server, and receives new parameters after aggregation.

Malware Image Conversion. Binary malware files are converted into grayscale images. Each byte value (0-255) is mapped to a pixel in the image, with the grayscale value corresponding directly to the byte value [8]. To construct the image, a fixed width is selected based on the sample size, and the byte stream is filled row by row into a matrix, forming an image with a specific width and flexible height. This process captures the structural, instruction sequence, and data distribution characteristics of the malware, which appear as unique textures and patterns in the image, providing effective input features for CNN. Since binary malware streams are executable across platforms, this method ensures broad applicability to various malware detection tasks without dependency on specific programming languages or operating systems.

CNN Feature Extraction. The converted malware images are fed into a CNN. Through a series of convolutional layers, pooling layers, and fully connected layers, the CNN extracts features such as edges, textures, and shapes. These features are then processed to identify potential malicious behaviors and attack patterns. Unlike traditional feature engineering methods, this approach eliminates the complexity of manually selecting features, instead learning latent features directly from raw image representations, resulting in an adaptive, automated detection process with reduced human bias.

Federated Learning Framework. In the FL framework, participating nodes train local models using their respective data and extract features from malware samples. Each node trains a CNN model locally and periodically shares the updated model parameters with a central aggregation server. Only model parameters are transmitted, ensuring data privacy and security. The central server aggregates the received parameters using a weighted average algorithm to form a global model, which represents the collective knowledge of all participating nodes. The updated global model is then distributed back to the nodes for further local optimization, iterating until convergence.

Improved Loss Function. To address data heterogeneity, the traditional FL loss function is optimized to consider both local data fitting and alignment with the global model. By introducing a regularization term based on parameter distance, the local model updates are guided towards the global model parameters, mitigating the impact of data distribution differences. This constraint ensures that the global model better accommodates the data distributions across all nodes, enhancing its overall robustness. Figure 2 illustrates the differences between our proposed method and FedAvg.

4 Experiments

4.1 Experimental Setup

Dataset. The experiments use the Big2015 dataset [11], which contains a large collection of binary malware files from multiple malware families. The dataset includes samples from 9 different malware families and exhibits significant class imbalance: certain families, such as Kelihos_ver3 and Lollipop, account for the majority of samples, while many smaller families have relatively fewer samples.

Baseline. The proposed method is compared against two baseline approaches:

CNN. A traditional convolutional neural network trained on centralized grayscale images, serving as a baseline for evaluating performance without FL.

FedAvg. The standard FL algorithm that aggregates model parameters across nodes using weighted averaging, tested in heterogeneous data scenarios.

Federated Learning Setup. To simulate real-world distributed learning, the dataset is divided among multiple clients, with each client training its model locally before aggregating with the global model. Key settings include:

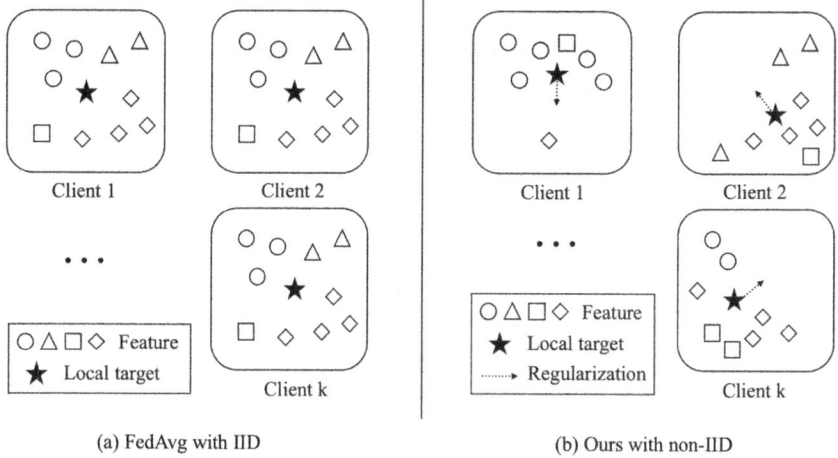

Fig. 2. Our approach mitigates data heterogeneity by improving the loss function, aligning local objectives with the global objective. (a) Under independent and identically distributed (IID) conditions, the FedAvg algorithm effectively aggregates results from all clients. (b) Under non-independent and identically distributed (non-IID) conditions, our algorithm incorporates a regularization term to guide local models toward the global model.

Number of Clients. 10 clients were configured for the experiments. The number of clients impacts the convergence speed and generalization ability of federated learning.

Communication Rounds. Total of 20 communication rounds were set to ensure sufficient training time. Each client performed local training during each round and synchronized with the global model.

Local Training Epochs. Each client conducted 5 gradient updates using local data during each training round.

Data Heterogeneity. Simulated using a Dirichlet distribution with $\alpha = 0.5$, where smaller α values represent more imbalanced partitions.

Experimental Environment. The experiments were conducted on a machine equipped with an NVIDIA GeForce RTX 4090 GPU, running Ubuntu 22.04 as the operating system. The implementation was developed in Python 3.10 using PyTorch 2.3 as the deep learning framework.

Evaluation Metrics To comprehensively evaluate the proposed method's performance, the following common classification metrics were used: accuracy, precision, recall, F1-Score.

4.2 Experimental Results

Results Without Data Heterogeneity. Under non-heterogeneous data conditions, the same training dataset was used for model training. The results are presented in Table 1, which compares the performance of CNN, FedAvg, and the proposed method across various evaluation metrics.

CNN. As a baseline method, CNN was trained using a centralized dataset. It demonstrated the effectiveness of image-based malware classification.

FedAvg. The traditional FL method that averages model parameters across clients, exhibited good convergence under non-heterogeneous data conditions and achieved comparable performance to centralized learning.

Ours. The experimental results show that the proposed FL approach achieved comparable performance to the baseline methods under non-heterogeneous data conditions, with faster convergence.

Table 1. Experimental results without data heterogeneity

Method	Accuracy	Precision	Recall	F1-Score
CNN	95.23%	94.79%	94.76%	94.57%
FedAvg	95.07%	95.54%	94.95%	94.89%
Ours	95.11%	94.83%	95.28%	95.05%

Table 1 shows that the proposed method maintains stability and achieves similar performance as CNN and FedAvg, demonstrating that FL does not inherently lead to performance degradation in malware detection under non-heterogeneous conditions.

Results With Data Heterogeneity. To evaluate performance in realistic FL scenarios, we introduced non-independent and identically distributed (non-IID) data to simulate data heterogeneity. The results are presented in Table 2.

FedAvg. Under data heterogeneity, FedAvg's performance significantly declined. Due to its simplistic averaging of model parameters, FedAvg struggled to adapt to client-specific differences, resulting in decreased generalization, slower convergence, and reduced overall performance.

Ours. The proposed method employs an optimized loss function to mitigate the negative effects of data heterogeneity. The results demonstrate that the proposed method maintained stable performance and outperformed FedAvg across all evaluation metrics.

From Table 2, it is evident that the proposed method outperforms FedAvg under heterogeneous conditions, highlighting its ability to address real-world challenges in FL scenarios.

Table 2. Experimental results with data heterogeneity

Method	Accuracy	Precision	Recall	F1-Score
FedAvg	82.34%	81.12%	82.09%	80.01%
Ours	89.61%	92.34%	88.11%	87.68%

Result Analysis. Based on the above experimental results, the following conclusions can be drawn:

1. Without data heterogeneity, CNN, FedAvg, and the proposed method all effectively performed the malware detection task, validating the feasibility of combining FL with image-based feature extraction for malware detection.
2. With data heterogeneity, the performance of the traditional FedAvg algorithm was significantly impacted by data heterogeneity. In contrast, the proposed method effectively mitigated the adverse effects of data distribution differences, maintaining stable performance and demonstrating superior robustness.

5 Conclusion

This paper proposed an FL-based malware detection method aimed at addressing the challenges posed by data heterogeneity in distributed environments. By converting binary malware samples into grayscale images and leveraging CNN, the proposed method achieved efficient feature extraction and cross-platform consistency. To alleviate the impact of non-IID data, an improved loss function with a regularization term was introduced to align local and global models, enhancing training stability and model robustness.

Experimental results on the Big2015 dataset showed that the proposed method outperforms traditional approaches under heterogeneous data conditions, achieving higher accuracy, precision, recall, and F1-score. Additionally, the proposed method exhibited faster convergence and better generalization, demonstrating its suitability for real-world distributed malware detection tasks. This study highlights the potential of combining FL with image-based malware detection techniques to tackle challenges related to privacy preservation and data heterogeneity.

Future research will focus on exploring more advanced aggregation strategies, such as adaptive and personalized FL algorithms, to further enhance model robustness and flexibility. Additionally, other malware representations, such as opcode sequences or API call graphs, will be incorporated to improve detection accuracy across diverse malware families.

Acknowledgments. This work was supported by the National Natural Science Foundation of China (No. 62172042).

References

1. Fang, W., et al.: Comprehensive android malware detection based on federated learning architecture. IEEE Trans. Inf. Forensics Secur. **18**, 3977–3990 (2023). https://doi.org/10.1109/TIFS.2023.3287395
2. Ferdous, J., Islam, R., Mahboubi, A., Islam, M.Z.: A review of state-of-the-art malware attack trends and defense mechanisms. IEEE Access **11**, 121118–121141 (2023). https://doi.org/10.1109/ACCESS.2023.3328351
3. He, D., Chan, S., Guizani, M.: Mobile application security: malware threats and defenses. IEEE Wirel. Commun. **22**(1), 138–144 (2015). https://doi.org/10.1109/MWC.2015.7054729
4. Hsu, R.H., et al.: A privacy-preserving federated learning system for android malware detection based on edge computing. In: 2020 15th Asia Joint Conference on Information Security (AsiaJCIS), pp. 128–136 (2020). https://doi.org/10.1109/AsiaJCIS50894.2020.00031
5. Kouliaridis, V., Barmpatsalou, K., Kambourakis, G., Chen, S.: A survey on mobile malware detection techniques. IEICE Trans. Inf. Syst. **103**(2), 204–211 (2020)
6. Li, T., Sahu, A.K., Talwalkar, A., Smith, V.: Federated learning: challenges, methods, and future directions. IEEE Signal Process. Mag. **37**(3), 50–60 (2020). https://doi.org/10.1109/MSP.2020.2975749
7. McMahan, B., Moore, E., Ramage, D., Hampson, S., y Arcas, B.A.: Communication-efficient learning of deep networks from decentralized data. In: Artificial Intelligence and Statistics, pp. 1273–1282. PMLR (2017)
8. Nataraj, L., Karthikeyan, S., Jacob, G., Manjunath, B.S.: Malware images: visualization and automatic classification. In: Proceedings of the 8th International Symposium on Visualization for Cyber Security, pp. 1–7 (2011)
9. Pinhero, A., et al.: Malware detection employed by visualization and deep neural network. Comput. Secur. **105**, 102247 (2021)
10. Rey, V., Sánchez Sánchez, P.M., Huertas Celdrán, A., Bovet, G.: Federated learning for malware detection in IoT devices. Comput. Netw. **204**, 108693 (2022). https://doi.org/10.1016/j.comnet.2021.108693, https://www.sciencedirect.com/science/article/pii/S1389128621005582
11. Ronen, R.: Microsoft malware classification challenge. arXiv preprint arXiv:1802.10135 (2018)
12. Zhao, Y., Li, M., Lai, L., Suda, N., Civin, D., Chandra, V.: Federated learning with non-IID data. arXiv preprint arXiv:1806.00582 (2018)

Author Index

C
Chen, Qunjian 144

D
Du, Wenbiao 74, 157

G
Gao, Yifan 53
Gao, Zhipeng 29
Guo, Weidong 13
Guo, Wenjie 41, 157

H
Han, Weijie 41
Hu, Jingjing 41
Hu, Sudan 121

J
Ji, Yi 66
Jiang, Chi 136

K
Kong, Lingming 41

L
Li, Runzhi 66
Li, Xueqiang 144
Liu, Daohua 1
Liu, Nan 29
Liu, Zeyang 74
Liu, Zixin 1
Luo, Xinyi 53

M
Mao, Baolei 66

P
Pang, Chenxi 96

S
Shi, Manhua 136
Sun, Xiangsen 1, 13
Sun, Zhihan 74

T
Tao, Ming 96, 109, 144

W
Wang, Dong 87
Wang, Jinglin 136
Wang, Liuting 157
Wang, Maoli 13
Wang, Xiaoliang 29
Wang, Yong 41
Wang, Yu 29
Wen, Haoyuan 41, 157
Wu, Peng 87
Wu, Yi 53

X
Xiao, Kaile 29
Xiao, Wei 29
Xie, Renping 96, 109
Xu, Hengye 109
Xu, Jiayi 53
Xue, Jingfeng 41, 74, 157

Y
Yang, Tengfei 74
Yang, Xiuqi 74
Yang, Yang 29

Z
Zhang, Hongwei 121
Zhang, Jian 144
Zhang, Ke 136
Zhang, Yin 136
Zhao, Zening 121
Zhu, Jun 87

Made in the USA
Monee, IL
03 May 2026